W9-BSU-041

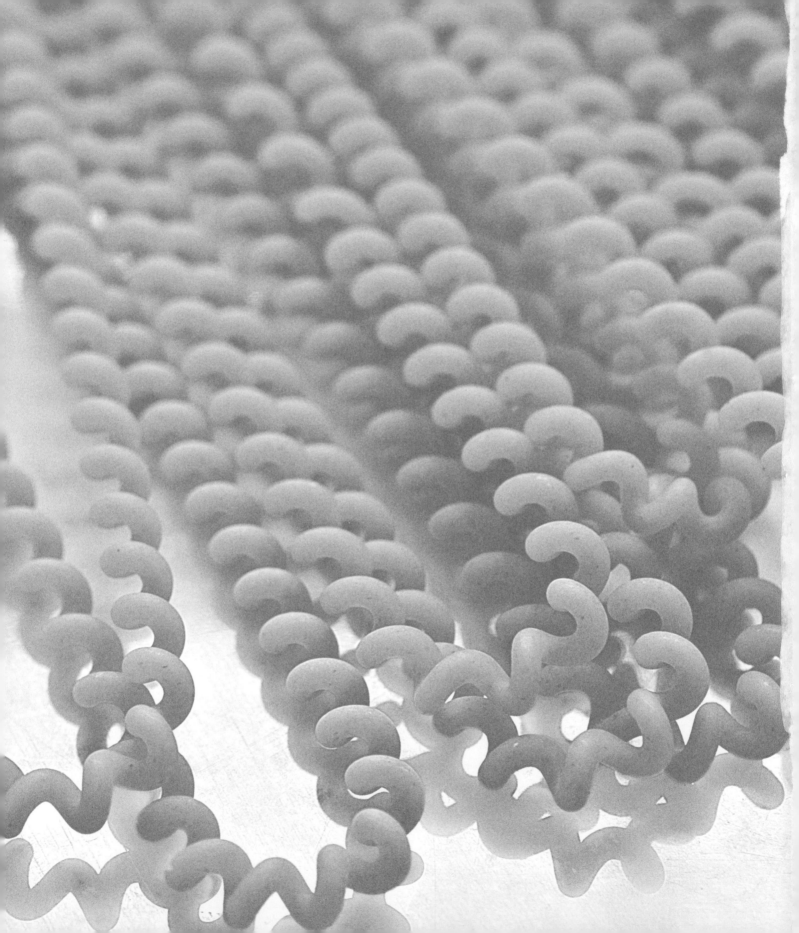

NIGELLISSIMA

ALSO BY NIGELLA LAWSON

HOW TO EAT
The Pleasures and Principles of Good Food

HOW TO BE A DOMESTIC GODDESS
Baking and the Art of Comfort Cooking

NIGELLA BITES
From Family Meals to Elegant
Dinners—Easy, Delectable
Recipes for Any Occasion

FEAST
Food to Celebrate Life

NIGELLA EXPRESS
130 Recipes for Good Food, Fast

NIGELLA CHRISTMAS
Food Family Friends Festivities

NIGELLA KITCHEN
Recipes from the Heart of the Home

NIGELLA FRESH
Delicious Flavors on Your Plate All Year Round

NIGELLISSIMA

EASY ITALIAN-INSPIRED RECIPES

NIGELLA LAWSON

PHOTOGRAPHS BY PETRINA TINSLAY

Clarkson Potter/Publishers

NEW YORK

Published in the United States by Clarkson Potter/Publishers,
an imprint of the Crown Publishing Group, a division of Random House, Inc., New York.
www.crownpublishing.com
www.clarksonpotter.com

CLARKSON POTTER is a trademark and POTTER with colophon is
a registered trademark of Random House, Inc.

Originally published in Great Britain by Chatto & Windus,
an imprint of the Random House Group Limited, London, in 2012.

Library of Congress Cataloging-in-Publication Data is available upon request

ISBN 978-0-7704-3701-5
eISBN 978-0-7704-3702-2

Printed in China

Book design by Caz Hildebrand
Jacket design by Ashley Tucker
Jacket photography by Petrina Tinslay

10 9 8 7 6 5 4 3 2 1

First Edition

CONTENTS

INTRODUCTION

IT WAS WHEN I WAS SIXTEEN or seventeen that I decided to be Italian. Not that it was a conscious decision; nor was it even part of the teenage armory of pretension—the battered Penguin Modern Classic stuffed conspicuously into a basket, the Anello & Davide tap shoes, the cult of the Rotring pen filled with dark brown ink—of the time. No: I simply felt drawn to it, to Italy. While doing other A-Levels (the British equivalent of high school examinations) I did a crash course in Italian and, before I knew it, I'd applied to read Italian at university. I did an entrance test in French and German—in the olden days you still sometimes had to do this—with a plea to swap French for Italian. Certain universities then, and I would guess still now, took a slightly condescending view toward the Romance languages: at Oxford, the authorities saw no reason why Spanish, Italian, or Portuguese couldn't be studied at degree level from scratch; if you knew Latin and French, they blithely assumed you were pretty well there, anyway.

At my interview, I talked of spending my gap year in Italy, and it came to pass that I did. I think I may have implied that my destination was along the lines of a stint at the British Council in Florence. And Florence was, indeed, where I went—at first—not as a student of culture, but as a chambermaid. I'd sworn to do anything to earn a living except clean restrooms, so of course that's what I ended up doing. But I did learn Italian—after a fashion. A year or so on, in a translation class at university—we had been given the task of rendering, orally, a piece of the *History of Western Philosophy*, or some such—my tutor said to me, "That's fine grammatically, Nigella, but I'm sure Bertrand Russell wouldn't have sounded like a Florentine greengrocer!"

I wish I sounded like a Florentine greengrocer now; I am afraid my Italian these days has the halted stammer of any smitten British tourist. But if I don't spend as much time in Italy as I'd like, I bring as much of Italy as I can into my kitchen. And that is what this book is about.

I fear I never write the introduction to a book without claiming that I had the germ of an idea for it way, way back. It's how I work, though: the books I really want to write are the ones I put off for longest. I will be charitable to myself here, and claim that it must be because I need to let them filter through and become part of me first. It is true that the book I have now written is not quite the one I originally intended. That's how it should be if the process of writing has any meaning. I had thought that one day I would write my "Italian book" and that it would concentrate on food as it is cooked in Italy. As someone who, since putting the project on the back burner, has bought a whole wall full of Italian cookbooks (about five hundred titles at the most recent count), I no longer felt so driven to write it. I also had a sense of embarrassment about my original idea; without the fearlessness (or arrogance) of youth, I blushed at the presumption of an English person's finger-wagging on the subject of authentic Italy—for all that I derive much pleasure as well as instruction from many Anglophone Italian cookbooks. And yet still I felt that Italian food was so central to me, and to how I cook, that I couldn't drop the project altogether.

In that family-run *pensione* in Florence where I worked as a chambermaid, I spent a lot of time with *Nonna*—the paternal grandmother, straight from Central Casting—in the kitchen. She didn't teach me to cook, but I learned from her. Actually, I cooked already but, being a child of the time in general, and of my Francophile parents in particular, my way in the kitchen was profoundly influenced by France and its cuisine. In that tiny little kitchen in Florence, I learned about pasta and how the sauce that dresses it must not swamp; I learned to cook meat on the stove top, and to make the simplest, scantest gravies with deglazed pan juices; I learned about *verdura*, cooked soft and served at room temperature, so unlike the crunchy vegetables that were strictly *comme il faut* in France-festishizing Britain at the time. I learned a lot more besides. I had very little money (chambermaiding is hardly lucrative, and a schoolfriend and I were sharing the position and hence also the accommodation and the wages) so eating out was limited. I mean, we did eat out a lot, but that mostly involved stretching a carafe of wine, a basket of that unsalted Tuscan bread, and a bowl of tortellini *in brodo* over an entire evening; luckily, when you're nineteen and female in Italy, you can pretty well get away with anything. When we ate in the evenings in our room with a view (squished together on a window ledge overlooking the Duomo) we could just afford between us a bottle of wine, a loaf of bread, 2 pounds of tomatoes, and some olive oil. And when our wages didn't stretch to wine, we drank the vodka and gin we'd bought duty-free on the way over, spritzed with dissolvable aspirin from our medicine bag; mixers, costing more than wine, were beyond our budget.

So, of course, it made sense to be in the kitchen, eating with Nonna. This was strictly prohibited by her son, but he and his wife—Ugo and Gabriella—were often at their farm in the country, and her grandson, Leonardo, was at school, so Nonna would invite me in for company, unaware that she was teaching me how to cook. She taught by example and involvement, the only way any of us really learn anything important. Thus, she drew me in, and from then on, I never wanted to be anywhere else.

But the recipes that follow are not those that issued from Nonna's kitchen: they are what I cook and, more important, how I cook, in mine. I've often joked that I pretend to myself that I'm Italian, but actually it is just that, a joke—against myself, more than anything—and I feel strongly that it is essential for me, in or out of the kitchen, to be authentic. What I am is an Englishwoman who has lived in Italy, who loves Italian food, and has been inspired and influenced by that: my food and the way I cook demonstrate as much.

So, no I don't claim that these recipes are authentically Italian, but authentic they are nonetheless. Food, like language, is a living entity: how we speak, what we cook, changes over time, historically and personally, too. As I've said elsewhere in these pages: usage dictates form. It has to. Quite apart from there being something hopelessly reductive about endless discussion of whether some recipe may be considered authentically Italian or not, it doesn't make real sense. Not only has "Italy" existed for a relatively short time (since 1861, to be precise) but customs change and, while tradition is to be cherished, the way we cook must evolve. In fact, one of the aspects that is most admirable about Italians and their food is that they manage to safeguard their culinary traditions—with all their anarchic variety—while remaining constantly interested in the new. (Not that this kind of culinary cultural embrace will surprise any Roman Empire obsessives.)

This quality, however, is entirely unregistered by many people, since it doesn't fit with our romantic idea of Italians or their cooking. Our picture of authentic Italian food is conveyed by an image of some glorified peasant past, when food was simple and good, and was enjoyed by large families around a kitchen table. The reality is that the peasant class did not own kitchen tables, often did not have kitchens, and frequently didn't have food. What we outside Italy tend to think of as Italian food is, most commonly, food from the Italian diaspora. In some very real sense it was the Italians who left who furnished the table for those who stayed behind. Their hankering after the produce of home created a huge industry, the vast Italian export business, which fed Italians abroad and enabled those in Italy to afford to eat similarly. And when émigré Italians who'd gotten used to the spoils of the soil from the Land of Plenty returned to their homeland, they brought back with them new habits and newly indulgent ways of cooking. At the same time, a worldwide market for Italian food was created. Italy (post-Rome) has never had much of an empire, but its culinary colonization of the entire world is now almost complete.

What is happening today in Italy is riveting. Where once was a country of regions with often little in common, and where culinary tradition was everything, for no other reason (we are not talking about France here) than that there was nothing else on offer, or nothing they had come across, now Italians are turning a greedy gaze outward. It is true that they still respect their traditions but—as noted above—Italians are suddenly learning and wanting to learn about other ways of cooking. Not least, this is due to the Internet and to global markets in television programs, which means that Italians, like the rest of us, see people on TV cooking cupcakes and muffins, or fiery Thai curries, in a way that wouldn't have been within the comprehension of earlier generations. I've gone a little further into this blossoming of non-Italian cooking in Italy (and specifically from the Anglo-American culinary canon), where relevant, at the beginning of certain recipes; and I do find it remarkable that one of my most interested audiences is Italian (at time of writing this, the highest number of non-Anglophone followers of my Twitter account come from Italy). Personally this is deeply gratifying, but I find it objectively interesting, too. What I admire about this newfound curiosity is that it doesn't come at the expense of the old. You are welcome to cook, for example, a dish of pasta with eggplants and tomatoes and feta (where "authentically" in Italy ricotta salata would be used) and no one will ridicule you for doing so; they may well try it themselves—provided you don't call it Pasta alla Norma. (And, by the way, you can find my own shamelessly inauthentic version on my website, should you want to.) In other words, innovation is not viewed with suspicion so long as there is no misappropriation going on. It is for that reason—among others—that I have tried to avoid giving recipes here Italian names. I am not attempting to pass off recipes as Italian. In most cases, it is the inspiration for, not the identity of, the recipe that comes, authentically, from Italy.

You could say that this book is just part of my long love affair with Italy and Italians, one that started as a heady teen romance and has weathered the ensuing years intact. But (compared with some of my others) this is a fairly slim book, and my passion is huge. I am aware, too, of the irony that the number of Italian recipes in all my other books combined exceeds the number of recipes in this, my "Italian" book.

I was, indeed, tempted to include some old favorites, but forbade myself: all the recipes that follow are newly published in book form, although three of the recipes included have been printed in *Stylist* magazine, another is adapted from a piece for *The Guardian*, and a further one has appeared on my website. It pained me, initially, not to present my Spaghetti Carbonara again, until I realized that, since it is freely available on my website, I could allow myself to move forward, as you say in that splendid foreign repository of Italianness, America.

But before I do, I should acknowledge that my version of this classic is not, in any case, authentic: I use pancetta, not *guanciale*, and I add cream. Also, I add wine (or, more usually, vermouth) and remain unapologetic (for all that I broke the rule by giving my recipe its Italian name). I have made many conquests with this recipe, all of them culinary, I hasten to add, and a lot of them Italian. What is accessible to me to cook with is both more limited and less limited (according to ingredient) than might traditionally have been the case. That's how cooking evolves. After all, we think of tomatoes as being an essential ingredient of Italian cooking and yet they are not originally Italian at all but from South America, and were introduced to Italy only in the sixteenth century.

Similarly, Italians, like all of us, now have access to ingredients that have never been part of their culinary traditions thus far and they cook with them; just as we cook with ingredients that would have been unknown to our ancestors. And, for me, it is in the acceptance, not denial, of this that authenticity actually lies.

• • •

Now, all this harrumphing may be heartfelt, but "*a tavola!*" as they say in Italy: time to eat! And, although I am the last person to want to come between a person and their food, I have to keep you from the table for just a little while longer. It's time for practicalities. So that all the recipes that ensue will make sense fully, I must discuss the contents of my kitchen cupboards with you. Don't worry, I am not going to tell you to store canned tomatoes and pasta or the other essentials that anyone who steps into a kitchen has already, but I do want to tell you what I need in order to make my daily (Italian-inspired) cooking life easier.

The first thing I have to say to you is **vermouth**. I have, in earlier books, written about my enthusiasm for **dry white vermouth**: it costs no more than wine, it comes with a screw-top and can be kept for as long as needed in a cupboard; thus, you can, in effect, create wine flavor in food without having to uncork a new bottle. I have now expanded this enthusiasm and my supplies, and rely all too readily on **dry red vermouth** (which is rubily mellow, and doesn't require the long cooking time that red wine needs to fuse itself with other ingredients); and I am ecstatic about my latest discovery, rosé or rather **rosato vermouth** (I have found only Italian variants so far), which is sensational in cooking, bringing a blossom-

VERMOUTH

fresh fruitiness to anything and everything, but is also pretty damn good, as it is, to drink, and makes for fine cocktails, too. Highly recommended.

MARSALA So, too, is **Marsala**, as many faithful readers will already know. This Sicilian fortified wine lends its distinct but flexible flavor to many a recipe that follows; please note that "Marsala" in any ingredients list generally means dry—not the sweeter "*all'uovo*," though when the recipe is for a dessert and not savory dish, you can of course use sweet Marsala; for my part, however, I find it less cupboard cluttering and more cost effective to use dry throughout.

SHALLOTS When you start reading the recipes in this book, you will notice that there is much evidence of what I have always known as a **banana shallot**, but which is these days often sold as an **echalion shallot**. I mentioned these most useful of alliums in *How to Eat* (1998) but I am newly enamored of them. The point is this: when you're strapped for time or energy, peeling, chopping, and cooking an onion can seem burdensome (even if it is embarrassing to admit). In *Nigella Express* (2007) I presented the labor- and time-saving properties of the scallion; now I want to urge you toward the banana shallot. I won't linger, but you do need to know that a banana shallot is much easier than an onion to peel (you just cut off each end, more or less, and the skin falls away), then you chop it, much as you would a scallion. And because it is sweet and tender, it cooks much faster than a regular onion. I find all the above things gratifying, but on top of all this there is the fact that the taste of a shallot is transformational, providing richness and depth, but delicately.

ANCHOVIES I feel I should hover around the subject of **anchovies** here, if only because so many favored recipes of mine start with a rich base of these, melting in a warm pan of **garlic-flavored oil** (another essential for me, even though it is not widely considered a creditable ingredient); and I do want to urge even those who think they don't like anchovies to try them once, cooked just to create a base of intense, rounded saltiness, and to give them a fair go. But I, too, wish to play fair and so, wherever I think that another ingredient could be used, or the anchovy be disregarded, I have said so in the introduction to the respective recipe.

The only recipe for which I have not offered an anchovy-opt-out clause is the Spelt Spaghetti with Olives & Anchovies (see **p.26**). I'm not saying you *couldn't* make this without anchovies, but it wouldn't be anything like this dish. Not that I want to sound unduly proscriptive (here or anywhere else), for I firmly believe that cooking is what we do while in the kitchen rather than while obeying a cookbook—this is not to discredit what I do, but to remind you that a recipe is always just a starting point.

Still, the mention of pasta prompts me to tell you what *my* starting point is, portionwise, at least. I reckon on 4 ounces dried weight of **pasta** per person, on average; there are variables of course, appetite and age chief among them. Other factors that come into play, when it comes to weighing out pasta, are what—if anything—else is being eaten and which kind of sauce partners it. Now, you will notice that the book is not divided into Antipasti (though some of these can be found in the chapter entitled "An Italian-Inspired Christmas"), First Courses, Second Courses, and so on: this is because I don't eat like that. When I make my supper, I make my supper, and it tends to comprise one course, whether that course be pasta or meat or, indeed, vegetables. I concede that many of the vegetable dishes are designed as accompaniments, but not all. Most of the recipes in the vegetable chapter are vegetarian, though not exclusively.

PORTIONS & COURSES

On the whole, I've tried to place the recipes here in the way that most clearly echoes how I cook and eat them at home. This is my way of explaining why not all pasta or pasta-related recipes are, in fact, included in the pasta chapter, though you'll find a list of other pasta recipes or suggestions on **p.48** at the end of the pasta chapter.

ORZO What I haven't done in the pasta chapter, however, is to give full rein to my enthusiasm for **pastina** (small, soup pasta) in general and **orzo** (the one that looks like rice, or more accurately, barley) in particular; all the other names for this type of pasta are listed on **p. 43**. I often make this as an effortless potato substitute, if that makes sense, and here's how. You cook the orzo, about ¼-⅓ cup per head as an accompanying starch, following the package instructions but check a couple of minutes before the pasta's meant to be ready. Before draining, reserve some pasta-cooking water and when the orzo is draining, melt a little butter in the saucepan, and whisk in a little of the starchy cooking water to help make an emulsion. Add salt and pepper to taste, tip in the drained pasta, and beat in a sprinkling of grated Parmesan to taste and as much of the pasta-cooking water as you need to make sure the pasta grains are just coated with a lightly flavorsome gleam of sauce.

PASTA-COOKING TIPS With this easy orzo, the pasta water comprises most of the sauce, but elsewhere in the book, you will find this technique of holding back some **pasta-cooking water** to help bind a sauce to the pasta—and it is a particularly Italian technique. Please, promise me that you will get into the habit of doing this every time you cook pasta. Indeed, you should make yourself incapable of draining pasta without first lowering a small cup into the cooking water to remove and reserve some for the sauce.

If it makes your life easier (not too much bubbling away on the stove), when you're feeding a lot of people, you can follow a pasta-cooking tip from Anna Del Conte: the Vincenzo Agnesi method, which reduces the risk of overcooking and is as follows. Bring your water to a boil, add salt, then tip in the pasta, stirring well to make sure it's all in and not clumped together. Once the water comes back to a boil, let the pasta cook for 2 minutes, then turn off the heat, cover the pan with a clean, thin kitchen towel (not a waffled-textured one) and clamp on a tight-fitting lid. Let the pasta stand like this for as long as the package tells you to cook it normally. When the time is up, drain the pasta, remembering to remove a small cupful of cooking water before doing so.

My only remaining word of wisdom on this subject is also from Anna Del Conte and it is that the water you cook pasta in should be as salty as the Mediterranean. Contemporary dietary mores could not run more counter to such a recommendation; you, of course, are free to act on my advice or ignore it, as you see fit.

BLACK RICE The only time that I am in accordance with the anti-salt brigade is when I cook rice, apart from when it's in a risotto. What I have mentioned within the book's pages (see **p.80**), but not given a recipe for, however, is a non-risotto rice, the **black Venere rice** from Italy that adds glamour, to be sure, but more important, is easy to cook and has a gloriously comforting aromatic flavor. I haven't offered a recipe, because you don't need one, but it would be helpful to have a method. So here goes. For 2–4 people (it will stretch to 4, but I love it left over to make for a very unItalian rice salad, so I cook no less if there are two of us eating) you need 1 cup of black rice to 1½ cups of cold water. Put both in a saucepan (salting if you wish) and when the contents of the pan come to a boil, clamp on a tightly fitting lid, turn the heat down to very, very low, and cook for 30 minutes. If, by that time, all the water is not absorbed, then turn off the heat, remove the lid, drape with a clean kitchen towel, clamp the lid back on, and leave to stand for 5–10 minutes. And you can leave it standing for up to half an hour.

● ● ●

Before I finally let you into the kitchen, there are a few things I am either honor or (disagreeably) duty bound to tell you, namely:

Always be sure to read a recipe right through before starting to cook.

The Ⓝ symbol above the list of ingredients in a recipe indicates that you'll find information in the Notes on **pp.264–267** about preparing ahead, freezing, or keeping.

I often use already grated Parmesan, even if it is shaming to admit it out loud. If you want to adopt this bad habit of mine, then do, but please be sure the cheese is fresh Parmigiano Reggiano or Grana Padano from Italy and comes in a resealable container to be kept in the refrigerator.

When you have people coming for dinner, make sure you get any ovens heated or pans of water filled and hot well in advance. I often do this quite a long time before. Once the pasta or vegetable water has come to a boil, I turn off the heat, but leave it with a lid on to keep warm. When it's time to eat, you can bring the water to a boil again, salting and proceeding with the recipe, without making everyone wait for 40 minutes to eat. (But see also tips for pasta cooking, opposite.)

All eggs used in these recipes are extra-large, organic, though sometimes, where mentioned, I use pasteurized egg white from a carton. Dishes containing raw or partially cooked eggs should not be served to those with weak or compromised immune systems, such as pregnant women, young children, or the elderly, unless you are using pasteurized egg, which can be bought in frozen, liquid, or powder form (and do check the carton to make sure they are indeed pasteurized).

When deep-frying, please regulate the temperature of the oil as instructed and keep a careful watch on your pan at all times: you must always be alert and vigilant.

All olive oil listed is regular (not extra-virgin), unless otherwise stated.

All milk for these recipes is full-fat whole milk.

Meat should, for preference, be organic.

For garlic, I use a fine-grade Microplane grater and generally grate the peeled garlic straight into the dish I'm cooking—no crushing or chopping required—but you can mince finely by hand and add it as usual, if you prefer.

If you don't have a cake tester, I suggest you do as the Italians and use an uncooked stick of spaghetti.

For specialty items, see my website **www.nigella.com**.

PASTA

I HAVE COME ACROSS MORE THAN ONE VERSION of "pesto Trapanese," the Sicilian pasta sauce from Trapani that differs from the more popularly known Genoese variety in a number of ways. Chief of these is that almonds, not pine nuts, are ground into the mix—a divergence whose origins (in common with a lot of Sicilian food) owe much to Arabic cooking.

Giorgio Locatelli, the London-based Italian chef and restaurateur, uses mint as his herb of choice for this; others go, as they more usually do up north, for basil; some use nothing more than tomatoes, garlic, and olive oil. The recipe below is rather more baroque in its sweep, which seems entirely right for a dish that is inspired by Sicily.

Throughout Italy, eaters do not grate Parmesan over pasta sauces that contain fish (or are very garlicky), so you should consider cheese here doubly ill-advised, unless you wish to substitute ¼ cup grated pecorino for the anchovies.

I like to use fusilli lunghi, which are like long golden ringlets (or, less poetically, telephone cords—and you can see them in their raw state on **p.49**) but, if you can't find them, simply substitute regulation-size fusilli (or indeed any pasta of your choice).

Since the sauce is unheated, it would be wise to warm the serving bowl first but, having said that, I absolutely adore eating this Sicilian pasta cold, should any be left over. It is so easy to make and, being both simple and spectacular, is first on my list for a pasta dish to serve when you have people round.

SICILIAN PASTA WITH TOMATOES, GARLIC & ALMONDS

SERVES 6 Ⓝ

1¼ POUNDS FUSILLI LUNGHI OR
  OTHER PASTA OF YOUR CHOICE
SALT FOR PASTA WATER, TO TASTE
8 OUNCES CHERRY OR GRAPE
  TOMATOES
6 ANCHOVY FILLETS
2 TABLESPOONS GOLDEN RAISINS
2 CLOVES GARLIC, PEELED
2 TABLESPOONS CAPERS,
  DRAINED
⅓ CUP SKINNED ALMONDS
¼ CUP EXTRA-VIRGIN OLIVE OIL
LEAVES FROM SMALL BUNCH
  BASIL (APPROX. 1 CUP, PACKED),
  TO SERVE

Put abundant water on to boil for the pasta, waiting for it to come to a boil before salting it. Add the pasta and cook following the package instructions, though start checking it a good 2 minutes before it's meant to be ready.

While the pasta is cooking, make the sauce by putting all the remaining ingredients, barring the basil, into a processor and blitzing until you have a nubbly textured sauce.

Just before draining the pasta, remove a cupful of pasta-cooking water and add 2 tablespoonfuls of it down the funnel of the processor, pulsing as you go.

Tip the drained pasta into your warmed serving bowl. Pour and scrape the sauce on top, tossing to coat (add a little more pasta-cooking water if you need it), and strew with basil leaves. ■

THIS IS ONE OF MY FAVORITE PASTAS, but I must start with a warning: it isn't as easy on the eye as on the palate; this is a dish made for pleasure not a photo op. In order for the zucchini to acquire the sweet, braised flavor they imbue the pasta with here, they are cooked to a squashy khaki.

This is how I prepare the zucchini: before dicing them, I peel away strips of skin, which gives them a striped look, see the photo on **p.22**. This habit is a maternal legacy that I don't expect you to inherit, too. So peel or don't peel, wholly or in stripes, as you see fit.

I like casarecce pasta, which for all that it means "homemade," is produced by most good pasta manufacturers and indeed is so common that I find it at my local supermarket. Casarecce are small, loosely rolled tubes with a gap—where the roll doesn't quite meet up along the side—which catches every bit of flavorsome sauce. The more colorfully named strozzapreti ("priest-stranglers") work in much the same way. Please don't be put off making this should either of these shapes elude you. My Italian friends blithely suggest, as an alternative, either penne or farfalle.

PASTA WITH ZUCCHINI

Put a pot of water on for the pasta, salting generously (or to taste) when it comes to a boil, then add the casarecce—cooking as per package instructions, though tasting a couple of minutes before they're meant to be ready—and get on with the sauce.

Put the garlic-flavored oil and chopped scallions in a heavy-based pan (that comes with a lid) on medium heat and cook, stirring, for 1 minute.

Add the diced zucchini and cook for 5 minutes, stirring every now and again.

Add the wine or vermouth, letting it bubble up, followed by 2 tablespoons of the chopped parsley, salt to taste, then lower the heat, cover with the lid, and cook for a further 5 minutes, by which time the zucchini should be gorgeously tender.

Before draining the pasta, remove a cupful of starchy cooking water.

Tip the drained pasta back into its pot, add the braised zucchini, or add the pasta to the pan of zucchini, along with 3 tablespoons grated Parmesan, and ¼ cup of pasta-cooking liquid. Combine thoroughly and taste to see if you wish to add more cheese or salt or pepper or, indeed, cooking liquid, then stir in the butter and most of the remaining parsley and divide between 2 warmed bowls, sprinkling with the rest of the parsley, and more Parmesan if wished, on serving. ■

SERVES 2

8 OUNCES CASARECCE PASTA

SALT FOR PASTA WATER, TO TASTE

2 TABLESPOONS GARLIC-FLAVORED OIL

4 SCALLIONS, THINLY SLICED

1 POUND ZUCCHINI (PREFERABLY ORGANIC), FINELY DICED

¼ CUP DRY WHITE WINE OR VERMOUTH

SMALL BUNCH FRESH PARSLEY, CHOPPED

3 TABLESPOONS GRATED PARMESAN, PLUS MORE (OPTIONAL) FOR SPRINKLING

SALT AND PEPPER, TO TASTE

2 TEASPOONS UNSALTED BUTTER

ALTHOUGH THIS RECIPE DOES NOT ITSELF issue from Italy, the inspiration is entirely Italian. One of my favorite things to eat is a risotto Milanese, sometimes called "risotto giallo"—or yellow risotto—and it occurred to me that pasta cooked similarly, or at least cooked to taste similar, would be perfect, and very easy. So here it is: spaghetti in an eggy, saffron-tinted, lightly cheesed, and creamy sauce; it is a bowlful of golden heaven. And see Note to the Reader on **p.xiii** about eggs before you start.

YELLOW SPAGHETTI

SERVES 2

¼ TEASPOON SAFFRON STRANDS

3 TABLESPOONS MARSALA

8 OUNCES SPAGHETTI

SALT FOR PASTA WATER, TO
   TASTE

2 EGGS

¼ CUP GRATED PARMESAN, PLUS
   MORE TO SERVE

2 TABLESPOONS HEAVY CREAM

SALT AND PEPPER, TO TASTE

1 TABLESPOON SOFT, UNSALTED
   BUTTER

Put plentiful water on for the pasta and at the same time put the saffron and Marsala into the littlest saucepan you have—such as one you'd melt butter in—and when the Marsala starts bubbling, take it off the heat and leave to steep.

When the pasta water comes to a boil, salt generously, then add the spaghetti and cook following the package instructions, though start testing 2 minutes early. You want to make sure it's *al dente*, as it will swell a little in the sauce later.

While the spaghetti is cooking, get on with the creamy sauce, by whisking together the eggs, cheese, and cream in a small bowl, adding a sprinkling of salt and a grinding of pepper.

Just before draining the spaghetti, remove a cupful of the starchy cooking liquid, then return the loosely drained pasta to its pan along with the butter and toss it over a low heat. Add 2 tablespoons of the pasta-cooking liquid to the saffron and Marsala in the little pan before pouring it over the pasta. Toss straightaway, working the sauce through the spaghetti, and watch the pale yellow of the spaghetti strands take on the deeper tint of the saffron; then remove the pan from the heat.

Now throw the egg, cheese, and cream mixture over the pasta, and toss to combine gently but thoroughly, before checking for seasoning and dividing between 2 warmed bowls or plates. Serve with more grated Parmesan on the side. ∎

"RAGOÛT" IS FRENCH; "RAGÙ," ITALIAN; and this meat sauce recipe is certainly inspired by the Sicilian combination of sweet lamb, dried wild mint, and crushed red pepper flakes, though I've added an Anglo note with a little red currant jelly (as well as the dash of Worcestershire sauce). If you were to have more time, then the sauce would benefit from being cooked at a lower heat for longer, but note I do not say "improved." This is perfect as it is, and is one of my go-to weeknight suppers.

I do love pappardelle, wide egg-rich ribbons, here, but mafaldine, these Neapolitan curly-edged pasta—like pappardelle with a party dress on—really make my heart sing.

CURLY-EDGED PASTA WITH LAMB RAGÙ

Put a large pot of water on to boil for the pasta; then warm the garlic-flavored oil in a small, heavy-based saucepan (with a lid), and cook the shallots, stirring, for 2 minutes.

Sprinkle in the herbs and red pepper flakes, stirring again in the hot pan before adding the meat and cooking for a couple of minutes, stirring to break it up with a wooden spatula or spoon, until it loses a bit of its pinkness.

Add the tomatoes, red currant jelly, Worcestershire sauce, pinch of salt, and some grindings of pepper, give a good stir, and bring to a bubble, then partially cover with the lid and simmer for 20 minutes.

Check the instructions on the pasta package and at the appropriate time, salt the boiling water and cook your pappardelle, making sure to check for readiness a couple of minutes before it's supposed to be done. Once cooked and not-too-efficiently drained, return the pasta to the pan and dress it with the lamb ragù. Sprinkle a little fresh mint, should you have some, onto each warmed bowl as you serve. ∎

SERVES 2

1½ TABLESPOONS GARLIC-
   FLAVORED OIL
1 ECHALION OR BANANA
   SHALLOT, CHOPPED
1 TEASPOON DRIED MINT
1 TEASPOON DRIED OREGANO
¼ TEASPOON CRUSHED RED
   PEPPER FLAKES
8 OUNCES GROUND LAMB
1 X 14-OUNCE CAN DICED
   TOMATOES
2 TEASPOONS RED CURRANT
   JELLY
1½ TEASPOONS
   WORCESTERSHIRE SAUCE
   (SUCH AS LEA & PERRINS)
PINCH SALT, PLUS MORE FOR
   PASTA WATER
FRESHLY GROUND PEPPER
8 OUNCES MAFALDINE OR
   PAPPARDELLE
FRESH MINT, TO SERVE
   (OPTIONAL)

I KNOW THIS SOUNDS LIKE A DR. SEUSS recipe (only without the elastic scansion) but it is, as the Italians say, "*sul serio*," no joke. The green factor is not crucial, but since this came about because I happened upon some spinach-dyed stubby coils of trottole—the pasta shape named after its supposed resemblance (I don't see it) to a spinning top—it feels right to me. Serendipity is only part of the story: I have also always had a thing about pasta and blue cheese, both separately and in conjunction. This recipe is in many ways an evolution of the Pasta with Gorgonzola, Arugula & Pine Nuts in my *Quick Collection* app, and indeed you could make any sort of mishmash of the two. The major developments here are that I felt the need—or rather a fancy—to sprinkle the deep green of the pasta with the paler pistachios, and I add no cream or mascarpone (as I used to) since a little pasta-cooking water, whisked into the cheese, makes it as creamy as you could wish for. This is not a dietary stance, but because the starchy water doesn't mute the palate-rasping piquancy of the Gorgonzola.

If you can't find trottole or, indeed, radiatori, which have a similarly corrugated form, do not despair. While I love the way the scant but fierce sauce cleaves to the shape, you do get some of that effect with the curl of fusilli.

GREEN PASTA WITH BLUE CHEESE

SERVES 2 HUNGRY PEOPLE

8 OUNCES TROTTOLE VERDE OR
  ANY CURLED PASTA OF CHOICE
  (SEE ABOVE)

SALT FOR PASTA WATER, TO
  TASTE

4 OUNCES GORGONZOLA
  PICCANTE, CRUMBLED OR
  CHOPPED

4 CUPS BABY OR SALAD SPINACH
  LEAVES (PACKED)

FRESHLY GROUND PEPPER,
  SLIGHTLY COARSER THAN
  REGULAR IF POSSIBLE

3 TABLESPOONS CHOPPED
  SHELLED, UNSALTED PISTACHIO
  NUTS

Heat water in a pot for the pasta, salting it when it comes to a boil, then add the pasta and cook following the package instructions, but checking 3 minutes before it's meant to be done. This needs to be really *al dente* because it will carry on cooking as you make the sauce.

Before draining the pasta, remove a cupful of pasta-cooking liquid, then tip the drained pasta back in the hot pan with 2 tablespoonfuls of the liquid, the crumbled cheese, and the spinach, and give a good grinding of coarse black pepper. Put the lid on the pan—off the heat, though back on the stove—and leave to stand for 2 minutes.

Remove the lid, turn the heat back on low, and stir the pasta, cheese, and spinach together, along with as much of the cupful of cooking liquid as you need—I find a scant ½ cup is about right—until the cheese is melted into a light sauce and the spinach, wilted.

Take off the heat, toss with about two-thirds of the chopped pistachios, and divide between 2 warmed bowls, sprinkling each bowl with the remaining nuts. Serve immediately. ∎

SOMETIMES I YEARN FOR OLD-FASHIONED PASTA, that's to say, the sort that comes in a creamy sauce, soft and slippery. Comfort is key here, but this doesn't mean I want blandness, and I exult in the husky depth and mellowness provided by the Marsala-soaked porcini. What's more, there's pasta, Parmesan, porcini, mascarpone (which has a long fridge life), and Marsala always at hand in my kitchen, so I know I'm always under 15 minutes away from a glorious and reassuring supper.

I do realize that 8 ounces of fettuccine is an inelegantly large amount for 2 people, given the egginess of the pasta and richness of the sauce, but mine tends to come in 8-ounce packages and, frankly, it seems silly to leave any in the package.

By the way, if you're not using egg pasta (which cooks more quickly), you should get the pasta on first and then cook the sauce while the pasta is bubbling away rather than as below.

FETTUCCINE WITH MUSHROOMS, MARSALA & MASCARPONE

SERVES 2

½ CUP DRIED PORCINI
¼ CUP MARSALA
¼ CUP WATER
½ CUP MASCARPONE
FRESHLY GRATED NUTMEG
GROUND PEPPER
2 TABLESPOONS CHOPPED
   FRESH PARSLEY, PLUS MORE
   (OPTIONAL) TO SERVE
SALT FOR PASTA WATER, TO
   TASTE
8 OUNCES EGG FETTUCCINE OR
   TAGLIATELLE
1 TABLESPOON UNSALTED
   BUTTER
SMALL CLOVE GARLIC, PEELED
¼ CUP GRATED PARMESAN

Measure the porcini into a tiny saucepan, such as one you'd melt butter in, then cover with the Marsala and water, put on the heat, and bring to a boil. As soon as it starts boiling, turn off the heat and leave to stand for at least 10 minutes. Put the water on for the pasta.

Measure the mascarpone into a bowl, adding a good grating of fresh nutmeg and ground pepper, and when the porcini have had their soaking, strain the contents of the mushroom pan into the bowl, letting the mushroom-Marsala liquid trickle over the mascarpone. Whisk or fork this together to combine.

Squeeze the porcini out over the bowl, then remove them to a chopping board, top with the parsley, and chop both together with a mezzaluna.

The pasta water should be boiling by now, so salt it and add the fettuccine, then move swiftly on with the sauce.

In a wok or similarly capacious pan, warm the butter and grate in (or mince and add) the garlic, stirring it over the heat for about 30 seconds, then mix in the chopped porcini and parsley and cook for a couple of minutes. Whisk in the contents of the mascarpone bowl and stir till it comes to a bubble, which should be a scant minute. Turn the heat off.

Reserve a small cup of the pasta-cooking water, then drain the pasta and tip it from the colander into the pan of mushroom-mascarpone sauce and toss to coat, adding a little pasta water to loosen the sauce should you want to.

Now add the Parmesan and toss again; you may want to add 2 tablespoonfuls at first, then the remaining 2 only to taste. Obviously, check seasoning, too.

Divide between 2 warmed bowls, scattering some more parsley over, if you would like. ■

MACARONI AND CHEESE IS THE QUINTESSENTIAL comfort-food supper; this version, while even simpler to make than the nursery staple, is altogether more elevated. The cheese sauce is almost instant: no roux at its base, just grated cheese mixed with a little cornstarch whisked into wine-lightened chicken broth. For this method, I have the maestro Heston Blumenthal to thank. The broth base stops the sauce—with its three cheeses and truffle butter or oil—from becoming unmanageably rich; the portion size helps, too. My decision to bake the pasta in little ramekins was originally made to speed up cooking time, certainly not to be chichi. Indeed, I usually avoid the individual-portion approach, feeling it not suited to eating at home. Here it works: cute meets cozy and becomes chic. Of course, it's partly the pennette that make it—think enchanting little pixie penne—but if you can't find them, use the small bulging crescents that are chifferi, or indeed regular elbow macaroni, instead.

MINI MACARONI & CHEESE ALL'ITALIANA

Preheat the oven to 400°F, or heat the broiler. Butter the 6 ramekins, and put a pot of water on to heat for the pasta. While you're waiting for the water to come to a boil, toss the grated Gruyère with the cornstarch in a bowl, and chop the mozzarella and let it stand somewhere to lose any excess liquid.

Salt the water once it's boiling, and cook the pennette until on the firm side of *al dente*: read package instructions and start checking 3 minutes before the pasta's meant to be ready.

Meanwhile, heat the vermouth (or wine) in a saucepan big enough to hold the pasta later, and let it come to a boil before adding the chicken broth. Let it come to a bubble again, then take it off the heat and whisk in the cornstarch-tossed Gruyère. The cheese will melt into a mass of gooey cheese strings.

Add the mascarpone to the pan and whisk again, then add the truffle butter/paste or oil— go slowly and taste—stirring it into the sauce.

Tip the cooked, drained pasta into the sauce and stir to coat. Then tumble in the chopped mozzarella, and stir again so that it is distributed throughout.

Ladle the cheesy pasta into the ramekins, trying to get an even amount of pasta and sauce in each. The sauce will seem very liquid but don't panic, as the pasta sucks it up in the oven. Sprinkle the Parmesan on top, dividing it equally between the 6 ramekins, and give a good grinding of white pepper to each one. Don't worry if black pepper is all you've got. It's more a matter of aesthetics (mine) than taste.

Bake for 10 minutes in the hot oven, or broil until golden on top, and let stand for 5 minutes, at least, before eating. ■

MAKES 6 RAMEKINS Ⓝ

SOFT BUTTER FOR RAMEKINS

1 CUP GRATED GRUYÈRE

1 TABLESPOON CORNSTARCH

4 OUNCES FRESH MOZZARELLA (NOT BUFFALO), CHOPPED

8 OUNCES PENNETTE, OR USE CHIFFERI OR ELBOW MACARONI

SALT FOR PASTA WATER, TO TASTE

¼ CUP DRY WHITE VERMOUTH OR WINE

1¼ CUPS CHICKEN BROTH

¼ CUP MASCARPONE

1 TEASPOON TRUFFLE BUTTER/ PASTE OR A FEW DROPS TRUFFLE OIL

3 TABLESPOONS GRATED PARMESAN

FRESHLY GROUND WHITE PEPPER, TO TASTE

I DO REALIZE THAT A DISH that needs an hour in the oven, might not, at first glance, seem to qualify for the epithet "quick," but I'm not trying to pull a fast one. All things are relative, and what makes this recipe feel so speedy is that there is no béchamel sauce—with its roux and patient stirring—involved, the meat sauce takes around 5 minutes, and the lasagna sheets are used straight from the package (no pre-boiling) and cook in the exaggeratedly liquid meat and tomato sauce. The recipe comes courtesy of an Italian informant of mine from Calabria, where sliced cooked ham and hard-boiled eggs are part of the local lasagna, and is known in Casa Mia as Lisa's Lasagna. This recipe comes courtesy of an Italian informant from Calabria, where sliced cooked ham and hard-boiled eggs are part of the local lasagna.

True, this is not as meltingly light a dish as it would be if you made the pasta yourself and rolled it out so thin you could read a newspaper through it, but it is reassuringly homespun and feels like cozy, safe-making food. The high carb content—you really can taste all the pasta layers wodged together—means it's a firm family favorite in my house: a tableful of teenagers make alarmingly light work of it. For the same reason, it is very good party food: I can't think of anything better to absorb excess alcohol. (It's also wonderful cold the next day as a hangover cure.) Should you wish to provide a vegetarian version, boost the number of hard-boiled eggs to 6, the mozzarella balls to a full pound, and dispense with the meat, stirring a couple of canfuls of diced tomatoes into the passata instead. Without the meat to bulk up the non-pasta part, it is certainly on the stodgy side, though that is not necessarily unwelcome. But you could certainly increase the cheese content—perhaps adding a stronger-tasting cheese, too. Don't be tempted to use buffalo mozzarella: not only would it be a waste of money, but the less expensive regular mozzarella seems to melt less stringily.

QUICK CALABRIAN LASAGNA

Preheat the oven to 400°F. Put the whole eggs into a saucepan of water, bring to a boil and let it boil for 7 minutes, then pour off the water and sit the pan under an abundantly flowing cold tap; turn it off and leave the pan filled with cold water in the sink until the eggs are cool enough to peel.

Warm the oil in a large, heavy-based saucepan (that comes with a lid), then add the onion, sprinkle with salt, and let it cook for a few minutes, until it begins to soften.

Add the meat and turn it in the pan just long enough for the raw red color to turn brown.

Add the wine or vermouth, then the passata, pouring the water into the empty passata can or carton and swilling it out into the pan. Bring to a bubble, then put the lid on the pan and cook at a robust simmer for 5 minutes.

Peel and thinly slice the eggs (which will crumble into a mess), and thinly slice the mozzarella; then put a deep, greased lasagna dish, measuring approx. 9 x 13 x 2 inches, onto a baking sheet and get ready for the grand assembly.

First, put a ladleful or so of very runny meat sauce into the bottom of the lasagna dish, to line the base, then arrange a layer of lasagna sheets—using about a quarter of them—on top, to cover the sauce—don't worry about a bit of overlapping.

Add another ladleful of sauce, just to wet the sheets, then add a layer of ham slices, using up a third of them, before dotting with a third of the egg and of the mozzarella slices.

Now add a second layer of lasagna sheets, then a couple of ladlefuls of sauce, followed again by a third of the ham, then egg, then mozzarella slices.

Repeat with a further layer of lasagna sheets, another 2 ladlefuls of meat sauce, then the remaining ham, egg, and mozzarella slices, before topping with a final layer of lasagna sheets.

Pour the remaining sauce over the top, sprinkle with the Parmesan and cover with aluminum foil—making sure the edges are sealed—and put in the oven still on the baking sheet, for 1 hour.

When the hour is up, remove the foil, to reveal the top layer runkled like a shar-pei made of pasta, and push a knife point through the lasagna to check it is soft—if not, re-cover it and return to the oven for about 10 minutes—then let it stand uncovered, out of the oven, for 15-20 minutes (although I love this barely above room temperature if I can bear, or have time, to wait—for up to 2 hours) before slicing into hearty slabs and serving. ■

SERVES 6–8

4 EGGS

2 TABLESPOONS OLIVE OIL, PLUS MORE FOR GREASING

1 SMALL ONION, PEELED AND CHOPPED

1 TEASPOON KOSHER SALT OR ½ TEASPOON TABLE SALT, OR TO TASTE

1 POUND GROUND BEEF

¼ CUP RED WINE OR VERMOUTH

1 QUART PASSATA (OR TOMATO SAUCE), PLUS 1 QUART WATER

8 OUNCES FRESH MOZZARELLA (NOT BUFFALO)

1¼ POUNDS LASAGNA SHEETS (DRIED NOT FRESH)

12 OUNCES COOKED HAM, THINLY SLICED

¼ CUP GRATED PARMESAN

IN THE SOUTH OF ITALY, savory fried or toasted bread crumbs are often known as *"il Parmigiano dei poveri,"* the Parmesan of the poor. These days, many high-toned restaurants think up ways to flavor bread crumbs and scatter them over costly dishes of pasta, but this doesn't detract from the time-hallowed peasant traditions behind this dish. And I always relish an opportunity to use up ingredients that would otherwise go in the trash can. I am not saying you must not buy bread crumbs (as long as they are not the ultra-sandy, excessively orange ones that come in plastic containers) but the idea of going out and buying bread crumbs for a recipe that is about scraping by with leftovers does make me feel a little queasy, even though I have been known to do it.

The thing to do is make bread crumbs with stale bread whenever it's at hand. Stash the bread crumbs in airtight bags in the freezer and use whenever needed, without thawing first. I am not totally old-school, though: I don't grate my stale bread to make bread crumbs, but blitz it in the food processor. When I measure my bread crumbs, I don't fuss too much about how level my cup measure is; how much or little you use here doesn't matter enormously. It's just not that kind of recipe.

SPAGHETTINI WITH LEMON & GARLIC BREAD CRUMBS

Bring water to a boil for your pasta, salting generously when it starts bubbling. Add the spaghettini, stir with a pasta fork or your equivalent, and let the pasta cook following the package instructions, tasting a couple of minutes before it's meant to be ready.

Warm the 1 tablespoon regular olive oil in a non-stick frying pan and add the lemon zest; it will sizzle fragrantly. Now add the bread crumbs and toast by stirring them in the warm pan until they turn a deep gold. Remove immediately to a cold dish.

Important step: before draining the pasta, remove a cupful of the starchy water. I often mention it, nearly always in fact, but here it is crucial.

Tip the drained pasta back into its own cooking pan, then add the extra-virgin olive oil and half the lemon juice and toss to combine in the hot pan until a lot of the liquid is absorbed. Add the red pepper flakes and salt (to taste) and grate in (or mince and add) the garlic, and toss again, adding some pasta-cooking liquid to help it amalgamate into a sparse but gleaming sauce. Season to taste and to check whether you want to add the remaining lemon juice.

Mix the chopped parsley into the toasted bread crumbs and add most of the bread crumb and parsley mix to the pasta, tossing well.

Divide between 2 warmed bowls and sprinkle the remaining lemony, parsley-flecked bread crumbs over each. ■

SERVES 2

8 OUNCES SPAGHETTINI
SALT FOR PASTA WATER, PLUS
  1 TEASPOON KOSHER SALT OR
  ½ TEASPOON TABLE SALT, OR
  TO TASTE
1 TABLESPOON REGULAR
  OLIVE OIL
ZEST AND JUICE 1 UNWAXED
  LEMON
½ CUP FRESH BREAD CRUMBS
2 TABLESPOONS EXTRA-VIRGIN
  OLIVE OIL
¼ TEASPOON CRUSHED RED
  PEPPER FLAKES
SMALL CLOVE GARLIC, PEELED
PEPPER, TO TASTE
SMALL BUNCH PARSLEY (APPROX.
  1 CUP, PACKED), CHOPPED

THERE IS NO TYPE OF MINESTRONE I don't like, but a green minestrone—one unsullied by tomatoes—is my favorite. The recipe that follows is a remarkably low-effort version with a generous yield: a minor episode of chopping is the prelude to a warming and sustaining meal for many.

I've got a couple of notes before gambolling to the recipe. I specify that the zucchini should be half-peeled, by which I mean taking a vegetable peeler and shaving the skin off in strips, so that you end up with dark- and light-green striped zucchini (see photo below). As I've mentioned before, you do not have to do likewise, but it's how my mother always peeled hers and I cannot do otherwise. As for the rest of the veggies, you can really use any you want, and do treat what's below as a guide, in which case work on a ratio—give or take—of 6 cups of water per 2¼ pounds of vegetables.

For normal weeknights, when you may have less of a crowd to feed, you might prefer to halve quantities, though you can still use the whole potato; leaving half a potato palely loitering in your refrigerator is pointless. But don't rush to downsize: I love this a day or two on, when the pasta's cooled in the soup and you're left with a thick vegetable stew stuffed with billowing soft pasta parcels to be reheated gently, but thoroughly.

TORTELLONI MINESTRONE

SERVES 8 Ⓝ

3 TABLESPOONS GARLIC-
   FLAVORED OIL
LEAVES FROM A FEW SPRIGS
   FRESH THYME OR 1 TEASPOON
   DRIED THYME
3 CUPS FROZEN PETITS POIS
2 LEEKS (APPROX. 8 OUNCES
   TOTAL), HALVED LENGTHWISE
   AND THINLY SLICED
1 BAKING POTATO (APPROX.
   8 OUNCES), PEELED AND FINELY
   DICED
1 STALK CELERY, FINELY DICED
2 LARGE ZUCCHINI (1 POUND
   TOTAL), HALF-PEELED AND
   FINELY DICED
8 OUNCES GREEN BEANS,
   TRIMMED AND CUT INTO SHORT
   LENGTHS
2 QUARTS COLD WATER
2 TEASPOONS KOSHER SALT OR
   1 TEASPOON TABLE SALT, OR
   TO TASTE
2 X 15-OUNCE CANS CANNELLINI
   OR FLAGEOLET BEANS,
   DRAINED AND RINSED
1 POUND FRESH SPINACH-AND-
   RICOTTA TORTELLONI
LEAVES FROM SMALL BUNCH
   BASIL (APPROX. 1 CUP, PACKED)
2 TABLESPOONS GRATED
   PARMESAN

Warm the oil in a large, heavy saucepan (that has a lid), stirring in the thyme.

Add the peas and turn them in the garlic-flavored oil, then tip in the prepared leeks, potato, celery, zucchini, and green beans and stir in the heat of the pan.

Pour in the water, add the salt, put the lid on the pan and let come to a boil, then—you will have to keep an eye, or certainly an ear, on it to tell when—remove the lid and let everything bubble cheerfully for 10–15 minutes or until the vegetables—check the potato particularly—are tender. You could let the soup stand at this stage; if I'm planning to press forward within an hour or so, I put the lid on to keep in the heat; otherwise it is better to let it cool swiftly before reheating.

Remove 3 ladlefuls of soup mixture, trying to scoop up more vegetables and less liquid, and tip into a blender (or a large bowl if you're using an immersion blender) and set this aside.

Add the drained, rinsed cannellini or flageolet beans to the pan and bring back to a boil, then add the tortelloni and bring it all up to a boil again. Turn off the heat.

Add the basil and Parmesan to the reserved vegetables in your blender or bowl and whizz to a vibrant green purée, then scrape this back into the pan, stirring it into the soup. Let it stand for 10–15 minutes before eating. ■

TRADITIONALLY IN ITALY, THERE IS ONLY one authentic whole wheat pasta dish, which is the Venetian *bigoli in salsa*: rough-hewn, buff-colored spaghetti dressed in an earthy onion and anchovy sauce. And I see now that the recipe below, while consciously inspired by a Sicilian pesto, similar to the sauce on **p.2**, only without the tomatoes, has much in common with the Venetian original. While this makes my concoction a rather unorthodox marriage between north and south (though historically Venice and Sicily share some notable qualities, not least the Moorish influence evident in both recipes), it is a convincing union. And I've since been delighted to see that La Loren herself created a similar recipe—the eponymous *Linguine con salsa Sophia*—in her book *Recipes and Memories*.

Here I use spelt spaghetti, as it's called on the label—though I use Italian spaghetti *di farro* interchangeably—and find its textured earthiness perfect with the pungency of the olive-sharp anchovies. And, in fact, it has a smoky, subtle strength that doesn't overwhelm less feisty sauces, either. Some regular whole grain pastas work well, here at least, but choose a high-quality Italian brand, unless you are in pursuit of claggy, heavy indigestibility.

The amount of pesto-like sauce you're making is so scant that you really do need an immersion blender, a relatively inexpensive and (for me) indispensable piece of gadgetry, unless you have a processor that comes with a small bowl to fit into it. Of course, to make this in the trad manner, you'd need a pestle and mortar, and should you have one and want to use it, ignore my recommendations on the machinery front and enjoy the elbow grease and authenticity.

There may seem to be an awful lot of anchovies in this. Indeed there are. But for those of us who love anchovies, there is nothing to complain about, and those who feel viscerally opposed to them would recoil at even half this amount.

I must say, finally, that the spelt spag—much like soba noodles—is also good cold, so any leftovers make for a perfect box lunch. It'll keep for 2 days in the fridge.

SPELT SPAGHETTI WITH OLIVES & ANCHOVIES

SERVES 2

8 OUNCES SPELT SPAGHETTI (OR *DI FARRO*)

SALT FOR PASTA WATER, TO TASTE

10 PITTED GREEN OLIVES

10 ANCHOVY FILLETS (FROM CAN OR JAR), DRAINED

1 CLOVE GARLIC, PEELED AND ROUGHLY CHOPPED

▶

Put a pot of water on to boil for the pasta. When the water comes to a boil, salt generously, or to taste, and add the pasta; my spelt spaghetti needs 8-9 minutes, so I set the timer for 7 and start testing for doneness then.

To make the sauce, put the olives, anchovies, garlic, pine nuts, parsley, lemon zest and juice, and olive oil in a small bowl and blitz with an immersion blender (or in your mini processor bowl). Don't worry about the odd unmashed pine nut (or olive); indeed, they are rather appealing.

Just before draining the pasta, remove a cupful of starchy cooking water and immediately add 2 tablespoons of it to the bowl of sauce, then give another brief blitz to combine those last ingredients.

Tip the drained pasta back into its pan, then pour and scrape the sauce on top and toss to mix, adding more of the cooking liquid if you feel you need the sauce to be looser.

Season to taste—you may want pepper or more lemon juice, but I can't see salt being necessary—then toss again and turn out onto a warm serving dish or divide between 2 plates or bowls. ■

2 TABLESPOONS PINE NUTS
LEAVES FROM SMALL BUNCH
  PARSLEY (APPROX. 1 CUP,
  PACKED)
ZEST AND JUICE OF ½ UNWAXED
  LEMON
¼ CUP OLIVE OIL
PEPPER (OPTIONAL)

THOSE UNUSED TO THE DARK CHARMS of spaghetti al nero should be warned, straight off the bat, that this is no first-date food: the sauce is the very devil's ink and I would rather not be observed, by any but the already committed, eating it. There is no absolute need to use black spaghetti, the sort that comes in malevolent Halloween bundles, as the sauce will tint any spaghetti it coats, but I found some black tonnarelli (like spaghetti, only square-cut rather than round) at one of my favorite Italian delis, and thought there could be nothing wrong in intensifying this desirable darkness.

I concede that 4 packets of squid ink (found at fishmongers or online) is an exuberant quantity, but I need flavor as well as color. And heat freaks can up the red pepper flakes at will. I find using canned San Marzano tomatoes—I bulk-buy them online and hoard them greedily—is the clincher here. They are always preferable, but for this sauce I would be tempted to insist upon them. The acidity of regular canned tomatoes can drown out the subtle sea scent of the squid ink.

All in all, this has to be quite the easiest, most exotic cupboard standby: a handful of spaghetti, a can of tomatoes, some packets of squid ink, garlic, a throaty glug of red vermouth, and a sprinkling of red pepper flakes—if you're fresh out of parsley, don't worry—is all you need to make a fierce but exquisite supper.

BACK-TO-BLACK SPAGHETTI

SERVES 2

8 OUNCES SQUID INK (OR REGULAR) SPAGHETTI

SALT FOR PASTA WATER, TO TASTE

1 TABLESPOON OLIVE OIL

¼ TEASPOON CRUSHED RED PEPPER FLAKES, OR TO TASTE

1 CLOVE GARLIC, PEELED

2 TABLESPOONS CHOPPED FRESH PARSLEY

1 X 14-OUNCE CAN WHOLE PEELED SAN MARZANO TOMATOES, DRAINED AND CHOPPED

¼ CUP DRY RED VERMOUTH

4 PACKETS SQUID INK

SALT AND PEPPER, TO TASTE

1 FRESH RED CHILI, FINELY CHOPPED (OPTIONAL)

Put water on for the pasta and, when boiling, salt to taste. Add the spaghetti, stir with a pasta fork or similar, and cook following the package instructions, though do make sure to test 2 minutes before it's supposed to be ready.

The sauce can safely be made while the pasta's cooking. Put the oil in a medium-sized saucepan along with the red pepper flakes and grate in (or mince and add) the garlic, then set it on a medium heat—stirring—till beginning to sizzle. Now stir in the chopped parsley.

Tip in the drained, roughly chopped tomatoes and give a good stir in the heat of the pan. Add the dry red vermouth, stir, and bring to a bubble, then let it simmer robustly for 3 minutes; it will reduce a little.

Turn off the heat and—I wear disposable vinyl gloves, *CSI*-style, for this—squeeze in the gloopy contents of 4 squid ink packets until you have a darkly, delectably menacing sauce in front of you.

Before draining the spaghetti, remove and reserve a cupful of water, then tip the drained pasta into the pan of black sauce, tossing to combine, and adding a spoonful or two of pasta-cooking water if you need the sauce to be more liquid. Divide between 2 warmed plates or bowls and sprinkle with some finely chopped red chili—for a devilish finish—or just scatter a little more parsley over them. ■

I HAVE ALWAYS BEEN EMPHATICALLY ANTI-TOMATO when it comes to seafood sauces, liking my spaghetti alle vongole and any similarly conceived dish strictly *in bianco*. (I should, at this point, refer you back to the Quick Calamari Pasta in *Kitchen*, where the sauce is, give or take, just squid rings sautéed in garlic and chilis and splashed up with white wine.) I don't renounce my previous preferences, but find I am now an enthusiastic consumer of the more southerly and less elegant red sauces, too. I certainly love the gutsiness of this fiery, tomatoey squid pasta. Rather like the Sausages with Beans & Roasted Red Peppers on **p.76**, it has all the swagger and gusto of old-fashioned gangster food, which is all the more astonishing since the recipe comes via the coolly northern and irreproachably chic Anna Del Conte.

SQUID SPAGHETTI

Put a large pot of water on to boil for the pasta.

Heat the oil in a heavy saucepan that can take the spaghetti later, then add the chopped shallot and a sprinkling of salt. Cook, stirring, for a few minutes over a medium heat.

Turn the heat down a little, then grate in (or mince and add) the garlic, sprinkle in the 3 tablespoons chopped parsley and the red pepper flakes, stirring for 30 seconds or so before adding the can of tomatoes.

Tip in the wine or vermouth, bring the sauce to a bubble, then leave to cook at a robust simmer for 10 minutes until slightly thickened.

At this point, you could salt the pasta water and cook your spaghetti, or you could stop here and reheat the sauce when needed.

Cook the spaghetti following the package instructions, though checking 2 minutes before it's due to be ready and remembering to remove a cupful of pasta-cooking water before draining.

When the sauce has had its 10 minutes, stir the prepared squid into it, and by the time the sauce comes back to a simmer, the squid should be tender and just cooked through, but do check.

Add a couple of tablespoons of reserved pasta water to the sauce, then tip the drained spaghetti into the squid sauce, adding more of the cooking liquid if you feel the sauce needs help to cling to the spaghetti strands. Sprinkle with some more parsley (but no cheese) on serving. ■

SERVES 4 ⓝ

3 TABLESPOONS OLIVE OIL

1 ECHALION OR BANANA SHALLOT, PEELED AND FINELY CHOPPED

SALT, TO TASTE

1 CLOVE GARLIC, PEELED

APPROX. 3 TABLESPOONS CHOPPED FRESH PARSLEY, PLUS MORE TO SERVE

½ TEASPOON CRUSHED RED PEPPER FLAKES

1 X 14-OUNCE CAN DICED TOMATOES

½ CUP DRY WHITE WINE OR VERMOUTH

12 OUNCES SPAGHETTI

1 POUND CLEANED SQUID, TUBES CUT INTO SHORT STRIPS AND TENTACLES INTO BITE-SIZED PIECES

THIS IS A REAL HYBRID OF A RECIPE; I'm afraid it might even, in Anna Del Conte's disapproving parlance, be called "Britalian." But I defend it, because I strongly believe that its honest evolution needs no apology. The inspiration lies in the fabulous pasta *con le sarde*, the traditional Sicilian pasta with sardines, capers, and currants or raisins (these, their Moorish legacy) and wild fennel. I wanted to make a faster version that came from our larder rather than the Mediterranean. Canned sardines just don't work for me, at least not in this context, but the English larder stalwart, smoked mackerel, begged to be tried, and—as not always with cooking—in this instance fortune truly did favor the brave. Dill, an herb that I feel is enormously underused (outside of Scandinavia), stands in for the almost-irreplaceable wild fennel.

What this emphatically is not is pasta *con le sarde*, to be sure. But in and of itself it works. More than that, it delights. And it happens to be an incredibly useful cupboard standby; I can never have too many of those.

By all means use fresh mackerel fillets, if you have a patient fishmonger ready to remove all the fine bones. Cook them quickly in the pan before you add the Marsala, then flake them when the sauce has bubbled a bit. But this is only a suggestion; I stick happily to the smoked mackerel option.

I grant you that salted capers, soaked in several goes of cold water then drained, are peppier than the kind of capers that come in jars in a vinegary brine, but I more often than not just reach lazily for the jar. The banana shallot is so easy to peel and quick to cook that I am happy to use it even on busy nights or when under stress, but I'd willingly suggest 4 fat or 6 thin sliced scallions if the banana shallot eludes you and a regular onion defeats you. I know those kinds of days, too.

PASTA WITH MACKEREL, MARSALA & PINE NUTS

SERVES 2
⅓ CUP GOLDEN (OR REGULAR) RAISINS
8 OUNCES LINGUINE
SALT FOR PASTA WATER, TO TASTE
2 TABLESPOONS OLIVE OIL
1 ECHALION OR BANANA SHALLOT, PEELED AND FINELY CHOPPED
¼ CUP MARSALA

▶

Put water on to boil for the pasta, then put the raisins into a cup and pour hot water from a recently boiled kettle over them, enough to cover.

Salt the pasta water when it boils and cook the linguine following the package instructions (though check a good 2 minutes before they're meant to be ready) and start on the sauce once the pasta's in and the water has come back to a boil.

Warm the oil in a frying pan, then cook the chopped shallot for about 2 minutes or until soft.

Add the Marsala and let it bubble, then straightaway add the mackerel flakes, the raisins (after squeezing out the water), the drained capers, and a few scant drops of red wine vinegar. As soon as the mackerel is warm, remove it from the heat. There will be almost no liquid left in the pan: this is a dry sauce, so be prepared.

Just before draining the pasta, remove a cupful of the starchy cooking liquid, which will be used to help the sauce amalgamate with the linguine later.

Put the drained pasta back into its own pan, then tip in the contents of the mackerel pan along with half the dill and half the pine nuts and a tablespoon or so of pasta-cooking liquid, and toss gently but thoroughly to combine. Taste to see if you want any more vinegar.

Divide between 2 warmed bowls and scatter the remaining dill and pine nuts on top. ■

2 FILLETS (6 OUNCES TOTAL)
  SMOKED MACKEREL, SKINNED
  AND FLAKED
2 TABLESPOONS DRAINED
  CAPERS
FEW DROPS RED WINE VINEGAR
HANDFUL FRESH DILL, TORN INTO
  FRONDS
2 TABLESPOONS TOASTED
  PINE NUTS

I HAVE NOTHING AGAINST THE SORT of unsauced shimp pasta that relies on the shrimp themselves, along with some chilis and maybe a splash of wine and some halved cherry tomatoes; indeed, I once wrote a recipe for just this. But, as with the Fettuccine with Mushrooms, Marsala & Mascarpone on **p.12**, at times I long for something less robust, more soothingly creamy. Actually, this recipe combines both virtues as, beneath the mascarpone-creamy sauce, lie the electric edginess of red pepper flakes and the acid tongue of tomato paste. Of course, it does amuse me that the sauce, whisked up pretty well instantly in a bowl, looks just like the Marie Rose you'd use to dress a classic shrimp cocktail, but its conception is no flight of whimsical fancy or culinary joke. And I'm also serious about the pink drink: I really do think it is worth investing in Martini or Cinzano Rosato, the Italian rosé vermouth. It gives the sauce a sweet blossominess that white vermouth or even rosé wine wouldn't quite convey. Still, brandy works in a retro way, too.

I generally use organic raw shrimp that I find at the supermarket, or else little cooked shrimp that come frozen. If you use frozen shrimp, they might come in slightly bigger bags, but just bung 'em all in. They will give off some water, but the thing about this pasta is that it sucks up almost as much sauce as you can throw at it, as you can see in the photograph.

Talking of which: yes, this is a rich sauce, and I've cooked more pasta (the egg pasta is particularly filling) than I would normally allocate per head, but that is mainly because these egg taglierini—think ultra-fine tagliatelle—tend to come in 8-ounce packages, and it seems bonkers to hold back any.

SHRIMP PASTA ROSA

SERVES 2

1 TABLESPOON TOMATO PASTE

¼ CUP MILK

¼ CUP MASCARPONE

1 TABLESPOON GARLIC-
    FLAVORED OIL

¼ TEASPOON CRUSHED RED
    PEPPER FLAKES

6 OUNCES RAW PEELED SHRIMP
    (OR SMALL COOKED SHRIMP)

5 TABLESPOONS MARTINI OR
    CINZANO ROSATO (SEE INTRO)

8 OUNCES EGG TAGLIERINI

SALT FOR PASTA WATER

Put copious water on for the pasta, adding salt later, when it comes to a boil.

In a bowl, whisk together the tomato paste and milk, then dollop on the mascarpone, whisk it in, and set to one side.

In a wok or large pan, warm the garlic-flavored oil and add the red pepper flakes, giving a stir in the heat, before tipping in the shrimp and stir-frying for a minute (or longer, if frozen), by which time they should be pretty well cooked through and hot.

Pour in the pink vermouth and let it bubble up excitedly. When it's reduced a little, add in the pink sauce from its bowl and cook, stirring, till it's hot throughout (and check that the frozen shrimp, if used, are cooked through and piping hot, too).

Meanwhile, add the taglierini to the salted boiling pasta water and cook it; this should take about 3 minutes. Be vigilant.

Drain the pasta, though not too well, then tip it into the pink sauce and toss gently but thoroughly to combine. Divide between 2 warmed plates or bowls and serve immediately. ■

I AM ONE OF THE FEW PEOPLE I know who does not like canned tuna, and so I surprise myself by the fact that I love this instant pasta sauce made with the stuff. Maybe it's the sharpness provided by the lemon, the heat of the red pepper flakes, the sprightliness of the scallions, and the tender pepperiness of the arugula, but this supper—the easy result of a quick forage in refrigerator and kitchen cupboard—is a regular fixture in my eating diary. As, I trust, it will be in yours.

SPAGHETTI WITH TUNA, LEMON & ARUGULA

SERVES 2

8 OUNCES SPAGHETTI

SALT FOR PASTA WATER, TO
  TASTE

1 X 6–8-OUNCE CAN TUNA IN
  OLIVE OIL (*VENTRESCA* IF
  BUDGET AND OPPORTUNITY
  ALLOW), DRAINED

ZEST AND JUICE 1 UNWAXED
  LEMON

½ CLOVE GARLIC, PEELED

3 SCALLIONS, THINLY SLICED

¼ TEASPOON CRUSHED RED
  PEPPER FLAKES, OR TO TASTE

½ TEASPOON KOSHER SALT OR
  ¼ TEASPOON TABLE SALT,
  OR TO TASTE

1 TABLESPOON EXTRA-VIRGIN
  OLIVE OIL

1 CUP ARUGULA (PACKED)

Put a big pot of water on to boil for the pasta and, once boiling, salt the water and add the spaghetti, cooking following the package instructions, though it's best to start checking 2 minutes before it should be ready.

While that's cooking, fork the drained tuna into a large bowl, and add the lemon zest and juice and grate in (or mince and add) the garlic.

Still using your fork, add and mix in the sliced scallions, then season to taste with the red pepper flakes and salt and, finally, add the extra-virgin olive oil, beating with your fork to combine.

Before draining the spaghetti, scoop out a little pasta-cooking liquid, then toss the drained pasta into the bowl of tuna, scallions, etc., and mix together really well, adding a spoonful or so of pasta-cooking water to bring some starchy creaminess to the sauce. Add the arugula leaves and gently work them through the pasta before dividing it between 2 bowls. ■

AT THE TIME OF WRITING, I confess you will need to go to an Italian deli or specialist food outlet for fregola, the sun-dried and toasted Sardinian couscous specified for this recipe. This is not an insurmountable obstacle, of course. What I suggest is that you buy a decent stock of the stuff (along with farro, see **p.44**, and any other more recondite pasta shapes you might be hankering after) in one go, so that you always have the wherewithal on hand.

I wouldn't substitute regular couscous for the fregola (or "fregula," as it is sometimes written), which is rather more like dense pasta peas than semolina grains, and thus most comparable to the larger Middle Eastern or Israeli couscous, which *could* be used in its stead. However, if you can't find fregola, I would suggest you try a chunky soup-pasta shape such as ditalini, which is more readily available.

Fregola itself, though, brings a distinct quality: when cooked, it certainly softens but also retains a singular chewiness and nuttiness, which is perfect in this light but clam-rich, spiced, and tomato-hued soup.

SARDINIAN COUSCOUS WITH CLAMS

Soak the clams in a large bowl of cold water, and sort through them, discarding any shells that remain open or are cracked or smashed.

Heat the oil in a large, heavy saucepan that comes with a lid, then add the chopped shallot, stirring for a minute, grate in (or mince and add) the garlic, and add the red pepper flakes, stirring again over the heat so that it sizzles, though not long enough to let the garlic brown.

Stir in the tomato paste, then add the broth and the vermouth and let it come to a boil.

Add the fregola—it should be covered completely by the liquid—and let it simmer, still uncovered, for 10–12 minutes (or as instructed on the fregola package).

Check that the fregola is nearly ready and then add the drained clams, and cover the pan with the lid. Let cook for 3 minutes at a fast simmer, then uncover the pan to check that the clams have opened. Any clams that, once cooked, stay closed should be discarded.

Sprinkle in the chopped parsley and stir to let everything combine before ladling into 4 warmed bowls to serve, sprinkling with a little more chopped parsley as you go. ■

SERVES 4

2–2½ POUNDS CLAMS, SUCH AS PALOURDES OR MANILA

2 TABLESPOONS OLIVE OIL

1 ECHALION OR BANANA SHALLOT, PEELED AND FINELY CHOPPED

2 CLOVES GARLIC, PEELED

½ TEASPOON CRUSHED RED PEPPER FLAKES

1 TABLESPOON TOMATO PASTE

3 CUPS LIGHT CHICKEN BROTH (MADE UP WITH LESS POWDER OR CONCENTRATE TO WATER THAN USUAL)

¼ CUP DRY RED VERMOUTH

1⅓ CUPS FREGOLA

3 TABLESPOONS CHOPPED PARSLEY, PLUS MORE FOR SPRINKLING

CRAB, LEMON, AND CHILIS: THESE, FOR ME, are the tastes of the Tuscan seaside. This fresh, sweet, spiky combo works as a pasta sauce (and indeed I've written one in an earlier book), as a salad, and as a topping for crostini (see **p.198**), such as I remember vividly from a summer holiday, years ago in Porto Santo Stefano. I can't remember how it morphed, in my kitchen, into a risotto, but it did, and convincingly so.

Had I time, I would certainly love to have the crab fresh from the sea in its shell, and the coral carapace in my kitchen to make a shellfish-scented broth. Or maybe I just kid myself. Still, it hardly matters, since I don't have the time and nor, I presume, do you, so I buy the crabmeat ready out of the shell, and tint and flavor a weak chicken broth (a concentrate made up to half strength) with saffron instead. It may seem to make more sense to buy ready-made fish stock, but I find it rudely invasive here.

At my local supermarket, I can buy both brown and white crabmeat separately; if you can't find, or stubbornly resist, the pâté-like brown meat, then increase the weight of the white to 8 ounces; and do give the white crabmeat a quick check for stray bits of shell before you start.

CHILI CRAB RISOTTO

SERVES 2 ⊘

1 QUART LIGHT CHICKEN BROTH (MADE UP TO HALF STRENGTH)

¼ TEASPOON SAFFRON STRANDS

2 TABLESPOONS GARLIC-FLAVORED OIL

4 SCALLIONS, THINLY SLICED

1 FRESH RED CHILI, SEEDED AND FINELY CHOPPED

1 CUP RISOTTO RICE

5 TABLESPOONS DRY WHITE WINE OR VERMOUTH

4 OUNCES BROWN CRABMEAT

4 OUNCES WHITE CRABMEAT

ZEST AND JUICE ½ UNWAXED LEMON, PLUS ½ LEMON TO SERVE

SALT AND PEPPER, TO TASTE

2 CUPS ARUGULA (PACKED)

Make up the broth, adding the strands of saffron, and put it in a saucepan over a low heat, to keep it hot.

Heat the garlic-flavored oil in a heavy saucepan, which has a lid, and when warm add the sliced scallions and most of the chopped chili and cook over a medium to low heat, stirring, for a minute or so.

Turn the heat up and add the rice, stirring it into the chili and scallions.

Add the white wine or vermouth and let this bubble up and be absorbed into the rice. Now add a ladleful of the hot, tinted broth and cook, stirring all the while, until it, too, is absorbed.

Turn the heat down and add another ladleful of hot broth and cook, stirring constantly, until it is absorbed into the rice, then continue in this surprisingly peaceable manner until all the broth is absorbed and the rice is cooked. I reckon on this taking around 18 minutes.

Take the pan off the heat, add the crabmeat and the lemon zest and juice and stir, then taste for seasoning. Now stir in the arugula , put the lid on, with the pan still off the heat, and let it stand for a minute. While you wait you can cut the untouched half lemon into quarters, so you can each spritz more juice into your bowl as you eat—though this is as much to avoid waste as anything else.

Divide the risotto gooily between 2 warmed shallow bowls or plates, sprinkle with the remaining chili, and set to lustily. ■

MANY YEARS AGO, I WROTE A RECIPE (never published in book form) for what I then styled "trompe l'œil risotto," using rice-shaped pasta, called variously orzo, risoni, semi de melone, or puntarelle. The version here is markedly altered, not least because rather than cooking the pasta and then dressing it in a creamy sauce so that it *looks* like risotto, here I actually cook the pasta much as I would if I were making a traditional risotto. But there are differences and they are all helpful ones. That you use less water to pasta than you would with rice probably doesn't interest you enormously. That you don't have to stir constantly and that the pasta takes only 10 minutes to cook are obvious benefits to the harried midweek cook.

You should also know that much as Italy respects its traditions, this way of cooking pasta— pasta *risottata*—is actually quite the new, cool thing, "*sciccoso*," as the recently coined Italian word (pronounced "chic-oso"), has it. When I've come across this way of cooking pasta in Italy, it's not in fact involved orzo or other rice-shaped pasta; the "risottata" part refers to the method, not the pasta or the end result. Pennette (see Mini Macaroni & Cheese all'Italiana, **p.14**) or macaroni or other similarly small pasta would also work, though cooking times may vary a little. But I love the rice-shaped pasta here most of all: the orzo oozes its starchiness out into the sauce rather than being flushed down the sink via the colander and—what's more—you need only the one pan. I advise that the pan be heavy: a small enameled cast-iron Dutch oven would be perfect although often as not I use a heavy-based saucepan.

Many Italian recipes don't specify amounts of water, merely instructing you to cover the pasta, just. I feel it's easier to begin only with an idea of how much water you'll need, but please regard this as a starting point only: you may need to add more if the pasta's absorbed all the water before it's cooked.

PASTA RISOTTO WITH PEAS & PANCETTA

Warm the oil in a heavy pan that will take everything later; a Dutch oven or saucepan of 10 inches diameter should be plenty big enough.

Add the pancetta and cook, stirring, until it becomes crisp and bronzed, then add the peas and stir for a minute or so until the frozen look leaves them.

Add the pasta and turn it about in the pancetta and peas then pour in the boiling water. Add salt (cautiously, especially if this is for children—the pancetta is salty, as is the Parmesan later); then turn down the heat and let simmer for 10 minutes, though check on it a couple of times and give a stir or two, to stop it from sticking and to see if you need to add a little more water from the kettle.

When it's ready, the pasta should be soft and starchy and the water absorbed. Beat the butter and Parmesan into the pan, check the seasoning, and serve immediately into warm waiting bowls. ■

SERVES 2 HUNGRY GROWN-UPS, OR 4 SMALL CHILDREN

2 TABLESPOONS GARLIC-
    FLAVORED OIL
6 OUNCES CUBED PANCETTA
1¼ CUPS FROZEN PETITS POIS
8 OUNCES ORZO PASTA
2½ CUPS BOILING WATER
SALT, TO TASTE
1 TABLESPOON SOFT BUTTER
2 TABLESPOONS GRATED
    PARMESAN
PEPPER, TO TASTE

FARRO RISOTTO WITH MUSHROOMS

I MAKE NO APOLOGY FOR THROWING such a little-known ingredient at you. You may not be aware of farro now, but believe me, once you've found it, cooked with it, eaten it, you will understand why I urge it upon you. Those who are already familiar with it need no convincing. (But do note that I'm talking here of farro *perlato*—pearled—and not "whole farro" with the husk still on.)

I stick to the Italian appellation, since the customary translation into English as "spelt" is not quite correct. It's not entirely unhelpful, as that's probably the nearest thing we've got, but actually farro is emmer wheat, an ancient grain and staple of the Roman Empire. In fact, I had a good mind to call this "Ancient Roman Risotto"; it would have a certain allure, at least for me who is obsessed by All Things Rome.

I don't suggest spelt as a substitute if you can't find farro, as spelt doesn't seem much easier to come by; instead, consider replacing the farro here with pearled barley. Mind you, I'm ready to start a campaign to make farro more widely known and available. What I love particularly is its nutty whole graininess but without the hessian-weave connotations.

It's true, it doesn't make a risotto (I don't call it a "farrotto," though I gladly call a pearled barley risotto an "orzotto") in the conventional succulently soupy sense; it is really more of a pilaf. But whatever it is, it works. The lack of gluten in the grain means it won't get sticky and starchy, and the upside here is that you don't need to stir while it cooks, as you do with risotto rice. You bung it into a pan, broth in, lid on—and you're done, pretty much. Regard this as a blueprint for further farro risotti but also consider the farro itself as a pastina substitute in soups.

Were I in Italy, in the right season of course, I'd plump for the gorgeous treat of fresh porcini, but my compromise (though none in flavor) is to use dried porcini boosted with crimini mushrooms which, when sliced, reveal beautiful bronze-edged white flesh, firm and compact. And the garlicky, thyme-scented, bosky smell of the mushrooms as they cook is heady heaven. If you find yourself in an Italian deli, do pick up some porcini bouillon cubes, but otherwise use vegetable or chicken broth here, depending on whether you need this to be vegetarian or not.

I cook this as a meal in itself, but it could as easily be brought out as a side dish. And it reheats wonderfully, so not only are leftovers (unlike with a conventional risotto) a positive blessing but you can cook it in advance, which makes it a real boon when you have people over for supper.

Cover the dried porcini with ½ cup of recently boiled water, then fill the kettle and put it on the heat again if you are making up the broth with concentrate, cube, or powder.

In a wide, heavy saucepan (that comes with a lid) add 2 tablespoons of the oil and the fine jade tangle of leek, and cook, stirring frequently, for about 5 minutes or until the leeks are softened.

Drain the porcini, reserving the soaking liquid, then chop them and add them to the pan.

Stir well, then add the farro and turn it gently but thoroughly in the pan. Tip in the Marsala and porcini-soaking water and let it bubble up.

Make up the broth as wished and add this to the farro pan, stir, bring to a boil, and then clamp on a lid, turn down the heat, and let it cook at a simmer for 30 minutes, until the farro is cooked and all the liquid absorbed.

While the farro is cooking, warm the remaining 2 tablespoons oil in a medium-sized frying pan and cook the sliced crimini mushrooms for about 5 minutes or until they begin to soften—they will first seem alarmingly dry—at which point add the thyme, grate in (or mince and add) the garlic, and cook for a further 5 minutes or until the mushrooms are juicy and soft. Remove from the heat if there is still time on the clock for the farro.

Once the farro is cooked, take it off the heat, too, and add the cooked mushrooms.

Stir in the ricotta and Parmesan—they will melt in the heat of the farro—until the farro is creamy, then sprinkle with parsley and serve. ■

SERVES 4–6 Ⓝ

½ CUP DRIED PORCINI

½ CUP RECENTLY BOILED WATER

¼ CUP OLIVE OIL

1 LEEK (WASHED AND TRIMMED), HALVED LENGTHWISE AND THINLY SLICED

2 ¾ CUPS PEARLED FARRO (*PERLATO*)

¼ CUP MARSALA

5 CUPS BROTH, VEGETABLE, CHICKEN, OR PORCINI

8 OUNCES CRIMINI MUSHROOMS, SLICED

LEAVES FROM A FEW SPRIGS FRESH THYME OR ½ TEASPOON DRIED THYME

1 CLOVE GARLIC, PEELED

¼ CUP RICOTTA

¼ CUP GRATED PARMESAN

APPROX. 3 TABLESPOONS CHOPPED FRESH PARSLEY, TO SERVE

AND SEE ALSO . . .

As mentioned in the Introduction, I have other pasta recipes not in this pasta chapter, but dotted about elsewhere, and these are:

Gnocchi Gratin on **p.131**; Pappardelle with Chestnuts & Pancetta on **p.212**; Hearty Whole Wheat Pasta with Brussels Sprouts, Cheese & Potato on **p.214**; Mountain Macaroni on **p.216**; Pasta & Lentils on **p.263**.

And—although it comes earlier in the book than some of the above, I do feel it needs solo star billing—Chocolate Pasta with Pecans & Caramel on **p.192**.

But there are suggestions I've made, too, for turning other recipes into pasta sauces and dishes, which you'll see when you come across Squid & Shrimp with Chili & Marjoram on **p.80**; Cod with Broccolini & Chilis on **p.82**; Chicken with Tarragon Salsa Verde on **p.94**; Cherry Tomatoes with Olives on **p.104**; Peas with Pancetta on **p.106**; Garlic Mushrooms with Chili & Lemon on **p.119**; Chili Tomato Sauce on **p.209**; and Spaghetti Spice on **p.235**.

MEAT, FISH & FOWL

LAMB CUTLETS WITH MINT, CHILI & GOLDEN POTATOES

THERE ARE FEW THINGS MORE CHEERING than a platter piled with food. This sentiment is not entirely fueled by greed: I always feel uplifted by a welcoming sense of plenty; I get pleasure from being able to bring good things to the table. The joy of this supper is that it is not just the eater who is cheered, but the cook, too—an essential deal, when you come to think of it.

If you put your halved baby potatoes on to steam before you get started on the lamb chops, you can fairly effortlessly rely on a proper meat-and-potatoes supper in around 20 minutes (plus a little marinating time). Steaming the potatoes is, for me, an important stipulation: a steamed spud is a sweet spud; more than that, cooked this way, rather than by boiling, the potatoes are dry when done, which makes them easy to fry to crisp bronzedness, without spitting, later. It's important, though, that you don't fill your pot with too much water first. If baby potatoes aren't around, then use a couple of baking potatoes, cut into ½-inch dice. Steaming here would be obligatory rather than merely desirable, as the potato chunks would dissolve into mush in boiling water.

As for what else to serve with this: as ever, I'd suggest strewing some arugula over the platter first (about 4 cupfuls should provide enough leafage to make this a salad rather than a garnish), but any leaves that are good and in season will do. I am always on for radicchio of some variety (and see **p.229**).

I concede that celery salt, essential component of Bloody Mary and condiment for gulls' eggs, is not an intrinsic part of the Italian larder, but celery itself is a pervasive back-note of the savory cooking of Italy, indeed it's one of the famous *odori*, the bunch of essential herbs and flavorings you can get from greengrocers there. If celery salt is not on hand, though, do not give it another thought: just sprinkle a little sea salt in its place.

Put the halved baby potatoes on to steam.

Get out a large dish—in which the lamb chops will fit in a single layer—and first pour into it the olive oil and sprinkle in the red pepper flakes, dried mint, and celery salt.

Using 1 lamb chop as if it were a wooden spoon, smoosh the oil with its sprinklings around a bit, so that it is rather better mixed, then place the lamb chops in a single layer, turn them instantly, and leave to marinate for 10 minutes.

Heat a large, heavy, non-stick frying pan—big enough (about 11 inches diameter) for all the chops to fit in—then duly place them all in it (the oil that clings to them from the marinade is plenty enough for them to fry in) and fry over a medium heat for 5 minutes. While the chops cook, check that the potatoes are tender, which they should be by now; in which case, turn the heat off under your steamer, pour off the water, and let the potatoes stand, drying, while they wait.

Using tongs (for ease), turn the chops over and cook for a further 3 minutes. If you are going to make this an entire one-plate meal, strew the bottom of a large serving platter with arugula, or any other leafage you desire, and when the lamb chops are cooked, but still juicily pink, remove them to the salad-lined (or, indeed, naked) plate. Obviously, cook for longer if you like your lamb well done.

Tip the steamed potatoes into the pan and fry for 3 minutes, then turn them over and fry for another 3 minutes, shaking the pan every now and again to make them tumble and turn in the hot, spiced fat.

Using a slotted spatula or similar, transfer the potatoes to the plate of chops and sprinkle with 1 teaspoon of kosher salt (I like these plenty salty, but if you have more austere tastes or are feeding small children, then decrease the salt or ignore the command altogether) along with the chopped parsley and mint. ◼

SERVES 4

1 POUND BABY WHITE POTATOES, HALVED BUT NOT PEELED

3 TABLESPOONS OLIVE OIL

½ TEASPOON CRUSHED RED PEPPER FLAKES

1 TEASPOON DRIED MINT

½ TEASPOON CELERY SALT

8 LAMB RIB CHOPS, FRENCHED

4 CUPS ARUGULA (PACKED), TO SERVE (OPTIONAL)

1 TEASPOON KOSHER SALT OR ½ TEASPOON TABLE SALT, OR TO TASTE

1 TABLESPOON CHOPPED FRESH PARSLEY

1 TABLESPOON CHOPPED FRESH MINT

THIS MAY BE A RECIPE THAT CONTAINS only a handful of ingredients and one, moreover, that takes scarcely 10 minutes from the time you kick off at the stove till dinner's on the table, and yet it conveys real richness of flavor and punchy elegance. There is something about the saltiness of anchovies with the sweetness of lamb that works with barely any effort on your part. I love the floral fragrance of the rosé vermouth at the end, but if you can't get ahold of that, a sweet—but not cream—sherry along with a sprinkling of lemon or orange zest should do the trick. Anchovy-phobes, poor creatures, can dispense with them but add salt, to taste, along with the vermouth.

I like this—yet again—with nothing more than some peppery arugula, but the fierce flavor of the deglazing juices really makes tomatoes zing, too. And I would never rule out some wilted spinach or good bread, either.

LAMB STEAKS WITH ANCHOVIES & THYME

Warm the garlic-flavored oil in a heavy, non-stick frying pan and fry the lamb steaks for about 2 minutes a side, or until they are as pink (or not) as you like.

Remove the steaks to a board lined with aluminum foil and turn up the ends so any meat juices that run out are contained.

Off the heat, add the anchovy fillets to the pan and stir until they start to break up and begin melting into the pan. Put it back on the heat and, still stirring, add the thyme leaves.

Now add the pink vermouth and let it bubble up in the pan, then pour in the juices that have collected from the lamb steaks, placing the steaks on a couple of warmed plates as you do so. Let the sauce continue boiling until it's thickened—30 seconds should do it—and pour it over the waiting steaks. Eat immediately and with gusto. ■

SERVES 2

1 TABLESPOON GARLIC-
  FLAVORED OIL
2 BONELESS LAMB LEG STEAKS
  (APPROX. 4 OUNCES EACH)
4 ANCHOVY FILLETS
LEAVES FROM A FEW SPRIGS
  FRESH THYME (APPROX.
  1 TEASPOONFUL)
¼ CUP MARTINI OR CINZANO
  ROSATO

A ROASTED, BONED, BUTTERFLIED LEG OF LAMB is just about the easiest, speediest way to cook a cut of meat. Plus, you dispense with all the difficult carving (I am an embarrassingly inept carver myself) as all you need to do is slice the boned meat once it's cooked, which even I can manage without stress.

I've cooked this a number of ways over the years—probably most often with rosemary and lemon and I am tempted to borrow the anchovy, thyme, and pink vermouth approach from the lamb steaks on the previous page, too—but this less in-your-face marinade highlights the sweetness of the lamb and imbues it with a definite but not intrusive flavor that makes it more universally appealing, which is a crucial factor when cooking for greater numbers.

I say marinade, but really, I just leave the lamb—which I get from my butcher, boned and butterflied—to steep in the pan while it comes to room temperature. From then on in, it's only a half-hour blitz in the hot oven, followed by a quarter of an hour's rest. It could hardly be simpler.

The heat of the oven, with the sugar in the vinegar, does mean that you will get scorched, even blackened, spots on the pan. This doesn't bother me unduly, but you might want to line the pan with aluminum foil first.

BUTTERFLIED LEG OF LAMB WITH BAY LEAVES & BALSAMIC VINEGAR

SERVES 8 Ⓝ

3 POUNDS (APPROX.) BONED AND
   BUTTERFLIED LEG OF LAMB
6 FRESH BAY LEAVES, SNIPPED,
   PLUS WHOLE LEAVES
   (OPTIONAL), TO SERVE
2 TEASPOONS KOSHER SALT, OR
   TO TASTE
¼ CUP OLIVE OIL
2 TABLESPOONS BALSAMIC
   VINEGAR
3 GARLIC CLOVES, PEELED AND
   SLICED THINLY

Preheat the oven to 425°F. Get out a shallow but sturdy roasting pan and put the butterflied leg of lamb in it, skin-side down.

Scatter with the snipped bay leaves and half the salt and pour the oil and vinegar over the lamb, then push the garlic slices into crevices where you can and lay the rest on top. Let marinate just until the lamb gets to room temperature.

Turn the lamb over, so it is now skin-side up, sprinkle with the remaining salt, and roast in the hot oven for 30 minutes.

Remove from the oven, tent with aluminum foil, and let it stand for 15 minutes: this will give you lusciously pink lamb; if you want the meat slightly less pink, then let it stand, under its foil, for 30 minutes.

I like to slice the meat and serve it in its piquant juices in the pan, but if you prefer—and for more formal occasions it does make sense—you can arrange the meat on a warmed serving platter and add a little boiling water (maybe an espresso cupful or so) to the juices in the pan before pouring them over the meat on the platter. A few more fresh bay leaves strewn over the meat will add to the aesthetic pleasure of the arrangement, too. ■

PORK CHOPS WITH FENNEL SEEDS & ALLSPICE

IN AN EARLIER BOOK, *FRESH*, I presented my domestic take on that aromatic Italian marketplace staple, *porchetta*, in the form of a boned and butterflied shoulder of pork, smeared with a paste made of onions cooked with garlic, fennel seeds, rosemary, bay, cloves, and peppercorns, to be rolled up, roasted, and, after its low and slow cooking, cut into melting slabs and eaten in a split ciabatta roll. What I give you here is the quick-time, pared-down version. Or, if I'm honest, not so much a version as an everyday recipe inspired by it. I'm happy with that: the *porchetta* needs around 30 hours for optimal results; the recipe below gives you a fennel-flavored, glossy-gravied supper in about 15 minutes.

I'd be all in favor of adding some rosemary (or sage) to the dredging mixture, but without the long time in the oven that a great big rolled joint of meat gets, you do need to oomph up the deeper, more aromatic spices, which means adding allspice to the pinch of cloves. The celery salt is authentic neither to Italy in general, as I've mentioned earlier, nor *porchetta* in particular, but it provides punch and flavorsome feistiness. Spicing may be a matter of taste, and one that withstands infinite variation, but I cannot be quite so relaxed about everything. So listen up: it is vital that the pork chops have some fat to them; I don't mean the strip that runs alongside the chops—you can trim that—but the marbling in the meat itself. Without this fat, the meat will be tasteless and as densely woven as a sweater that's gone through the hot wash by mistake (and about as good to eat). Pork in the UK and US, especially in supermarkets, is reared to be indigestibly lean. Luckily, there is the beginning of a backlash. Be part of it.

It's also important that the pan you use is a neat fit for the chops; any bit of pan that is over the heat but uncovered with meat will just start to make your kitchen smoky. I find a 9-inch frying pan perfect here; it helps that it is heavy and non-stick.

And a last bit of fine-tuning: I do know that the amounts of flour, modest as they are, will give you some left over but, if there is any less, it is too difficult to dredge the pork chops properly. I am not an advocate of waste, indeed I disapprove very fiercely of even a hint of it, but I can live with throwing away a spoonful of flour.

I'd suggest with this, if you have time, mashed potatoes (along with some steamed spinach or green beans); as it is, I gladly refer you to the Mock Mash on **p.136**.

Cut the rind and most of the outer fat off the pork chops. A terrible shame, I know, but the fat is unlikely to cook in time. (As said above, it is the filigree network of fat in the meat that you need here.)

Mix the flour, spices, and seasonings, including a good grinding of pepper, in a small, flat dish and dredge the pork chops thoroughly all over.

Leave the chops sitting in their floury dish while you warm the garlic-flavored oil in a heavy frying pan, preferably non-stick, in which the 2 chops fit snugly. Duly add and cook the pork chops for 5 minutes on one side, making sure the heat is not so hot that the chops burn.

Turn the chops over and cook for another 5 minutes, then pour in the Marsala and give the chops a further 5 minutes on a low-medium heat, testing to see they are cooked through before removing them to a couple of warmed plates.

Give the sauce a swirl in the pan over the heat, checking to see that it has thickened and become a rich, glossy chestnut, then pour it over the chops. Serve immediately. ■

SERVES 2

2 PORK RIB CHOPS, NOT TOO
  LEAN (SEE ABOVE)
3 TABLESPOONS FLOUR
2 TEASPOONS FENNEL SEEDS
½ TEASPOON GROUND ALLSPICE
½ TEASPOON CELERY SALT
PINCH GROUND CLOVES
FRESHLY GROUND PEPPER
2 TABLESPOONS GARLIC-
  FLAVORED OIL
5 TABLESPOONS MARSALA

PORK LOIN WITH PARMA HAM & OREGANO

ONE DAY I WOULD LOVE TO learn a bit of butchery, but in the meantime I am more than happy, grateful even, to defer to the experts. That's to say, I ask my butcher for a loin of pork, requesting that, once boned and with the rind off, it weigh around 3 pounds, and then I throw in that I want it opened out "like a book," as I want to stuff it and roll it up.

Sometimes, I have to take a knife to it myself just to open up one end part, if I feel there is an uneven chunkiness. I am not going for professional uniformity, but I need a slab of meat with room to have some thin slices of ham lining the inside and that can then be rolled into a log and tied. Probably it's better I don't try to explain any more here. You'll see the end result in the picture opposite.

It's certainly a simple recipe to do. And that's why it's here, despite the fact that it needs about 1¼ hours to cook. The thing about this is that it is quick to stuff and roll and then you've got nothing to do, which means it is perfect for keeping you calm and your guests contented when you have people over for dinner.

Furthermore, the end result provides a gravy that more or less makes itself. The onions, which are sliced to provide a podium for the pork—a flavor platform—drip their juices into the pan as the meat roasts, and from the meat, too, come the intense drips of Parma ham, oregano, and garlic. As the meat rests, I throw vermouth and hot water into the pan, and because vermouth (unlike wine) doesn't need mellowing out, you can at this stage just walk away and let the liquid do its work without you.

I love to set these flavorsome rounds on a bed of peppery arugula—and I know this suggestion is one you hear often from me. To make life even rosier, may I suggest some plain green beans and Mock Mash (see **p.136**) alongside?

And there's one more thing. You may have noticed that I said the pork loin should be derinded. However, you do still want the rind, or I certainly do. Although cracklings may not be renowned as an Italian delicacy, the *ciccioli* (pronounced, rather enchantingly, "cheecholli")—as Italian pork cracklings (give or take) are known—make for a very fine aperitivo-accompanying morsel (my vote here goes to Prosecco, tinted orange with Aperol). What I like to do, before the pork gets its roasting, is to cook the rind in the oven, preheated (see **p.65**), for 30 minutes on a rack above a pan, then I break up the pieces and put them out on a few saucers, sprinkled with kosher salt, for people to crunch on and keep their dentists in business. Speaking of which, if you've got your pork from the butcher, you should take the bones that have been removed, too, and cook them in the pan with the rolled pork. I like to gnaw on these privately: cook's treat.

Preheat the oven to 400°F. Open up the loin of pork, ready for stuffing, by laying it out in front of you vertically so that the thick part is on the left (I'm right-handed). Now, starting at the top, cut through this thick part of the loin, all the way down, so that you can open it out to the left like a book. This will give you a larger surface area to lay the filling on.

Grate or mince the garlic cloves, and spread the pungent purée all over the meat. Then take the leaves from a few sprigs of oregano and dot them about too; keep the stalks.

Lay the pieces of ham horizontally over the pork loin; this way it will roll up more easily as the roll will follow the long length of the ham slices.

Sprinkle the red pepper flakes over the ham and then roll up the loin, starting from the opened end side, keeping as tight a roll as you can. Secure the meat with string at 1¼- to 1½-inch intervals, knotting the lengths of string firmly. If you're using stationer's string rather than cook's twine, dampen it first. I wish I could instruct you as to how to tie proper knots, but I do very bad knots myself. If you have the offer of a friendly hand—or rather finger—to hold the knot down as you tie it, take it gratefully.

Cut the onion into thick slices without peeling it, and sit them in the bottom of a roasting pan to make the flavor platform for the pork. Add the reserved stalks from the oregano, sit the loin on top and drizzle with the oil.

Cook for 1¼ hours; when it's cooked, the juices must run clear when you put a skewer into the center and a meat thermometer should read 160°F.

Transfer the pan to a heatproof kitchen surface, immediately pour the vermouth and boiling water into the pan, and scrape all around the bottom of the pan so any oniony, meaty stuck-on bits dissolve into this instant gravy. You can let the meat rest in this sauce for 15 minutes or so.

When you are ready to slice the pork, remove it to a board and warm the gravy (removing the onion bits) if it's cooled. Cut the meat into approximately ¾-inch slices; in other words, thick enough for the slices to keep their shape and hold the filling. Discard the string as you go. This size cut should give you 10 good slices plus the misshapen end pieces.

Arrange these sturdy slices on a bed of arugula with the gravy served separately in a little jug, or just sit them on a warm platter and pour over them a little gravy or any extra juices the meat has made. Take some more oregano leaves and strew them over the pork slices before serving. ■

SERVES 6

3 POUNDS BONELESS AND
   RINDLESS LOIN OF PORK
2 FAT CLOVES GARLIC, PEELED
FEW SPRIGS FRESH OREGANO,
   PLUS MORE TO SERVE
4 OUNCES PARMA HAM, THINLY
   SLICED
¼ TEASPOON CRUSHED RED
   PEPPER FLAKES
1 ONION, UNPEELED
2 TABLESPOONS OLIVE OIL
¼ CUP DRY WHITE VERMOUTH
¼ CUP BOILING WATER

VENETIAN STEW

THERE IS AN OLD VENETIAN DISH called, in dialect, *Manai*, that is the inspiration for this. And I emphasize the word "inspiration": *Manai*, which broadly speaking involves polenta with beans, bacon, and local raisins, is the fruitful starting point for my pink-hued stew, with its beans and bacon and radicchio (my innovation, but it does come from Venice), echoing the cinnamon-rose colors of the *palazzi* that line the Grand Canal.

I suspect that the original stew would have used speck (think along the lines of smoked bacon) rather than the unsmoked pancetta, but either will do. If you can, though, do buy a good Italian can of borlotti beans as the juice they come in is usable; the gloop in cheaper supermarket private-label brands can be disconcertingly smelly and frankly unfit for consumption. Still, if the only beans you can find need to be rinsed vigorously, you will have to add more water to make sure the beans are covered as they cook. That in turn will make for a runnier stew, so maybe mash some of the beans at the end just to help thicken it.

I adore this salty stew ladled in bowls over a mounded pile of sweet yellow polenta. Or you could consider the Mock Mash on **p.136**, though some unsalty Italian bread with it is enough for me; either way, this is a pretty well instant, soothing, and substantial supper.

SERVES 2

2 TABLESPOONS RAISINS

½ CUP BOILING WATER

2 TEASPOONS GARLIC-
 FLAVORED OIL

6 OUNCES PANCETTA CUBES
 OR DICED SPECK OR JAMON
 SERRANO

1 ECHALION OR BANANA
 SHALLOT, FINELY CHOPPED

½ TEASPOON GROUND CUMIN

1 X 15-OUNCE CAN BORLOTTI
 BEANS

½ HEAD RADICCHIO (APPROX.
 5 OUNCES), FINELY SHREDDED

FOR THE POLENTA

2¾ CUPS WATER

1 TEASPOON KOSHER SALT OR
 ½ TEASPOON TABLE SALT, OR
 TO TASTE

⅔ CUP INSTANT POLENTA

2 TABLESPOONS GRATED
 PARMESAN

1 TABLESPOON UNSALTED BUTTER

Put the raisins into a cup or bowl and pour the ½ cup boiling water over them.

Put 2¾ cups water in a saucepan for the polenta and set it on to boil.

Heat the garlic-flavored oil in a heavy frying pan of about 11 inches in diameter (that has a lid) and cook the pancetta (or other) cubes for 3–5 minutes, stirring every now and again, then add the chopped shallot and cook for another 3–5 minutes, until the pancetta is bronzed and the shallot soft.

Stir in the cumin (not Italian, but Venice was the hub of the spice trade so I allow its inauthentic addition) then add the raisins with their soaking water and let it bubble up before tipping in the borlotti beans and their liquid (but see introduction above if your bean gloop is unusable).

Bring to a boil, then add the shredded radicchio and, once the stew starts bubbling again, turn off the heat, put on the lid, and get on with the polenta.

Add salt (to taste) to the now bubbling polenta water, then stir in the polenta, pouring it into the pan in a steady but gentle stream, and cook till smooth and thickened. I use more than the usual ratio of water to polenta here, as I want the finished polenta creamy not set. Once it is cooked, take the pan off the heat and beat in the Parmesan and butter, seasoning to taste. Decant into a warmed serving bowl.

Check the bean stew seasoning, then bring it to the table with the golden polenta. ◼

ITALIANS ARE VERY GOOD AT FINDING WAYS of elevating the less costly cuts of meat in their cooking. Although beef pizzaiola emanates from Naples, you'll find it (and, more commonly, veal as well as fish steaks cooked this way) throughout Italy. It's a cheerful, punchy little number, taking its name, as is self-explanatory, from the fact that it tastes rather like a pizza topping. Tomatoes, oregano, and garlic are pretty much always in evidence, with frequent sightings of olives and capers; I like to add anchovies and a sprinkle of crushed red pepper flakes, too.

Originally, cheap slices of meat or fish would have been cooked in the sauce whose acidity would have tenderized tough meat. But although I keep faith with the thrifty origins of the recipe by making 12 ounces of steak feed up to 4 people, I don't buy my meat cheap, and I fry the thin slices of steak first, wrap them in aluminum foil to keep them warm, and then rustle up the sauce in the hot pan. Actually, I have used humanely raised veal escalopes here, and pointedly so. There is such widespread revulsion at the idea of eating veal, but it is crucial to know that humane organizations say it is okay to eat veal, so long as it is humanely raised (and sometimes labeled as "rose veal"); otherwise countless animals are needlessly destroyed. It is time to rethink our prejudices. Lecture over. And whether beef or veal, all in all, this takes about 5 minutes to cook, so even if you're not saving money, you're certainly saving time.

BEEF PIZZAIOLA

Warm the garlic-flavored oil in a non-stick frying pan that will contain all 4 steaks or escalopes snugly; I use one with a diameter of 11 inches.

When the oil is hot, fry the steaks or escalopes over a high heat for 30 seconds a side (for medium-rare, longer if you must), then take the pan off the heat, transfer the steaks to a large piece of aluminum foil and make a loose but tightly sealed package. I don't salt the meat at this stage, as I would do normally, since the oil-cured olives are intensely salty. If using regular pitted olives, add a pinch of salt to each steak.

Put the pan back on the heat and add the anchovy fillets, stirring and squishing them down with a wooden spoon or similar until they start to dissolve into the oil. Stir in the dried oregano and red pepper flakes.

Now tumble in the halved tomatoes along with the olives and capers and the red vermouth, and cook for 2 minutes. Add the water and cook for 1 further minute.

Acting fast, while the sauce is cooking, unwrap the steaks, slice and arrange them on a platter, pouring the juices that have collected in the foil into the pan. Now pour the contents of the pan over and sprinkle with the parsley.

Serve immediately, and if you want to feed 4 rather than 2, I'd simply add more than one side dish, remembering that the piquancy of the sauce already helps it to go further. ∎

SERVES 2–4

1 TABLESPOON GARLIC-FLAVORED OIL

4 THIN-CUT NEW YORK STRIP STEAKS OR HUMANELY RAISED VEAL ESCALOPES (APPROX. 12 OUNCES)

4 ANCHOVY FILLETS

1 TEASPOON DRIED OREGANO

¼ TEASPOON CRUSHED RED PEPPER FLAKES

8 OUNCES CHERRY TOMATOES, HALVED

¼ CUP PITTED BLACK OLIVES, PREFERABLY OIL-CURED

2 TABLESPOONS DRAINED CAPERS

2 TABLESPOONS DRY RED VERMOUTH

2 TABLESPOONS WATER

1 TABLESPOON CHOPPED FRESH PARSLEY, TO SERVE

THE FRENCH AND THE AMERICANS may be proud of their steaks but, for me, the Italians win hands down. Nothing can compare to a *tagliata* (pronounced "tallyata") in its full glory: a vast, juicy, rare steak, big enough for a tableful of people, cut into thin slices (*tagliare* simply means to cut) and served most often over arugula and with some Parmesan shaved on top. I've given recipes for just such a dish before, but it seemed to me that it might be possible to downsize a little, making this a more easily accomplished dish for a midweek meat feast.

That's to say, instead of going to the butcher and asking for a huge hunk of steak cut specially, you can make 1 supermarket strip steak (it still should be good meat, or don't bother) stretch to feed 2 of you with no suggestion of scrimping; and the "marinade" is really a post-cooking dressing, so can happily be used as such. This is fabulously fiery, and the cherry tomatoes somehow serve as both condiment and accompaniment. Of course, you could add potatoes—steamed would be good to stab with a fork and use to soak up the piquant juices, though the Tuscan Fries on **p.138** are the greedy person's obvious choice—but I am happy with nothing more than some bread alongside. My son (whose absolute favorite this is) thinks likewise.

TAGLIATA FOR TWO

SERVES 2

2 TABLESPOONS EXTRA-VIRGIN OLIVE OIL, PLUS SOME FOR OILING

½ TEASPOON CRUSHED RED PEPPER FLAKES

1 TEASPOON DRIED OREGANO

JUST UNDER A TEASPOON KOSHER SALT OR ½ TEASPOON TABLE SALT, OR TO TASTE

2 TEASPOONS RED WINE VINEGAR

1 NEW YORK STRIP STEAK (APPROX. 12 OUNCES)

8 OUNCES CHERRY OR GRAPE TOMATOES, HALVED

FEW SPRIGS FRESH OREGANO, TO SERVE (OPTIONAL)

Heat a grill pan, or cast-iron or heavy non-stick frying pan.

In a small dish that can take the steak snugly later, combine the extra-virgin olive oil, red pepper flakes, dried oregano, salt, and red wine vinegar.

Oil the steak lightly and put it in the hot pan and cook for 2 minutes on each side, then remove it to the dish of spicy marinade and sit the cooked steak for 2 minutes a side in the dish. Your steak will be rare, but that's the way it's meant to be—although if you want to cook it for longer, I won't stop you.

Remove the steeped steak to a board, ready for slicing, and while it sits there, arrange the cherry tomatoes, cut-side down, in the marinade dish. Cut the steak into thin slices on the diagonal and arrange on a serving dish or 2 dinner plates.

Smoosh the tomatoes around in the marinade, then pour them, and the marinade, over the ribbons of meat. Add a few leaves of fresh oregano, if you can get them, and serve immediately. ■

MEATZZA

OF ALL THE RECIPES IN THIS BOOK (and, of course, this statement is made prior to publication) this is the *numero uno* so far, in terms of repeat requests and general all-round joyous reception it gets at home. (I concede that since my on-hand sample demographic is the teenage market, factors are skewed in its favor.) It amuses. But then, a culinary pun, it is intended to amuse: it looks like a pizza, but its base is made out of meatball mixture, moreover a meatball mixture you don't have to roll into balls but can simply press into a pan, rather like a juicy disc of meatloaf, or *polpettone*.

I first came across this idea in the form of Giuliano Hazan's Meat Pie Pizza Style (though mine is a characteristically lazy, simplified version) in his book *Every Night Italian*, but it was the great Ed Victor, consumer of bonnes bouches and producer of bons mots (if you'll forgive my French) who named it Meatzza.

I have been struggling with the problem of conveying this particular pun in Italian, and the best I can come up with (so far) is *polpettizza* but maybe this isn't a particularly Italian joke, anyway. Quite rightly, Italians take their traditions seriously, but I am untroubled and hope they will be, as this is seriously delicious. What's more, I find it more and more helpful in the repertoire as so many children—small children at any rate—seem to be kept on strict wheat-free diets by their parents these days; this is why I've given the option of replacing the bread crumbs with oatmeal, and very well it works, too. All in all, it is just about the perfect children's supper. My own children favor a Meatzza Margherita so I've kept it simple, but of course you could add any other toppings you like.

SERVES 4–6

1 POUND GROUND BEEF

3 TABLESPOONS GRATED PARMESAN

3 TABLESPOONS BREAD CRUMBS OR QUICK-COOKING OATMEAL (NOT INSTANT)

3 TABLESPOONS CHOPPED FRESH PARSLEY

2 EGGS, LIGHTLY BEATEN

1 CLOVE GARLIC, PEELED

SALT AND PEPPER, TO TASTE

BUTTER, FOR GREASING

1 X 14-OUNCE CAN DICED TOMATOES, DRAINED

1 TEASPOON GARLIC-FLAVORED OIL

1 TEASPOON DRIED OREGANO

4 OUNCES FRESH MOZZARELLA (NOT BUFFALO), HALVED THEN SLICED

FEW LEAVES FRESH BASIL

Preheat the oven to 425°F.

In a large bowl, using your hands, combine the beef, Parmesan, bread crumbs or oatmeal, parsley, and eggs. Grate in (or mince and add) the garlic and add some salt and pepper. Do not overwork it, just lightly mix together, or the meat will become compacted and dense.

Butter a shallow, round baking pan of about 11 inches diameter and turn the meat into it, pressing the mixture lightly with your fingers to cover the bottom as if the seasoned ground meat were your pizza crust.

Make sure you've drained as much runny liquid as possible out of your can of diced tomatoes, then mix the tomato with the garlic-flavored oil, oregano, and some salt and pepper, and spread, using a rubber spatula, lightly on top of the meat base. Arrange the mozzarella slices on top, and then put in the oven for 20–25 minutes, by which time the meat should be cooked through and lightly set and the mozzarella melted.

Remove from the oven and let it sit for 5 minutes, then adorn with some basil leaves and bring it to the table before cutting into wedges, like a pizza. ■

THERE IS ALWAYS GREAT JUBILATION IN MY HOUSE when meatballs are on the menu, and with this recipe it is easy to rustle them up in minutes. Instead of making up a meatball mixture with ground meat or meats, Parmesan, garlic, parsley, and egg, I simply squeeze the stuffing out of about a pound of Italian sausages and roll it into cherry-tomato-sized balls. It's not so much that the making process is simplified, it's that this recipe is easier on the shopping and fridge-stocking front. I'm not sure that, now, my children don't prefer this version.

SHORTCUT SAUSAGE MEATBALLS

Squeeze the sausage meat from the sausages and roll small cherry-tomato-sized meatballs out of it, putting them onto a plastic wrap–lined baking sheet as you go. Your final tally should be around 40.

Heat the oil in a large, heavy pan or flameproof Dutch oven and add the meatballs, frying them until golden; as they become firmer, nudge them up in the pan to make room for the rest, if you can't fit them all in at first.

When all the meatballs are in the pan and browned, add the scallions and oregano and stir about gently.

Add the wine or vermouth and diced tomatoes, then fill half of one of the empty cans with cold water and tip it into the other empty can, then into the pan. The can-to-can technique is just my way of making sure you rinse out as much of the tomato residue as possible.

Put in the bay leaves and let the pan come to a fast simmer. Let cook like this, uncovered, for 20 minutes, until the sauce has thickened slightly and the meatballs are cooked through. Check the sauce for seasoning, adding some salt and pepper, if you like.

During this time you can cook whatever you fancy to go with the meatballs, whether it be pasta, rice, whatever.

Once the meatballs are ready, you can eat them immediately or let them stand, off the heat but still on the stove, for 15 minutes. The sauce will thicken up a bit on standing. Should your diners be other than children who balk at green bits, sprinkle with parsley on serving. ■

SERVES 4, *MAKES APPROX. 40 MEATBALLS*

1 POUND HOT OR SWEET ITALIAN SAUSAGES

2 TABLESPOONS GARLIC-FLAVORED OIL

4 FAT OR 6 SPINDLY SCALLIONS, THINLY SLICED

1 TEASPOON DRIED OREGANO

¼ CUP WHITE WINE OR VERMOUTH

2 X 14-OUNCE CANS DICED TOMATOES, PLUS WATER TO RINSE ½ CAN

2 BAY LEAVES

SALT AND PEPPER, TO TASTE

CHOPPED FRESH PARSLEY, TO SERVE (OPTIONAL)

THIS IS ANOTHER RECIPE THAT USES ITALIAN SAUSAGES, and I specify them advisedly; being 100% meat and loosely packed, they cook much faster than other sausage types, which can be more densely woven and fine textured. I've used regular Italian *salsicce* below but, given that this recipe already has a bit of the gangster food air about it (I feel I should be called Knuckles Lawsoni and be packing a piece when I eat it), here might be the place to choose the spicier hot sausages, instead.

Feel free to use whatever canned beans you have in the cupboard; borlotti or cannellini would be just fine, too. Similarly, standard canned tomatoes can replace the cherry tomatoes. Don't be tempted, however, to omit the roasted red peppers. Their flavor—the sweetness and smokiness—is essential.

SAUSAGES WITH BEANS & ROASTED RED PEPPERS

SERVES 4

1 TABLESPOON GARLIC-
  FLAVORED OIL
1 POUND HOT OR SWEET ITALIAN
  SAUSAGES (5–6 IN NUMBER)
¼ CUP DRY RED VERMOUTH
2 X 15-OUNCE CANS BUTTER
  BEANS, DRAINED
1 X 12-OUNCE JAR (APPROX.
  8 OUNCES DRAINED WEIGHT)
  ROASTED RED PEPPERS,
  DRAINED AND SCISSORED INTO
  BITE-SIZED PIECES
1 X 14-OUNCE CAN CHERRY
  TOMATOES IN JUICE
3 BAY LEAVES
SALT AND PEPPER, TO TASTE

Heat the garlic-flavored oil in a shallow, flameproof Dutch oven or heavy saucepan that comes with a lid, and brown the sausages, bearing in mind that Italian sausages do not color hugely.

Take the pan off the heat for a moment, and pour in the red vermouth, then put it back on the heat and let the vermouth bubble up a bit, before adding the drained beans, the drained, snipped peppers, and the can of tomatoes.

Now, take the emptied can of tomatoes and half-fill with water, then throw this in, too, before adding the bay leaves, and salt and pepper to taste.

Bring to a bubble, then turn the heat down to low, clamp on a lid, and let it simmer for 15 minutes, until the sausages are cooked through.

Remove the lid, turn up the heat a bit, and simmer robustly for 5 further minutes, until the sauce has thickened slightly.

Now, take off the heat altogether, then—using tongs, for ease—remove the sausages to a cutting board and cut them into thick slices, on a gentle diagonal if you can. You can leave them whole, but they go further sliced. Return the sausage slices to the pan and dish out from there, *or* ladle the beans into shallow bowls, adding the sliced sausages on top. Either way, serve with hunks of bread for people to *fare la scarpetta*—dunk—as they eat. ■

I AM FULLY EXPECTING A PHONE CALL from the 1980s asking for its menu back, but in my defense this is simple, superfast (to prepare), and sensational (to eat, which is what counts) and I am not suggesting you serve it with kiwi fruit disks or a raspberry vinaigrette.

What I do is slice the cooked monkfish thickly, so it holds its shape, and arrange these chunky medallions (I am keeping period here) on a platter, or couple of plates, lined with rubied radicchio leaves: they make for exquisite bite-sized wraps.

All in all, were you in the market for a romantico little dinner, this would be the recipe I'd steer you toward.

MONKFISH WRAPPED IN ROSEMARY, LEMON & PARMA HAM

Preheat the oven to 425°F.

Scatter the chopped rosemary and the lemon zest onto a cutting board, and then roll the monkfish fillets in the delicate mixture. The dampness of the fish should make everything stick.

Wrap the monkfish fillets with the cat's-tongue-pink prosciutto, rather as if you were putting on a ham bandage, letting the thin pieces overlap a little so that the fish stays covered.

Drizzle the oil in a shallow roasting pan and place the Parma-ham-covered fish in the pan. Roast for 15 minutes or until the fish is just cooked.

Take the pan out of the oven, transfer the fish to a board, and let it rest for 2 or 3 minutes, while you arrange a bed of red leaves on a serving platter (dribbling a little extra-virgin olive oil and squeezing some lemon juice over the salad, if wished). Then carve the fish into chunky diagonal slices, taking care to keep the ham in place around it (this is not as difficult as it sounds), place these on the leaves, and serve immediately. ∎

SERVES 2

2 SPRIGS ROSEMARY, LEAVES
   STRIPPED AND CHOPPED
ZEST ½ UNWAXED LEMON
2 MONKFISH TAIL FILLETS
   (APPROX. 6 OUNCES EACH)
3 OUNCES PARMA HAM OR
   PROSCIUTTO DI SAN DANIELE,
   THINLY SLICED
1 TABLESPOON OLIVE OIL
RADICCHIO OR OTHER RED
   LEAVES, TO SERVE (OPTIONAL)
EXTRA-VIRGIN OLIVE OIL AND
   LEMON JUICE, TO SERVE
   (OPTIONAL)

SQUID & SHRIMP WITH CHILI & MARJORAM

IF I DIDN'T HAVE A SPEEDY SEAFOOD SUPPER in an earlier book (*Kitchen*), that surely would have been the title of this recipe. This is nothing if not a fast feast: I reckon that if you get all the bits and pieces out in front of you, ready to go, you can get this cooked in around 5 minutes. Not that there is a great deal to get ready: 1 chili and a handful of herbs to chop, plus a little light grating of garlic and lemon zest. I buy the shrimp already peeled and the squid cleaned and cut into rings.

Indeed, if you keep a package of shrimp and some squid in your freezer (always advisable) and then stick them in the refrigerator to thaw before you go off to work in the morning, you can be moments away from a really elegant and luscious supper once you get back, which makes this an instant de-stressor in the face of midweek entertaining.

If you want to make this a smaller supper for ordinary, everyday eating (though, tasting like this, it is never quite going to be *ordinary*), you can simply halve the quantities of seafood, or use only the squid or only the shrimp.

If time allows, then I love to serve this along with plain, boiled Italian black rice (see **p.xii**), which I advise for its drama as well as its sauce-soaking capacity. But if you want to stretch the amounts below to feed more people, then cook a package of spaghetti and toss the lemony, chili-flecked, and marjoram-scented seafood through it, making sure you use a little pasta-cooking water to help the sauce emulsify.

In summer, or when ease and speed are major considerations, simply line a platter (with a lip to stop any lemony juices escaping) with arugula.

Marjoram—*maggiorana* in Italian—has a more tender leaf and slightly sweeter scent than the oregano it is related to, but nothing dreadful would happen were you to use oregano instead.

SERVES 4

3 TABLESPOONS OLIVE OIL

1 RED CHILI, SEEDED (IF WISHED) AND FINELY CHOPPED

ZEST AND JUICE 1 UNWAXED LEMON

1 CLOVE GARLIC, PEELED

FINELY CHOPPED LEAVES (APPROX. 3 TABLESPOONS) FROM SMALL BUNCH PARSLEY

FINELY CHOPPED LEAVES (APPROX. 2 TABLESPOONS) FROM SMALL BUNCH MARJORAM

12 OUNCES PREPARED SQUID (THAWED IF FROZEN), SLICED INTO RINGS

20 (APPROX. 12 OUNCES TOTAL) RAW PEELED EXTRA-LARGE SHRIMP (THAWED IF FROZEN)

1 TEASPOON KOSHER SALT OR ½ TEASPOON TABLE SALT, OR TO TASTE

Warm the oil in a wok or similarly wide, capacious pan, then add the chopped chili (with seeds if you like it fiery) and lemon zest, turning them as they sizzle in the hot oil. This is a moment of fragrant joy.

Now grate in the garlic, or mince and add it, along with about a third of the chopped parsley and marjoram, and give a quick stir, before tumbling in the prepared squid and shrimp. Stir-fry in the pan for 2–3 minutes, until the seafood is just cooked through.

Add the juice of half the lemon and most of the remaining herbs and cook, stirring, for another 30 seconds or so. Taste to see if you need any salt or more lemon juice, before turning the seafood out onto a warm platter and scattering it with the last remaining bits of chopped parsley and marjoram. ∎

COD WITH BROCCOLINI & CHILI

THIS STARTED LIFE AS A COZILY TRADITIONAL pasta with broccoli, the sort that I've eaten in people's homes in Italy, but never seen unembellished on a restaurant menu. (That is not for everyone: the broccolini is cooked until beyond tender and, though flavorsome, also—it must be said—an unglamorous, sludgy green.) I do think it's time people got to grips with the Italian way of cooking vegetables—those reared on French traditions would call it overcooking—and embraced this savory softness, but until you do, this recipe is the way to go.

Paired, as it is here, with the cod rather than pasta, the broccolini gets a shorter time in the pan, developing all the depth of flavor *without* the floppiness of texture or drabness of tone. It's also a quick and easy way of making a party out of everyday ingredients: I've given quantities for two people eating, but doing this as part of a midweek supper party menu would work, too.

The broccolini is quite a revelation like this, and I say that as someone who already has a bias toward brassicas. You cook anchovy fillets in oil, melting them into a sauce with chilis and garlic, and then toss in broccolini and let the leggy vegetables cook in scant water and a generous splosh of vermouth. (If you've got a bottle of white wine open, by all means use that, instead.) Because I use the broccolini as a condiment as much as an accompaniment—tumbling it on top of the cooked cod fillets—it doesn't matter if the fish breaks up or flakes too much as you transfer it from pan to plate, making this an altogether very unstressy undertaking. There is a great deal of broccolini—it is broccolini with cod rather than cod with broccolini, really—but that's the way I like it.

Oh, and it doesn't have to be cod: please use any fish that's local and not too delicate. Or by all means revert to the original inspiration, the pasta *con i broccoli*. This is simplicity itself: for two people, cook the broccolini exactly as opposite but for just over twice as long, about 15 minutes, and then use it to dress 6 ounces (you don't need any more) pasta, stirring in an espresso-cupful of pasta-cooking liquid to the soft-stewed broccolini first. I like frilly edged pappardelle torn into short lengths before being cooked, although spaccatelle (think C-shaped, not-quite-completed tubes) are the traditional shape used. With either accompaniment, or indeed alone, broccolini cooked this way is utterly addictive, as I'm sure—I certainly hope—you'll find out.

Last word: anchovy-haters could use 2 slices of bacon, chopped, in their place.

In a wok (or other very wide, deepish pan) that comes with a tightly fitting lid, warm 2 tablespoonfuls of the oil, and then add the anchovy fillets, stirring them over a low heat until they seem to dissolve into the oil.

Grate in the garlic (or mince and add it), add the ¼ teaspoon red pepper flakes, and stir them in the warm oil for about 30 seconds, before adding the broccolini and stirring some more to combine.

Add the vermouth or wine and let it bubble up, then add the water, letting it bubble, too; now clamp on the lid, turn down the heat to its lowest setting, and let it cook slowly for 7 minutes, until the broccolini is tender-crisp (plus 2–3 minutes longer if your broccolini is short and stubby).

Meanwhile, heat the remaining tablespoon of oil in a small frying pan and fry the cod; depending on thickness and on how cold it is before it goes in the pan, it should need 2–3 minutes per side, plus 1–2 minutes' standing time on a warmed platter.

Once the cod and broccolini are ready, season the broccolini to taste then tip it out of its pan on top of the cod pieces on their platter and sprinkle with a pinch more of red pepper flakes or some chopped fresh red chilis for a dot of exuberant color, if wished. I can't but help, once I've got the white of the cod and the green of the broccolini, going for the full *tricolore*. ◼

SERVES 2

3 TABLESPOONS OLIVE OIL

4 ANCHOVY FILLETS

1 CLOVE GARLIC, PEELED

¼ TEASPOON CRUSHED RED PEPPER FLAKES, PLUS MORE TO TASTE

8 OUNCES BROCCOLINI, TRIMMED

¼ CUP DRY WHITE VERMOUTH OR WHITE WINE

¼ CUP WATER, FROM A RECENTLY BOILED KETTLE

2 COD FILLETS (APPROX. 6 OUNCES EACH, NO MORE THAN 1 INCH THICK), PREFERABLY SKINLESS

SALT AND PEPPER, TO TASTE

FRESH RED CHILI, SEEDED AND CHOPPED (OPTIONAL), TO SERVE

WHENEVER I'M IN AN ITALIAN RESTAURANT and see "zucchini fritti" on the menu, I order them. There is something irresistible about those string-thin zucchini fries in their light batter, and I had wanted to give a recipe for them here. But you only have to make a small batch once to see why you'd go to a restaurant to eat them. The Italian practice of frying bite-sized mouthfuls of fish and seafood does, however, lend itself to home appropriation, as long as amounts are modest, so I've borrowed the traditional zucchini fritti batter and used it to provide a filigree coating for sweet-fleshed shrimp and wafer-thin lemon slices—exquisite to eat, and both charming and chic—instead. I can't bear ever to waste even a teaspoonful of batter, so I let any remnants lacily drape over some sage and parsley leaves to scatter on top at the end. The result is simply (and I *mean* simply) Italian tempura.

ITALIAN TEMPURA SHRIMP

SERVES 2 *AS A DINNER, OR MORE AS AN APPETIZER*

⅓ CUP FLOUR

1 TEASPOON OLIVE OIL

APPROX. ¼ CUP WARM WATER, FROM A TAP

1 EGG WHITE (FINE TO USE FROM A CARTON)

APPROX. 1½ QUARTS FLAVORLESS VEGETABLE OIL, FOR FRYING

1 UNWAXED LEMON

15 RAW PEELED EXTRA-LARGE SHRIMP (APPROX. 8 OUNCES TOTAL), PATTED DRY

4–6 SMALL FRESH SAGE LEAVES, NOT BIG TOUGH ONES (OPTIONAL)

FEW SPRIGS FRESH PARSLEY

Whisk the flour and olive oil briefly in a bowl, then start to add your ¼ cup of warm water, pouring in a little at a time, whisking until you have a smooth batter the consistency of heavy cream. You may need more or, indeed, less water to reach this point.

In a separate bowl, whisk the egg white until it is thick and holding its shape (you can do this easily enough by hand with only one egg white). Fold the egg white into the batter, and then refrigerate for about 30 minutes.

When the time's almost up, heat the oil in a smallish saucepan, then halve your lemon lengthwise and cut one of the halves across into wafer-thin slices. Cut the remaining half in two, and add to the serving plate for squeezing over the shrimp (if wished) when eating.

To check the oil is hot enough, drop in a cube of bread and if it sizzles quickly, you're ready to go—that's 350°F, should you want to know. Watch your pan carefully all the time.

Get out another bowl and pour a small amount of batter in it—about 3 tablespoons' worth—then add 4 or 5 shrimp, turning with a small spatula to coat them.

Carefully lower the coated shrimp, one by one, into the hot oil, then fish them out with a perforated spoon as soon as they turn a pale gold (this will take less than 1 minute) and put them straight onto a plate lined with paper towel. Since I've specified an odd number of shrimp, you could let the first one cool slightly and cut it to check it's cooked through.

Continue with all your shrimp, decanting a little batter into the separate bowl to coat each batch. Do the same with the lemon slices, although they will take only a few seconds to cook.

Then quickly dredge the herbs, first the sage (if you have the small leaves) and then the parsley, in the batter and fry these. They'll crisp up pretty much at once, so remove them fast and take the pan off the heat.

Tumble all the tempura-coated shrimp and lemons onto a warmed platter, sprinkle the batter-crisped herbs on top, and serve instantly. ∎

I WAS READING THE COMMUNITY RECIPES on my website one evening, when I came across one for Tuscan Steak Tartare. I liked the sound of it, but I knew that it would not be something I'd make at home. It's entirely illogical, to the point of nonsensical, but, for some counterintuitive reason, I feel more comfortable doing raw meat in a restaurant. Equally illogically, I don't feel the same way about fish, and that is how my Tuscan Tuna Tartare came into being.

I have a proviso: I have to get the fish from a fishmonger, not the supermarket. Moreover, I do inform him first that I will be eating it raw, and thus require sashimi-grade tuna. I find it easier if the tuna comes in slices about ½ inch thick, but this is not imperative. What *is* crucial is that when you chop it, you *really* chop it, whether it be with a knife or a mezzaluna: *never, ever* grind it or put it in a processor.

For me, this is the perfect summer supper with a girlfriend. I'm thinking crisp, cold white wine or rosé first (and during), then toasted bread, be it hearty farmhouse slices or small white-toast triangles, with. I really, really love this, though, with some searingly hot Tuscan Fries (see **p.138**) but then of course it's no longer a no-cook supper. To end, some perfect white peaches. Or, if you insist, the Licorice Pudding on **p.152**. What happiness just the idea of all this brings.

TUSCAN TUNA TARTARE

Arrange the arugula on 2 dinner plates or a serving platter, like a messy wreath, with some of the leaves falling into the center, too.

Using a sharp knife, cut the tuna into small chunks and then (with a mezzaluna, if you have one), chop it finely.

While the tuna is still on the cutting board, zest the lemon over it and add the sliced scallions, capers, salt, and a good coarse grinding of pepper. Mix gently and briefly with your hands, and then carry it over to the center of the waiting plate(s) in a messy heap.

Drizzle the olive oil over the arugula and the tuna, and squeeze half the lemon over the circling frame of arugula. Don't spritz the tuna yet or it will whiten. Cut the remaining piece of lemon in half so that each person can have a wedge to squeeze over their tuna as they eat. ■

SERVES 2

2 CUPS WILD ARUGULA (PACKED)
12 OUNCES RAW SASHIMI-
  QUALITY TUNA
1 UNWAXED LEMON
1 FAT OR 2 THIN SCALLIONS,
  THINLY SLICED (CUT FAT
  SCALLION LENGTHWISE FIRST)
2 TABLESPOONS DRAINED
  CAPERS
1 TEASPOON KOSHER SALT OR
  ½ TEASPOON TABLE SALT,
  OR TO TASTE
GROUND PEPPER
2 TABLESPOONS EXTRA-VIRGIN
  OLIVE OIL

EVERYBODY LOVES A "TRAY BAKE." It's not just the ease—though I admit that's a great part of it—but how cooking everything together makes the flavors juicily commingle. There are no official writings on tray bakes in Italy, or none that I am aware of, but one-pot cooking is as old as the Tuscan hills, so this recipe makes perfect sense to me and to everyone (Italians included) who has eaten it.

It is "Italian" in its flavorings—the rosemary and lemon that waft gorgeously through the house as you cook—and in deference to the Italian sausages I use in it. You can go for the milder sausages, sold as "sweet," or the chilified hot sausages, as you please. If you would prefer to use a whole chicken, butchered into portions, rather than just the thighs, I'd go along with that, too. What I wouldn't recommend here is boneless chicken, especially not breast fillets.

So that's the chicken and the sausages. What I need to tell you most urgently though is that the potato chunks soak up the meaty, lemony juices as they cook. So set your mind not to expect crunchy roasted potatoes, but rather soft-soused chunks, scorched crisp at the corners.

I use a large, shallow roasting pan, in which everything below fits. It's a tight fit, but nothing suffers. Otherwise, use 2 quarter-sheet pans; it's important that they be low sided, as a deep pan will stop the meat and potatoes from browning desirably. This is not just an aesthetic consideration; it will have an impact on texture, too.

For all that there are potatoes included, I do like this with bread. I also like lentils alongside (but only if there's no bread on the table) and if that appeals to you, too, check out the recipe on **p.128**. And for an instant accompaniment, consider a couple of jars of roasted red peppers, drained and dressed with good olive oil, red wine vinegar, and parsley. *Buon appetito!*

ITALIAN TRAY BAKE

SERVES 4–6 ◊

3 LARGE YUKON GOLD POTATOES (APPROX. 1¾ POUNDS TOTAL), UNPEELED AND CUT INTO 1-INCH CHUNKS

8 CHICKEN THIGHS, BONE IN AND SKIN ON

8 ITALIAN SAUSAGES (APPROX. 1¾ POUNDS TOTAL)

▶

Preheat the oven to 425°F.

Put the potatoes into a sheet pan or large, shallow roasting pan and add the chicken thighs and sausages. If using 2 pans, divide everything between them (and also swap the pans over and turn them round halfway through cooking time).

Arrange about 4 sprigs of the rosemary among the chicken and sausages, then finely chop the needles of another 2 sprigs, to give you about 2 teaspoons of finely chopped needles, and sprinkle these onto the chicken pieces.

Zest the lemon over everything, and season with the salt and a good grinding of pepper. Drizzle with the oil and bake for 50–60 minutes, or until the chicken skin and sausages are golden and the potato pieces are cooked through. It's fine to let all of this stand for up to 30 minutes once cooked, prior to serving. ■

SMALL BUNCH (6 OR 7 SPRIGS)
  FRESH ROSEMARY
ZEST 1 UNWAXED LEMON
1 TEASPOON KOSHER SALT OR
  ½ TEASPOON TABLE SALT
GROUND PEPPER
¼ CUP OLIVE OIL

I LOVE THE ITALIAN "POLLO AL MATTONE" (which means "chicken cooked with a brick"), and although I am given to believe it is Italo-American rather than old-country authentic, I have been recently admonished and told it is in fact a dish that originates with the Etruscans. Hmm. Does it matter? It is a glorious creation: salty, lemony, and either fiercely peppery or afire with crushed red pepper flakes.

The particular pollo al mattone I love dearly is the incredibly tender, melting-fleshed, super-lemony, and thyme-scented version served at Sfoglia, in New York. Inspired by a recent visit, I knew I had to make it my own, and this is what I'm now giving you. In a domestic oven, I feel this works best, with 2 Cornish hens rather than one chicken, which makes it not quite chicken under a brick, but you get the gist. This is not an instant recipe by any means, but it is a very simple one. It is certainly streamlined from the original, if that counts. And even if it doesn't, I wouldn't feel happy keeping it from you.

CHICKEN UNDER A BRICK

SERVES 2

2 CORNISH HENS

ZEST AND JUICE 2 UNWAXED
    LEMONS

8 SPRIGS THYME

1 TEASPOON KOSHER SALT OR
    ½ TEASPOON TABLE SALT, OR
    TO TASTE

½ TEASPOON COARSELY
    GROUND PEPPER OR CRUSHED
    RED PEPPER FLAKES

¼ CUP OLIVE OIL

2 CLOVES GARLIC, PEELED

2 ALUMINUM FOIL-COVERED
    BUILDERS' BRICKS

Cut along the backbone of each Cornish hen to open them out flat: you can do this with a pair of strong kitchen scissors.

Zest and juice the lemons into a large resealable bag, then pull off the thyme leaves, dropping them in too.

Sprinkle in the salt and either grind in the pepper or shake in the red pepper flakes, then pour the oil into the bag, and, finally, grate in (or mince and add) the garlic.

Add the spatchcocked Cornish hens, then seal the bag before squidging the marinade all over the flattened birds as efficiently (and agreeably) as you can. Put the bag of birds on a dish and pop it into the refrigerator and leave for a day or overnight.

When you are ready to cook the Cornish hens, preheat the oven to 400°F, and let them come to room temperature.

Heat a grill pan or roasting pan that can go into the oven and on the stovetop. Then take the birds out of the marinade (reserving it for later) and place them skin-side down on the grill pan or in the roasting pan.

Place the bricks on top of the birds and let them cook over a moderate heat for 5 minutes.

Immediately place the Cornish hens in the oven, bricks still on top, and cook for 15 minutes.

Take the pan out of the oven and, wearing oven mitts, carefully remove the bricks before turning the Cornish hens over. Pour the reserved marinade over the flattened birds, then put the bricks back on top and roast in the oven for another 15 minutes, until the juices run clear.

Take the Cornish hens out of the oven, carefully remove the hot bricks, then carve each bird into 4 pieces, drizzling with any intense pan juices. Bread and a green salad is all I need on the side. ∎

ON THE WHOLE, I'D DESCRIBE MY ITALIAN TASTES as having more of a northern than southern affiliation; it's the non-Mediterranean Italy that has always lured me, not least at the table.

Having said that—and maybe it's the mellowness of age—I seem to be warming to the sunnier approach, cheerfully cooking with tomatoes and roasted red peppers and finding myself unfamiliarly delighted with the result. This stew says it all, really: it has spirit-lifting southern gusto, and the rich sweetness of the roasted red peppers (a kitchen cupboard must-have for me) keeps the acidity of the tomatoes in check.

If I make this for my children for supper, I most often serve it with a bowlful of orzo pasta (see right); when it's for me, though, some wilted spinach and gorgeous bread are the only accompaniments I require.

CHICKEN WITH TOMATOES & PEPPERS

Pour the oil into a small, flameproof Dutch oven or heavy-based pan—I use my old enameled cast-iron one with an 8-inch diameter—and cook the chopped shallot, stirring frequently, until soft: this should take about 3 minutes; an onion may take longer.

Add the chicken pieces along with the dried oregano and turn them in the hot pan. Add the Marsala and watch it bubble up, then promptly add the canned tomatoes and the salt.

Half-fill the empty tomato can with water and pour it into the pan, rinsing out as much of the tomato residue as you can.

Drain the roasted red peppers and snip with scissors—for ease—into bite-sized pieces and add to the pan, then bring to a boil before turning down the heat and letting cook at a steady simmer, uncovered, for 20 minutes until the sauce has thickened slightly and the chicken is cooked through. Decant into a bowl, or bowls, or just leave in the pan, if you prefer, and serve. ■

SERVES 3–4

1 TABLESPOON GARLIC-FLAVORED OIL

1 ECHALION OR BANANA SHALLOT, OR 1 SMALL ONION, PEELED AND FINELY CHOPPED

1 POUND SKINLESS, BONELESS CHICKEN THIGHS, CUT INTO BITE-SIZED PIECES

1 TEASPOON DRIED OREGANO

2 TABLESPOONS MARSALA

1 X 14-OUNCE CAN DICED TOMATOES, PLUS WATER TO RINSE OUT CAN

1 TEASPOON KOSHER SALT OR ½ TEASPOON TABLE SALT, OR TO TASTE

1 X 12-OUNCE JAR (APPROX. 8 OUNCES DRAINED WEIGHT) ROASTED RED PEPPERS

CHICKEN WITH TARRAGON SALSA VERDE

TARRAGON, THE GORGEOUSLY NAMED "DRAGONCELLO," is actually little used in Italy, despite the country's immoderate passion for all things anise. You find tarragon used only here and there, mainly in Tuscany; indeed, it is sometimes referred to as *erba di Siena*, the herb of Siena.

Its chief appearance in those parts is in the *salsa al dragoncello*, where the herb is pounded with bread crumbs and garlic and then emulsified with olive oil to produce a fragrant sauce customarily served with plain boiled meats. To be honest, I'm not sure I had that in mind when I first made this: all I wanted was to create a version of that fabulously spiky Italian green sauce, tweaked to suit chicken, which for me (and I hope this display of frankly French influence is forgiven in Italy) means tarragon.

Even though I've always been open about my preference for thigh meat (tastes more and costs less), I specifically need the tender delicacy of the breast meat here. I find that organic corn-fed breast cutlets, with the skin still on, make for the most succulent slices later.

There are many good ways to eat this. Obviously hot—or after 10 minutes' post-roasting rest—is the first port of call (with some green beans or a crisp salad and either baked potatoes or steamed baby ones), but in summer I am happy to let the chicken cool to room temperature, or somewhere hovering around it (covered and out of the sun, for up to 45 minutes), before slicing them and blitzing up the sauce. And any slices that are left over can, with the sauce and some cooked, drained, and cooled fusilli, be turned into a strangely compelling (not terribly Italian) pasta salad.

I always feel slightly silly giving exact measures for herbs, but I do so to give guidance. Generally a small bunch of fresh herbs yields about a cupful of leaves (loosely packed). It's really all about proportions though: the amount of tarragon in the sauce should be a quarter of the amount of parsley. It may seem odd to pick out the smaller quantity of the herb as the defining feature of this sauce, but a little tarragon goes a long way. Use too much and a slightly musty farmyard scent is evoked; pitched perfectly, as here, and you get a fragrant herbal hit, at once light and refreshing and warmly mellow.

Preheat the oven to 425°F.

Pour 1 tablespoon of the oil into a shallow ovenproof dish or roasting pan in which the chicken breast cutlets will fit snugly and then arrange them in there skin-side up. Tuck 2 sprigs of tarragon in between the chicken pieces, add a good grinding of pepper and dribble another tablespoon of oil over them, then pop them in the oven for 20–30 minutes, or until the skins are golden and the flesh tender.

Take out of the oven, and let the cooked chicken stand for 5–10 minutes in the pan while you prepare the sauce.

Put the parsley and tarragon leaves, along with the scallions, lemon zest, salt, and 3 tablespoons olive oil, into a suitable receptacle and, using an immersion blender, whizz to a paste, adding the lemon juice and remaining 3 tablespoons olive oil slowly as you blend. Leave for a mo, while you slice the chicken.

Cut the chicken into thickish—½ inch or so—slices (if you need it to go further, then slice more thinly) and arrange on a platter.

Pour any juices that have collected in the pan into the tarragon salsa and whizz again with your immersion blender, tasting for seasoning before dribbling the sauce over the tender sliced chicken. ■

SERVES 6–8
FOR THE CHICKEN
2 TABLESPOONS OLIVE OIL
4 CHICKEN BREAST CUTLETS
   (PREFERABLY ORGANIC AND
   CORN-FED), WITH SKIN ON
SMALL BUNCH FRESH TARRAGON
   (2 SPRIGS FOR CHICKEN PLUS
   MORE LEAVES FOR SAUCE)
PEPPER (PREFERABLY WHITE
   COARSELY GROUND), TO TASTE

FOR THE SAUCE
LEAVES FROM SMALL BUNCH
   FRESH PARSLEY (PACKED)
   (APPROX. 1 CUP)
LEAVES FROM SPRIGS FRESH
   TARRAGON (PACKED)
   (APPROX. ¼ CUP)
1 SCALLION (INCLUDING GREEN
   PART), ROUGHLY CHOPPED
ZEST 1 UNWAXED LEMON AND
   JUICE ½ LEMON
1 TEASPOON KOSHER SALT OR
   ½ TEASPOON TABLE SALT, OR
   TO TASTE
⅓ CUP OLIVE OIL

A ROAST CHICKEN ALWAYS FEELS CELEBRATORY; indeed, a roast chicken always *is* celebratory. The vibrantly colored and intensely flavored vegetables that are cooked alongside here seem only to underline this, offering their own brightness and brio, sunny in taste as well as mood.

If you had a really huge roasting pan—and a really huge oven to put it in—you could happily double the amount of vegetables; as it is, think of the soft tangle of leeks and bell peppers, punctuated by the salty olives, more as an accompanying sauce. The chicken will feed 4, and could stretch to 6 but that will give you only a spoonful of the vegetables each. I add a crisp green salad and a Pugliese loaf, or any other good bread I can use to soak up the scant but flavorsome vegetables and their juices. My children like some simply cooked soup pasta—orzo or miniature bow ties—dressed in a little butter or olive oil and served alongside, as well.

ITALIAN ROAST CHICKEN WITH BELL PEPPERS & OLIVES

SERVES 4-6

1 CHICKEN (APPROX. 3 POUNDS, OR SLIGHTLY MORE), PREFERABLY ORGANIC AND CORN-FED
1 UNWAXED LEMON, CUT IN HALF
4 SPRIGS ROSEMARY
3 LEEKS, WASHED AND TRIMMED
2 RED BELL PEPPERS
1 ORANGE BELL PEPPER
1 YELLOW BELL PEPPER
⅔ CUP PITTED OIL-CURED BLACK OLIVES
¼ CUP OLIVE OIL
KOSHER SALT AND PEPPER, TO TASTE

Preheat the oven to 400°F. Untruss the chicken, sit it in a roasting pan, and put the lemon halves and 2 of the rosemary sprigs into the chicken's cavity.

Cut each leek into 3 logs, then slice lengthwise and add to the pan. Now, remove the core and seeds of the bell peppers and slice them into strips, following their natural curves and ridges, and add these to the pan.

Tumble in the olives, and now pour the olive oil, mostly over the vegetables but a little over the chicken, too. Add the remaining rosemary sprigs to the vegetables, along with some salt and freshly ground pepper, to taste, and, using a couple of spoons or spatulas, gently toss the vegetables about to help coat them with the oil and make sure everything's well mixed up.

Sprinkle some salt over the chicken and put it in the oven for about 1-1¼ hours, by which time the chicken should be cooked through, and its juices running clear when you cut into the flesh with a small sharp knife at the thickest part of the thigh joint. The vegetables should be tender by now, too, and some of the leeks will be a scorched light brown in parts.

Remove the chicken to a cutting board and, while it rests (for about 10 minutes), pop the pan of veggies back in the oven, switching the oven off as you do so.

Cut the chicken up chunkily, transferring the pieces to a large warmed platter. Now take the pan back out of the oven and, with a slotted spoon or spatula, remove the vegetables to the large platter and when all is arranged to your aesthetic delight, pour over it all the bronze, highly flavored juices that have collected in the pan. ∎

VEGETABLES & SIDES

I REMEMBER, WHEN I WAS IN the south of Italy, eating eggplant that had been roughly chopped, sprinkled with dried wild oregano, doused with olive oil, and then roasted with a little garlic and a lot of red onions. Indeed, a friend of mine from Campania says this is the way her mother always cooks eggplants, sometimes throwing chopped potatoes into the oven pan at the same time.

This, below, is my version: quicker, yes, but I also like the way it can be eaten as an appetizer or part of an antipasti table, and even as an entrée course, sprinkled with some ricotta salata (the deliciously salted, semi-dried kind) or crumbled feta, or as an accompaniment to meat and fish. If you are adding cheese, then sprinkle it over before topping with the onions, which are turned a glorious, luminescent puce by their red-wine vinegar marinade (an old and favorite trick of mine).

BABY EGGPLANT WITH OREGANO & RED ONION

SERVES 6, *AS A SIDE DISH*
1¼ POUNDS BABY EGGPLANT
3 TABLESPOONS REGULAR
   OLIVE OIL
2 TEASPOONS DRIED OREGANO
1 SMALL RED ONION, CUT INTO
   THIN HALF-MOONS
3 TABLESPOONS RED WINE
   VINEGAR
1 TEASPOON KOSHER SALT OR
   ½ TEASPOON TABLE SALT, OR
   TO TASTE
¼ CUP EXTRA-VIRGIN OLIVE OIL
1 CLOVE GARLIC, PEELED
1½ TABLESPOONS COLD WATER
FEW SPRIGS FRESH OREGANO
   (OPTIONAL)

Preheat the oven to 475°F.

Slice the baby eggplants in half lengthwise, keeping the stalks on; this is an aesthetic consideration, nothing to do with flavor, but humor me.

Pour the 3 tablespoons regular olive oil into a very shallow roasting pan, sprinkle in the dried oregano, add the eggplants, cut-side down, and swirl them gently around. Then turn them so they are cut-side up and put the pan in the hot oven for 15 minutes, by which time they should be tender and turning gold in parts.

As soon as the eggplants are in the oven, put the fine half-moons of red onion in a bowl and cover with the red wine vinegar and salt.

Remove the cooked eggplants to a platter, and now whisk into the vinegary onions the extra-virgin olive oil, then grate in (or mince and add) the garlic and, finally, whisk in the cold water.

Pour this over the warm eggplants, using your hands to arrange the glowingly pink onion over them evenly, then leave it all for about half an hour to cool to room temperature before you eat, scattering with fresh oregano, if you have any, when serving. ■

I CAN FEEL SLIGHTLY SELF-CONSCIOUS fiddling about with traditional pesto recipes, when in its authentic original it is surely unbeatable. But having had such uplifting results with—admittedly still traditional—Sicilian variants (see, in particular, **p.2**), I decided that the uninhibited approach had something going for it—hence the substitution of pistachios for pine nuts in the pesto here. And, frankly, this was born to go with the green beans: it's a riot of verdigloriousness!

It's up to you whether you go with this, or revert to the standard model. I should tell you that when I make this for my only slightly picky children, I leave the nuts out altogether. And perhaps I shouldn't be telling you, but if you use a couple of spoonfuls of store-bought pesto, instead—so long as it's made fresh in an Italian deli—it's not the end of the world. There is no good argument, really, for not making this, however. It is just so easy—providing you have a simple, inexpensive immersion blender—and gives your everyday vegetables a bit of dinner-party dash.

GREEN BEANS WITH PISTACHIO PESTO

Put a saucepan of water on for the beans, adding salt when it starts to boil.

To make the pesto, put the pistachios, Parmesan, basil, and olive oil in a small bowl. Grate in (or mince and add) a little bit of the garlic—about a quarter of a clove—throwing the remaining piece of garlic into the bean water. Using an immersion blender, blitz the pesto ingredients to a thick green paste.

Cook the beans to taste (check after 4 minutes), and, before draining, spoon a little of the cooking water (1 or 2 tablespoons is all you need) into the pesto bowl and blitz quickly to mix again with your immersion blender.

Drain the beans (discarding the rogue garlic clove), and toss them in the bowl with the pesto, then transfer to a serving bowl, and take them fragrantly to the table. ■

SERVES 6–8, *AS A SIDE DISH*

1½ POUNDS TRIMMED GREEN BEANS, CUT IN HALF OR INTO SHORT LENGTHS

1 TEASPOON KOSHER SALT OR ½ TEASPOON TABLE SALT, OR TO TASTE

3 TABLESPOONS SHELLED, UNSALTED PISTACHIOS

3 TABLESPOONS GRATED PARMESAN

LEAVES FROM SMALL BUNCH FRESH BASIL (APPROX. 1 CUP, PACKED)

3 TABLESPOONS EXTRA-VIRGIN OLIVE OIL

1 CLOVE GARLIC, PEELED

WHERE DO I START WITH THIS? You can see at a glance that it is extraordinarily simple, but the full-on flavors have a gratifying complexity that is not reflected in either the length of the ingredients list or the time and technique needed to make it. Moreover, it easily lends itself to being turned into a sauce for pasta (in which case, consider adding some shredded or diced mozzarella) or for meat and also fish.

My own preferences are markedly—as ever—for the less than ubiquitous oil-cured pitted olives, but you could use any pitted (or unpitted, for that matter, if your guests are forewarned) black olives you wanted. I also feel the floral scent of the pink vermouth is the best balance for the acid tang of the tomatoes, but am not troubled unduly by the idea of your using either red or white vermouth in its place.

And have I said, by the way, how great this is, eaten alone, not to accompany anything, but just with a hunk or three of bread to dunk in it, too?

CHERRY TOMATOES WITH OLIVES

SERVES 4–6, *AS A SIDE DISH* Ⓝ

3 TABLESPOONS GARLIC-
FLAVORED OIL

2 TEASPOONS FINELY CHOPPED
FRESH ROSEMARY

1 POUND CHERRY OR GRAPE
TOMATOES, HALVED

¼ CUP MARTINI OR CINZANO
ROSATO

⅓ CUP OIL-CURED PITTED BLACK
OLIVES

3 TABLESPOONS CHOPPED
FRESH PARSLEY

SALT AND PEPPER, TO TASTE

Put the garlic-flavored oil and chopped rosemary into a thick-bottomed, non-stick wok—or wide, heavy pan—that comes with a lid, and put it on a low to medium heat to warm up, letting the rosemary sizzle fragrantly in the oil for 30 seconds.

Add the halved cherry tomatoes and cook, stirring gently, for about 1½ minutes, by which time the tomatoes will start softening and oozing their viscous juices.

Add the pink vermouth and bring to a bubble, then clamp on a lid and let it cook away for a further minute.

Remove the lid, stir in the olives, and let it bubble uncovered for another minute, letting the juices reduce a little. Stir in most of the parsley and season to taste, then pour into a warmed serving dish, leaving it to stand for 10 minutes if you can, as the juices will thicken and the flavors mellow.

Sprinkle with the remaining parsley and serve. ∎

PEAS WITH PANCETTA

I LOVE THE WAY ITALIANS COOK PEAS; indeed I love the way they cook all their *verdura*. Sometimes I think that the Anglo tendency to champion crunchy vegetables (often on the challenging side of *al dente*), is a form of subconscious overcompensation for the shamefully suppressed British past of under-seasoned and over-cooked greens—the Waterlogged Cabbage Era. Now, these peas are not cooked for an unreasonably long time, but just long enough—around 20 minutes—for them to soften and sweeten; and if their vibrant green has left them by the time they're ready to eat, know that the vividness of taste more than makes up for any drabness of tone.

If you're cooking for vegetarians, or don't want to include the pancetta for any number of reasons, that's fine, too; but in that case I would add another chopped shallot and—without the flavorful fat so generously yielded by the pancetta—also another couple of tablespoons of garlic-flavored oil at the beginning, as well as adding some vegetable bouillon powder, or similar, to the water later.

And about that: I know it does seem there is very little liquid for a great deal of peas. That's on purpose: the peas are braised in the scant liquid (remember that as they thaw, they give up more of their own, too) and not drained at the end, but rather served in their intense savory syrup. The trick is to use a pan that you think will be too small. I bring out one of my favorite eBay buys—an old 8-inch Le Creuset Dutch oven—and squish everything in. If you do use a larger pan, then you may need more water, but do not add any more than just enough to cover the peas.

Leftovers can be simply recycled as they are (transfer to an airtight container, cool as quickly as possible, cover, and refrigerate for up to 2 days), and reheated gently in a pan; or, if you have only a little left, as a sauce for pasta—penne, tagliatelle, whatever you feel like—with or without the addition of cream; if you have a fair amount left, then add water, bring to a boil, and cook some soup pasta, such as ditalini, in the pea and pancetta broth until soft, then let it stand, off the heat, for 5–10 minutes before serving.

The mint is an English touch, to be sure, but then—as the great 21st-century philosopher Lady Gaga, has it—"Baby, I was born this way."

Warm the garlic-flavored oil over a medium heat in a smallish, heavy saucepan or flameproof Dutch oven (see introduction, left) that comes with a lid, and fry the pancetta—stirring every now and again—until it is nearly, but not quite, crisp (about 5 minutes).

Add the chopped shallot and cook for another 2 minutes or so, stirring, until the pancetta cubes are crisp and the shallot soft. Stir in the dried mint.

Tip in the frozen peas and turn them in the pan a little (if you're using the requisite small pan you won't be able to do much more than nudge them with your wooden spoon) then, after a couple of minutes or so, when the frozen look has left the peas a bit, turn up the heat, slosh in the vermouth or wine, and when you hear it begin to bubble, pour in the water to cover the peas.

Bring to a boil, then turn down the heat to low, cover, and simmer for 15 minutes.

Remove the lid, turn up the heat, and let it bubble away for 5 minutes, so that the sweet and salty juices reduce and thicken a little.

Remove from the heat, and—if time and patience permit—let the peas stand, with the lid still off, for 15 minutes before serving. At which time, stir in most of the chopped fresh mint and parsley and then sprinkle the little remaining quantity over the top. I often put out a perforated spoon as well as a regular serving spoon so that those who want the sweet, sticky gravy can have it, and those who don't can let it drain back into the pan as they help themselves. ■

SERVES 6–8, *AS A SIDE DISH* Ⓝ

1 TABLESPOON GARLIC-FLAVORED OIL

8 OUNCES CUBED PANCETTA

1 ECHALION OR BANANA SHALLOT, PEELED AND FINELY CHOPPED

1 TEASPOON DRIED MINT

6¼ CUPS FROZEN PEAS, UNTHAWED

5 TABLESPOONS DRY WHITE VERMOUTH OR WHITE WINE

2 CUPS WATER (OR JUST ENOUGH TO COVER THE PEAS)

2 TABLESPOONS CHOPPED FRESH MINT

2 TABLESPOONS CHOPPED FRESH PARSLEY

IN THE NORTH OF ITALY, you will often find sage-scented squash tossed over pasta, and I often do the same myself. Here, I'm happy enough to enjoy the squash solo.

I eat this two ways: the first pretty well as is, as a substantial and goldenly glowing vegetable course; but if I have no room in the oven while the entrée is roasting, I cook this first, leave it in the pan, and then, on serving, transfer it to an arugula-lined platter and add a dribble or two of extra-virgin olive oil along with the lemon and pine nuts. I've always got time and the taste for an *insalata tiepida,* or warm salad.

To bolster it into an entrée course you can go any number of ways but, most commonly, I either toss the hot roasted butternut with some lentils (see the recipe on **p.128**) and then sprinkle with sage, but leave out the pine nuts; or I add small dabs of Gorgonzola all over the warm salad of arugula and butternut before sprinkling it with the toasted pine nuts.

ROAST BUTTERNUT WITH SAGE & PINE NUTS

Preheat the oven to 425°F.

Don't peel, but halve and seed the butternut and cut into large, fork-sized pieces, about 1½-inch wedges.

Drizzle the oil into a shallow roasting pan and arrange the pieces in the pan, skin-side down.

Tear the leaves off 2 of the sprigs of sage and arrange them around the butternut chunks. Bake in the oven for about 40 minutes, or until the butternut is tender and cooked through.

Heat a small frying pan, pop in the pine nuts, and shake them about for a couple of minutes until golden and toasted, and don't leave the pan till they're done.

Transfer the baked butternut to a platter or shallow bowl. Squeeze the lemon juice over it, sprinkle with salt and pepper to taste, and scatter with the toasted pine nuts.

Finally, tear off the leaves from the remaining sprig of sage to decorate, and serve. ∎

SERVES 4–6, *AS A SIDE DISH*
1 LARGE BUTTERNUT SQUASH
  (APPROX. 2¼ POUNDS)
2 TABLESPOONS OLIVE OIL
3 SPRIGS FRESH SAGE
3 TABLESPOONS PINE NUTS
JUICE ½ LEMON
KOSHER SALT AND PEPPER,
  TO TASTE

BRAISED FAVA BEANS, PEAS & ARTICHOKES WITH THYME & MINT

THE INSPIRATION FOR THIS IS STRAIGHTFORWARD: what we have here is simply the lazy person's *vignarola*. *La vignarola*—for some reason often called *vignole* in British and American restaurant versions—is the soft, sweetly fragrant Roman spring stew of young fava beans, peas, and violet-tipped artichokes; truly, it's a beautiful thing. It's also, made traditionally—properly, you could say—enormously labor intensive. I don't, however, feel ashamed of this streamlined, shortcut, out-of-a-package version. No, I exult in it. Besides, if you're in Rome in April (and it's worth it to eat this in seasonal *situ*) you'll see small bags of shelled peas, shelled fava beans, and prepared artichokes for sale in all the markets. I just happen to keep my little bags of the above in the freezer.

I do, nonetheless, like to buy the herbs fresh. I have made it with dried mint and thyme (bolstered with some fresh parsley) but, for best results, use fresh mint, fresh thyme: they make the stew really sing for your supper.

Traditionally, *guanciale* or pancetta would be among the ingredients but, although as a general rule I believe—as one of my favorite book titles has it—*Everything Tastes Better with Bacon*, here I prefer not to go the whole hog.

A couple of notes about the holy trinity of vegetables used here: I buy frozen artichoke bottoms (not to be confused with artichoke hearts) from Middle Eastern stores and stash them (along with the baby fava beans and the peas) in the freezer so that I can always make this without notice; but you can equally well use those that come in jars in oil (drained). The weight I give is because of the package size I use, so don't be constrained by it. And I know I said this is a lazy take, but I do like my fava beans skinned. This is not hard work, and rather satisfying: you thaw the beans, then it's the work of moments to squish them so that the vivid green beans shoot out, free of their tough outer casing. You don't have to follow suit.

I often make this in advance, but only slightly, preferring to eat it a few beats above room temperature. But if you preferred, you could make it a couple of days in advance and reheat it gently later (see Notes on **p.264**).

Should you have any left (though I wouldn't count on it), this makes for the basis of a wholly heavenly risotto *primavera*. (Just follow the method of the Chili Crab Risotto recipe on **p.40**, omitting the chili and saffron, and using 1 quart vegetable broth in place of the chicken broth. Add whatever leftover vegetables you have, at the point where the crab is added to the crab risotto.)

Warm the garlic-flavored oil and butter in a heavy, flameproof Dutch oven that comes with a lid, then add the leaves from about 5 sprigs of the thyme and cook for 30 seconds or so, before adding the frozen peas.

Cook, stirring, until the frozen look leaves the peas—no more than a couple of minutes—then tip in the fava beans and the artichoke slices and stir gently to mix, before adding the white wine or vermouth and the water.

Bring to a bubble, then add salt and pepper to taste, clamp on the lid, turn down the heat, and let it simmer for 15 minutes, or until all the vegetables are sweetly soused and tender. You can then hold them like this—with the lid on but heat off—for 10–15 minutes, if you like.

Stir in the chopped mint and parsley and the leaves from another 4 sprigs of thyme just before serving. And, if you want, dribble in some extra-virgin olive oil as well. ∎

SERVES 6–8 Ⓝ

2 TABLESPOONS GARLIC-
FLAVORED OIL

1 TABLESPOON BUTTER

SMALL BUNCH FRESH THYME

4 CUPS FROZEN PETITS POIS,
UNTHAWED

1½ CUPS FROZEN FAVA BEANS,
THAWED AND POPPED OUT OF
THEIR SKINS

12 OUNCES ARTICHOKE
BOTTOMS, CUT INTO APPROX.
½-INCH SLICES WHILE
PARTIALLY FROZEN

¼ CUP DRY WHITE WINE OR
VERMOUTH

¼ CUP WATER

KOSHER SALT AND PEPPER,
TO TASTE

2 TABLESPOONS CHOPPED
FRESH MINT

3 TABLESPOONS CHOPPED
FRESH PARSLEY

EXTRA-VIRGIN OLIVE OIL, TO
SERVE (OPTIONAL)

THIS IS ONE OF THOSE RECIPES that, while not quick to cook, is the work of easy minutes to make. Also, because it's best warm rather than hot, you can cook this before getting on with anything else, thus freeing up the oven later, should you need it.

I know that having to peel more than 2 pounds of onions doesn't seem like light work, but if you quarter them first, the peel almost falls off. And I never worry about a bit of it here and there in the pan, anyway. I prefer to use smallish red onions, but if you can only find large ones, then cut them into eighths rather than quarters.

This recipe can easily lend itself to being part of a buffet-type arrangement for parties, but is a wonderful supper or lunch accompaniment to roast lamb or, for that matter, any lamb. I also love it alongside a platter of (very unItalian) grilled halloumi. If you want it to be an entrée in itself, then crumble or dab over it the cheese of your choice—ricotta salata (the lightly salted, semi-dried version), fresh ricotta, Gorgonzola, Taleggio—just as it comes out of the oven, but before you add the uplifting and scented splendor of the basil.

ROAST RED ONIONS WITH BASIL

SERVES 6–8, *AS PART OF A MEAL* Ⓝ

2¼ POUNDS RED ONIONS (PREFERABLY SMALL), QUARTERED THEN PEELED

½ CUP OLIVE OIL

1 TEASPOON FENNEL SEEDS

1 TEASPOON KOSHER SALT OR ½ TEASPOON TABLE SALT, OR TO TASTE

1 TEASPOON BEST-QUALITY BALSAMIC VINEGAR, OR TO TASTE

LARGE BUNCH FRESH BASIL (APPROX. 4 CUPS PACKED)

Preheat the oven to 400°F.

Tip the quartered onions into a roasting pan, pour the olive oil over them, then scatter with fennel seeds, tossing the onions in the pan to coat them thoroughly; then put the pan in the oven for 1 hour, by which time the onions should be soft and cooked through.

Remove from the oven, sprinkle with the salt, and drizzle the balsamic vinegar over the onions, then toss them gently and leave (for up to 1 hour) to come to room temperature, though you can eat this hot if you prefer.

On serving, add the basil leaves, torn from their stems, and toss again, seasoning to taste. There is a lot of basil, but think of it as a salad leaf, here, not mere decoration. ∎

HERE IS MY ITALIAN VERSION, you could say, of creamed spinach. Actually, it tastes rather like the ricotta and spinach mixture that's used to stuff pasta; of course, given the ingredients, this is scarcely surprising.

For me this is the perfect accompaniment to a grilled steak or roast chicken but then I could spoon this soft, eggy spinach down, swooningly, just as it is.

SPINACH BAKED WITH RICOTTA & NUTMEG

Preheat the oven to 400°F, and butter a small ovenproof dish: I use a vaguely oval one with a capacity of about 3 cups.

In a wok or wide, heavy pan, warm the olive oil with the garlic clove and cook until the garlic is bronze.

Over a low heat stir in the spinach, bearing in mind that, though it will look at first as if you can't fit it all in, cooked spinach reduces to a fraction of its raw volume.

Turn up the heat, throw in the wine or vermouth, and toss gently until the spinach has wilted—which will take around 30 seconds.

Remove from the heat and stir in the Parmesan and ricotta and season to taste, adding a good grating of nutmeg.

Beat in the eggs, then transfer the eggy spinach to your buttered oven dish—I leave the garlic clove in just out of laziness, but you could remove it at this point—and bake in the oven for 10 minutes, until just set. Let it stand for at least 5 but no longer than 15 minutes, before serving. ◾

SERVES 2, *AS A SIDE DISH*
BUTTER FOR GREASING
1 TABLESPOON OLIVE OIL
1 CLOVE GARLIC, PEELED
10 CUPS (PACKED) (APPROX.
   12 OUNCES) BABY SPINACH
   LEAVES, WASHED AND DRIED
2 TABLESPOONS WHITE WINE OR
   VERMOUTH
3 TABLESPOONS GRATED
   PARMESAN
2 TABLESPOONS RICOTTA
FRESHLY GROUND PEPPER AND
   SALT, TO TASTE
FRESHLY GRATED NUTMEG
2 EGGS, BEATEN

THIS RECIPE IS A HODGEPODGE, REALLY. I do equate Savoy cabbage—*verza*—very much with Italy, but then again, whenever I eat it I also think of how my mother used to cook it, halfway between stir-fried and braised, with caraway seeds. The fennel seeds are my way of conjoining the two. On top of that, the potatoes I add give it something of an Italo-Irish spin. You don't need to bother with the potatoes: I used not to; but I did it once, as I had a spare spud around, and couldn't then go back. Nor do you absolutely need the cheese at the end. I add the gooey blobs of Taleggio only when I'm making this as a meal in itself, and if Taleggio eludes you, use any soft but full-bodied cheese that's easier to come by locally: Camembert would be the most obvious option.

Any leftovers, you may like to know, make for a gorgeous frittata the next day. For about 1 cup of cabbage and potato mixture, use 2 eggs, whisk and add to the leftovers, then tip them into a buttery frying pan and once the underside is cooked, give it a flash under a hot broiler to cook the top. I happen to adore cold frittata, so a bonus of this recipe could also be a cooked box lunch for later in the week (but make sure, if that's your plan, that the frittata is cooled, covered, and refrigerated quickly).

SAVOY CABBAGE WITH POTATOES, FENNEL SEEDS & TALEGGIO

SERVES 4–6 Ⓝ

2 TABLESPOONS OLIVE OIL
8 OUNCES POTATOES (APPROX.
   1 LARGE POTATO), UNPEELED,
   CUT INTO ½-INCH DICE
6 SCALLIONS, SLICED
2 TEASPOONS FENNEL SEEDS
1 HEAD SAVOY CABBAGE
2½ CUPS HOT WATER, FROM A
   RECENTLY BOILED KETTLE
SALT AND PEPPER, TO TASTE
7 OUNCES TALEGGIO CHEESE,
   RIND REMOVED (OPTIONAL)

Heat the oil in a large pan or heavy wok (my preference) that has a lid, then add the diced potatoes and cook in the hot oil, stirring frequently, for 10 minutes, by which time the potatoes will be more or less cooked through.

Stir in the scallions and fennel seeds and cook, stirring, for a further minute.

Meanwhile, shred the Savoy cabbage (by hand, with a knife). Then, when the potatoes have had their 10 minutes, add the cabbage, turning it in the hot pan—I like to use a spatula or spoon in each hand for this, like tossing a salad—and making sure the potato is mixed into it. Pour in the hot water, adding salt and pepper to taste, then give the pan a quick stir, clamp on the lid, turning the heat down, and let it simmer for 10 minutes or until the potatoes and cabbage are cooked through.

Remove from the heat, then pinch out blobs of Taleggio (if using) and let them drop into the pan, stirring as you go so that the cheese melts into the cabbage. But if the pan you've cooked everything in can't be brought to the table, then warm a bowl, and tip the cabbage and potatoes mixture into it first, before adding the cheese, and toss well so that it melts and mixes in the serving dish. ■

THIS IS, IN EFFECT, NOTHING OTHER than the *funghi trifolati* you find all over Italy in the autumn. Perhaps I have been a bit more exuberant with the lemon, but it really brings out the rich, sweet meatiness of the mushrooms. And although *funghi trifolati* means, literally, truffled mushrooms, that isn't to indicate that truffles are included but, rather, that the porcini mushrooms resemble truffles.

I'm not really sure they do, much as I love the image, and anyway, porcini mushrooms are neither easily nor cheaply come by in the UK, and so I use any mixture of mushrooms I can get hold of. (Don't forget that mushrooms should be wiped with a damp cloth or a sheet of paper towel, never washed.) The larger mushrooms I slice; others I quarter, halve, or leave whole as I see fit; and although I do remove the stems, I then slice and throw them in, too, where I can.

As an entrée, this is wonderful alongside a big bowlful of golden polenta (cooked following the package instructions), the paler Mock Mash, or indeed the Gnocchi Gratin (see **pp.136** and **131**) and I wouldn't rule out the Saffron Orzotto (**p.134**) as a supper-party partner, either. Stirred through a tangle of egg tagliatelle, they would be sublime, too.

GARLIC MUSHROOMS WITH CHILI & LEMON

Pour the oil into a heavy saucepan or flameproof Dutch oven that comes with a lid, and put it on a low to medium heat. Add the parsley, lemon zest, and red pepper flakes and grate in (or mince and add) the garlic, and let them sizzle fragrantly, but briefly, as you don't want them to burn or, really, do anything other than infuse the oil with their heady scent.

Turn up the heat, add the mushrooms, sprinkle with the salt, and give a gentle stir to try to mix in the flavored oil, then clamp on the lid. Turn the heat down to low and let everything simmer for 10 minutes. Although the mushrooms look dangerously dry as you put the lid on, when you remove the lid after these 10 minutes, you will see that they have given off quite a bit of liquid.

Now add the juice of the lemon, give everything a vigorous stir, then put the lid back on for another 10 minutes' simmering until the mushrooms are tender. It's wise to have a look once or twice during that time—just lift the lid and give a bit of a stir.

Scatter a little more parsley over the mushrooms, and serve. ∎

SERVES 4–6
¼ CUP OLIVE OIL
¼ CUP CHOPPED FRESH PARSLEY, PLUS MORE TO SERVE
ZEST AND JUICE 1 UNWAXED LEMON
½ TEASPOON CRUSHED RED PEPPER FLAKES
1 FAT CLOVE GARLIC, PEELED
1¾ POUNDS MIXED MUSHROOMS (SEE INTRO ABOVE FOR PREP. NOTES)
1 TEASPOON KOSHER SALT OR ½ TEASPOON TABLE SALT, OR TO TASTE

IN BRITAIN WE TEND TO CONSIGN Brussels sprouts too readily to the Christmas culinary canon. It's true, of course, that they are a winter vegetable, thriving on frost, as anyone who has painfully picked them on icy mornings can attest.

I am slotting them in here, rather than in the Christmas section, not simply because I am happy to eat them roasted, nuttily like this, whenever I can, but because trying to find last-minute oven space as you're about to serve up Christmas lunch could be enough to push one over the edge on a day that already has enough stress and tension. Of course, if you are blessed with a double oven, then augment quantities as needed and go for it.

I have specified smallish sprouts, by which I mean those that are still neatly and tightly furled rather than looser-leaved and blowsy.

ROAST BRUSSELS SPROUTS WITH ROSEMARY, LEMON & PECORINO

SERVES 4–6, *DEPENDING ON OTHER SIDE DISHES*
2 TABLESPOONS GARLIC-FLAVORED OIL
1 TEASPOON FINELY CHOPPED FRESH ROSEMARY NEEDLES
ZEST 1 UNWAXED LEMON (JUICE OPTIONAL)
1 POUND SMALLISH BRUSSELS SPROUTS, TRIMMED AND HALVED
2 TABLESPOONS GRATED PECORINO OR PARMESAN CHEESE
SALT AND PEPPER, TO TASTE

Preheat the oven to 425°F.

Put the garlic-flavored oil in a shallow roasting pan, add the chopped rosemary and the finely grated lemon zest, then tumble in the halved sprouts and smoosh everything about in the pan to coat as best you can, before roasting in the oven for 20 minutes.

Taste (being careful not to burn your mouth), to check that the sprouts are cooked through—though a bit of resistance (in this vegetable instance) is not a bad thing—and roast them another 4–5 minutes if they're not quite done; then remove the pan from the oven.

Decant the sprouts into a warmed serving bowl, sprinkle with the pecorino, then toss to combine well before adding salt and pepper to taste. If you want to add some lemon juice, from the lemon you zested earlier, do. ■

WITHOUT THE LEMON, THIS IS MY children's favorite way of eating broccoli; they have been known to whoop with pleasure when seeing it on the kitchen table. Strange but true. I prefer it with the edge of lemon cutting across the rich saltiness of the Parmesan but, with or without, this does add a bit of Mambo Italiano to the Sunday lunch or weeknight dinner vegetable menu.

For the Cod with Broccolini & Chili on **p.82** I've specified 8 ounces of broccolini for two people; here I've reckoned that it will feed four. This is partly because of the cheese that's added, but mostly because I tend to bring this out as one of a couple of side dishes to accompany roasted meats or at any rate some entrée more robust than a modest cod fillet.

As an entrée for 2, divide between 2 bowls and top each with a poached egg.

BROCCOLINI WITH PARMESAN & LEMON

Put a pan of water on for the broccolini, adding salt to taste when it comes to a boil, and cook the broccolini until the stalk is tender. Drain and return to the pan, adding the lemon zest and juice, then toss to coat.

Transfer the broccolini to a warmed bowl and add the shaved Parmesan. There's no absolute need to do this—you could add the cheese to the broccolini in the pan—but it helps with the dishwashing later. Either use a vegetable peeler to shave off strips or—if laziness dictates—use some already shaved, from a container found in the refrigerated section of grocery stores.

Add the olive oil and toss well so that some of the cheese flakes start melting into the broccolini. Before serving, add pepper—and salt if wished, though it's unlikely any will be needed—to taste. ◼

SERVES UP TO 4, *DEPENDING ON WHAT ELSE IS ON THE TABLE*

8 OUNCES TRIMMED BROCCOLINI

ZEST AND JUICE ½ UNWAXED LEMON

¼ CUP SHAVED PARMESAN (FRESHLY SHAVED OR STORE-BOUGHT)

1 TABLESPOON EXTRA-VIRGIN OLIVE OIL

SALT AND PEPPER, TO TASTE

THIS RECIPE DOESN'T EXACTLY EMANATE FROM Sicily, but the Moorish flavorings, with the saffron and that mixture of sweet raisins and salty olives, most definitely do. I like the addition of (Sicilian) Marsala, but you can use water in its place, adding the saffron and its water to the raisins and theirs. As ever, I go for oil-cured pitted black olives, but you can use black or green, pitted or unpitted, spiced or not. I have been known, *in extremis*, to use those retro anchovy-stuffed green ones. I'm not sure this quite counts as a salad, but I've settled on that nomenclature since I like to eat it at a whispering breath above room temperature, or even cold. I often do this salad when I have people over, as it really demands to be prepared ahead, which can make life easier as kick-off approaches.

SICILIAN CAULIFLOWER SALAD

SERVES 4–6, *AS A SIDE DISH* Ⓝ

1 HEAD CAULIFLOWER (APPROX. 2 POUNDS)

1 TEASPOON KOSHER SALT OR ½ TEASPOON TABLE SALT, PLUS MORE TO TASTE

2 BAY LEAVES

½ TEASPOON SAFFRON THREADS

¼ CUP WATER, FROM A RECENTLY BOILED KETTLE

½ CUP GOLDEN (OR REGULAR) RAISINS

5 TABLESPOONS MARSALA

1 ECHALION OR BANANA SHALLOT, PEELED AND FINELY CHOPPED

1 TABLESPOON LEMON JUICE

¼ CUP EXTRA-VIRGIN OLIVE OIL

¾ CUP OIL-CURED BLACK OLIVES

3 TABLESPOONS PINE NUTS

SMALL BUNCH FRESH PARSLEY, CHOPPED

Break the cauliflower into florets and put these in a saucepan that comes with a lid. Cover with cold water, add the salt and bay leaves, put the lid on, set the pan on a high heat and bring to a boil; then drain immediately, discarding the bay leaves, and hold the colander bearing the cauliflower under a running cold tap for a moment, before putting it to one side. This will take the edge off the heat, but the cauliflower will still be warm.

Meanwhile, as the cauliflower is heating up in its water, put the saffron threads into a small bowl and pour the ¼ cup of recently boiled water over them. Let steep.

Put the raisins into a small saucepan with the Marsala and bring to a boil, then immediately remove from the heat.

Put the still-warm cauliflower into a large serving bowl.

Add the chopped shallot to the saffron water, then whisk in the lemon juice and carry on whisking while you add the olive oil—a small hand whisk is all you need for this.

Add the raisins (with any Marsala that clings to them and any left in the pan) and the olives to the cauliflower, then pour the dressing over them, scraping every drop out, and—first putting on a pair of disposable vinyl gloves, *CSI*-style—use your hands to toss to combine. Of course you can use external implements, if you prefer. Season to taste.

Let your salad come to room temperature (about 30 minutes to 1 hour, or less if you want it warmer) and, while you wait, heat a small frying pan, put in the pine nuts, and shake them about for a couple of minutes until golden and toasted. Don't leave the pan.

Toss most of the toasted pine nuts and chopped parsley through the salad and scatter what's left on top. This turns just about anything into a feast. ∎

SHOULD I FEEL BASHFUL ABOUT GIVING a recipe that involves little more than opening a can? Well, if I should, I don't. I can't apologize for speed or ease when the outcome is so enduringly pleasurable.

Even if there are only two of us eating, I still like to make this amount, as it's perfect the next day, cold, and with the addition of some good tuna from another can, makes for a great box lunch or speedy supper.

CANNELLINI BEANS WITH ROSEMARY

In a non-stick frying pan placed over a medium to low heat, warm the oil, then add the rosemary and lemon zest and let them sizzle aromatically, as you stir, for about 30 seconds.

Now grate in the garlic (or mince and add it) and stir for another 30 seconds, making sure the garlic doesn't color. Put in the beans with some rinsing water still clinging to them, stirring gently but thoroughly enough to coat the beans in the fragrant oil.

Squeeze in the lemon juice and add salt and pepper to taste, then cook, stirring occasionally, until the beans are hot through—this shouldn't take more than a couple of minutes. Taste for seasoning.

Decant to a warm serving bowl and drizzle with a little extra-virgin olive oil, if wished. ▪

SERVES 2–4 Ⓝ

2 TABLESPOONS REGULAR
  OLIVE OIL
1 TEASPOON FINELY CHOPPED
  FRESH ROSEMARY
ZEST AND JUICE 1 UNWAXED
  LEMON
1 SMALL CLOVE GARLIC, PEELED
2 X 15-OUNCE CANS CANNELLINI
  BEANS (OR OTHER BEANS OF
  YOUR CHOICE), DRAINED AND
  RINSED
SALT AND PEPPER, TO TASTE
APPROX. 1 TEASPOON EXTRA-
  VIRGIN OLIVE OIL (OPTIONAL)

IF YOU HAVEN'T AS YET COME across the small, bronzy-gold Castelluccio lentils from Umbria, you have a treat in store—and I use that last word advisedly here, as I always keep a package or two of these on hand. Like the French Puy lentils, they are smaller than the generic green or brown lentils, and also—it should be said—more expensive. But, in the same way as their French counterparts, these Umbrian lentils are less earthy and more delicate in flavor than the generic ones and keep their nuttiness and texture better on cooking, too. I adore Puy lentils, and there is something appealing about their slate blue-black coloring, but the antique gold of a bowl of Castelluccio lentils brings a Renaissance opulence to any meal.

I should say that, as often as not, I include *cubetti di pancetta* in any dish of lentils I make, but not always, and it seems sensible to give the recipe without it, and offer you the option. If you do want to add the pancetta—or any bacon, frankly—for 3 cups lentils, I use 6 ounces cubed pancetta and reduce the garlic oil at the beginning to 1 tablespoon.

This is a go-to recipe in my repertoire, because I find that if I make this—and though it's not instant, it's definitely low-effort—I can dispense with potatoes or any other starch, which lightens the load when entertaining. And these lentils can be made in advance, and then either reheated or served at room temperature, depending on how ahead of yourself you want to get.

Of course, you can use other lentils, but they don't quite capture the celebratory flourish of the Castelluccio gold.

ITALIAN GOLDEN LENTILS

SERVES 6–8, *AS A SIDE DISH* Ⓝ

3 TABLESPOONS GARLIC-
   FLAVORED OIL
1 LEEK, WASHED, TRIMMED,
   HALVED LENGTHWISE AND
   THINLY SLICED
2 TEASPOONS DRIED THYME
3 CUPS CASTELLUCCIO LENTILS,
   RINSED AND DRAINED
APPROX. 1 QUART COLD WATER
3 DRIED BAY LEAVES
SALT AND PEPPER, TO TASTE
CHOPPED FRESH PARSLEY OR
   CHIVES, TO SERVE (OPTIONAL)
EXTRA-VIRGIN OR CHILI OIL, TO
   SERVE (OPTIONAL)

In a medium-sized saucepan, with a heavy base—or in a flameproof Dutch oven—that has a lid, warm the garlic-flavored oil over a medium heat and stir in the pale jade strips of leek. Cook, stirring, for 2–3 minutes, then add the thyme and give a quick stir, before tipping in the lentils. Toss briskly but cautiously, so that the lentils are turned in the leeks and oil.

Pour in the water so that it comes ¾–1 inch above the lentils, then add the bay leaves, turn the heat up, and let everything come to a boil. Clamp on the lid, turn the heat down to low, and let it simmer gently for 30 minutes, or until the water is absorbed and the lentils are cooked, but not soft. If the lentils are old (I have been known to keep them till beyond their best-before date, though I don't advise it), you may need to give them longer. Season to taste and remove the bay leaves, then toss the lentils through with a little chopped parsley, or some chives, if wished, and sprinkle some more on top before serving.

I like to put a bottle of extra-virgin olive oil or chili oil, or indeed both, for people to drizzle over the lentils as they eat, and I recommend you do, too. ■

IN *KITCHEN*, I CAME UP WITH THE IDEA of frying gnocchi to make near-instant mini roasted potatoes, and I still immodestly exult in it. (To recap: just fry gnocchi, so long as they're fresh and chilled rather than frozen, in hot oil for about 4 minutes a side.) But I knew that there were other routes to be taken. Gnocchi are, after all, just potatoes and so it seemed that a dinner-party gratin that didn't involve more than 2 minutes' preparation could be possible. And I'm here to tell you now that it is indeed possible. And I don't know why I said just "dinner party." Yes, this recipe makes short work of any midweek entertaining, but I love this for everyday family suppers, too.

I make this gratin, for preference, only with the freshly made kind of gnocchi that can be found in the refrigerated section of grocery stores. They come (or do near me) in packages of 14 ounces but, if you find them in packages of 1 pound, simply use two of those instead. I have even used three 14-ounce packages of gnocchi with the same amount of sauce without trouble.

As for the sauce: I mix the mascarpone and milk in a bowl first—otherwise I risk spraying my stove with everything—but if you're prepared to proceed more patiently and slowly, mix them in the Dutch oven on the stove before you turn on the heat.

There would be nothing to stop you upping the cheese or adding some white truffle paste (or butter or oil) to the sauce as per the Mascarpone Mash on **p.132**, either.

GNOCCHI GRATIN

Preheat the oven to 400°F, and put a saucepan of water on for the gnocchi.

Whisk the mascarpone in a bowl with the milk, then warm it in a shallow, flameproof Dutch oven or gratin dish wide enough to fit the cooked gnocchi in later, in more or less a single layer.

Once the mascarpone mixture starts bubbling, turn off the heat, stir 3 tablespoons of the grated Parmesan into the sauce, and then whisk till it melts. Add a good grinding of pepper and grate in some nutmeg, stir, then taste, and add salt only if you feel it needs it. Take the pan off the heat.

Salt the boiling water for the gnocchi and cook them following the package instructions.

Drain the gnocchi and add to the sauce, turning them well, but gently, to coat, and once they are in an even layer in the dish, mix the remaining Parmesan with the bread crumbs and sprinkle this on top.

Bake for 15 minutes, by which time the gratin should be bubbling and golden on top.

Remove from the oven and let it sit out for 5–10 minutes, to cool a little before serving. Don't let it stand for any longer than 15 minutes, or too much of the gloriously gooey sauce will be absorbed. ■

SERVES 6, *AS A SIDE DISH*
1 CUP MASCARPONE
¼ CUP WHOLE MILK
¼ CUP GRATED PARMESAN
FRESHLY GROUND PEPPER
FRESHLY GRATED NUTMEG
1 TEASPOON KOSHER SALT OR
  ½ TEASPOON TABLE SALT,
  OR TO TASTE
2 X 14-OUNCE PACKAGES
  GNOCCHI
2 TABLESPOONS BREAD CRUMBS

I JUST LOVE THESE MASHED POTATOES: they're gloriously rich and yet fluffily light in texture. Normally, I like my mashed potatoes plain, considering it a neutral starchy blanket and not an emphatic flavor purveyor in its own right. I mean, obviously, I always load it up with butter and cream, but that doesn't counter my argument. Here I do without butter or cream, but before you rejoice in or scorn my supposed dietary restraint, let me tell you that mascarpone does the job of both. A sprinkling of Parmesan balances the creamy mellowness with spiky saltiness. Were I to leave it here, I think these mashed potatoes would still pass muster as plain. But I don't leave it here: I add white truffle paste or truffle butter. If you don't have either, use white truffle oil, though only a drop or two. The paste (which seems to last for yonks in my refrigerator) does have more of a natural truffle taste, but (unlike many) I don't absolutely condemn the use of white truffle oil. I have been known to use it myself.

Neither adding mascarpone nor truffle paste came as a revelation to me, but what *did* was this cooking method (courtesy of one of my favorite websites, food52.com), which involves steaming rather than boiling the potatoes. And because you're using a potato ricer later—I always do, incidentally—you don't even have to peel them. I should admit to simplifying their process from there on in.

When I have people over, I cook this slightly in advance, then trickle a film of whole milk over the top (as my mother taught me), cover with aluminum foil, and keep it warm in a low oven, probably somewhere just below 200°F for 45 minutes and no longer than 1 hour. The result: ultra-easeful pleasure all round. And should you be lucky enough to have a small amount left over, I recommend a gentle reheat with the addition of a little milk stirred in, to be eaten—for pure, private joy—with either a poached or soft-boiled egg squished on top. You know it makes sense.

MASCARPONE MASHED POTATOES

SERVES 4-6 Ⓝ

2¼ POUNDS YUKON GOLD POTATOES (UNPEELED, IF YOU HAVE A RICER), CUT IN 2-INCH CHUNKS

½ CUP WHOLE MILK

3 TABLESPOONS MASCARPONE, AT ROOM TEMPERATURE

1 TEASPOON KOSHER SALT OR ½ TEASPOON TABLE SALT, OR TO TASTE

▶

Put the unpeeled potato chunks in a steamer above a saucepan of boiling water, filled just about 3 inches deep, and steam them until soft; I find this takes about 20 minutes. The scant amount of water will not boil dry in this time and the potatoes will not get too wet.

Remove the steamer part, pour out all the water from the pan, and then put the steamer with the cooked potatoes back on the now dry, hot pan, with the lid off, to stand for 10 minutes to dry out.

Then remove the top part and, in the bottom pan of the steamer, warm the milk but do not let it boil. Stir in the marscarpone and the salt.

Purée the potatoes using a ricer over the pan of warm milk, and give a good beat or two with a wooden spoon, whipping in some air as you do so.

When smooth, beat in the Parmesan and white truffle paste or truffle butter, tasting as you go: you may wish to add half the quantity of truffle paste, taste, and then decide for yourself if you want to add the rest. And remember: if using truffle oil, add the merest drop or two and proceed with caution. Eat, however, with heady abandon. ■

1½ TABLESPOONS GRATED PARMESAN

1 TEASPOON WHITE TRUFFLE PASTE OR TRUFFLE BUTTER

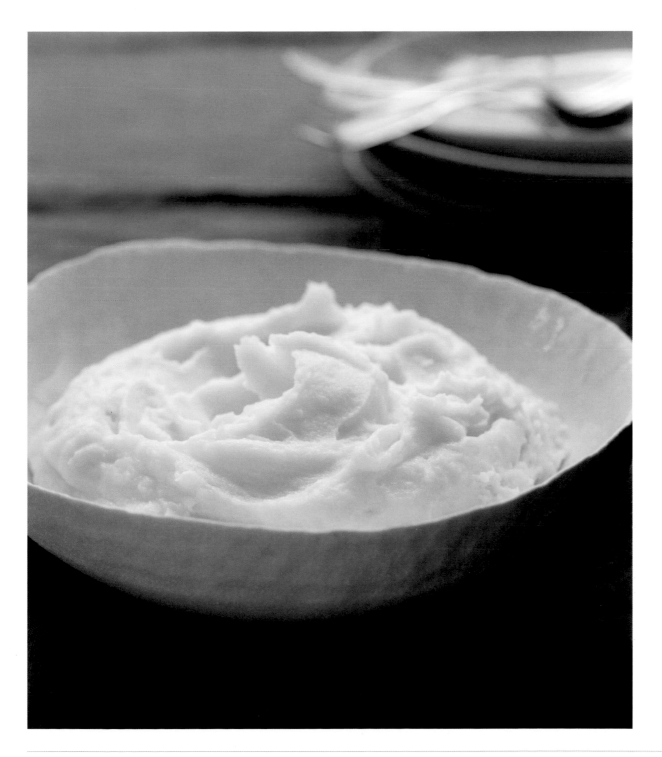

THERE IS A REASON WHY THIS orzotto—think risotto, only made with barley, *orzo* in Italian—is huddling among the vegetables rather than being offered up with the pasta: I make it almost exclusively as a potato substitute, that's to say as a starchy accompaniment to a roast chicken or ham or bowl of meatballs and any number of stews.

It's incredibly simple to make, since, unlike risotto, there is almost no stirring involved, and it can easily be done ahead of time. On reheating, you may want to add a little more liquid first, and perhaps—to stir through at the end with the Parmesan—a couple of spoonfuls of mascarpone. In fact, if you would like a creamier texture, I suggest you add the mascarpone the first time around.

My children are genetically predisposed to barley, but luckily this dish seems to win everyone over. It's just so charming to look at, as well as addictive to eat. The saffron-soused grains of barley positively ooze sunniness. I leave you with this thought: in my house there is a faction that insists on eating this with ultra-thin slices of pancetta, fried to a crisp, crumbled on top.

SAFFRON ORZOTTO

SERVES 4, *AS A SIDE DISH* Ⓝ
3 CUPS WEAK CHICKEN OR
   VEGETABLE BROTH
¼ TEASPOON SAFFRON THREADS
2 TABLESPOONS GARLIC-
   FLAVORED OIL
1 ECHALION OR BANANA SHALLOT,
   OR 1 SMALL ONION, PEELED AND
   FINELY CHOPPED
1⅓ CUPS PEARLED BARLEY
2 TABLESPOONS DRY VERMOUTH
   OR WHITE WINE
2 TABLESPOONS GRATED
   PARMESAN
SALT AND PEPPER, TO TASTE
2-3 TABLESPOONS MASCARPONE
   (OPTIONAL)

First, make up the broth in a pitcher. (I don't use homemade, but just add good broth concentrate or bouillon powder to boiling water.) And use slightly less broth concentrate or powder to water than advised on the package, to ensure that saltiness is kept at bay. Add the saffron, stir, and set aside for a moment.

In a shallow, heavy pan or flameproof Dutch oven, about 10 inches diameter and— important—that has a lid, warm the garlic-flavored oil over a medium-low heat, then add the chopped shallot and cook for a couple of minutes, stirring. You don't want this to color. If using an onion instead of a shallot, you may need to cook it for nearer 5 minutes.

Turn up the heat and add the barley, stirring it in the hot pan for a minute, then add the vermouth or wine and stir again.

Add the hot saffron broth, clamp the lid on, then turn the heat down to low and let the orzotto simmer gently for 20-30 minutes, or until the barley is cooked through and tender and most of the liquid absorbed. Do add a little extra boiling water if the liquid is absorbed before the barley is tender enough. Remove the lid, stir, and take the pan off the heat; if you wanted, you could let it cool now, cover, refrigerate, and leave it for a day or two (see Notes on **p.265**). Otherwise, stir in the Parmesan and season to taste. Should you fancy adding the mascarpone, now would be the time to do it. ∎

ON THE ONE HAND, THIS IS an entirely non-Italian concept; on the other, its inspiration and derivation come hot-foot from Italy. Let me explain. I was making *gnocchi alla Romana* one day (think little round patties made with semolina) and before they'd been cut out, while I still had the mixture in front of me ready to cool, Lisa—who works with me and is Italian—walked past, dipped in a finger, tasted some, and said, "What lovely mashed potatoes!"

I went on, waited for the mixture to cool so that I could cut out my patties, laid them out like roof tiles, dusted with Parmesan, and baked them. All good. But I couldn't help feeling afterward that I could dispense with a major part of the activity: hence this, my mock mash. I know it sounds spooky—especially to those of us reared on semolina pudding at school, even those among us who have affection for the memory—but this is more wonderful than you could imagine. It's as fast as it is easy to whip up, so I wouldn't prepare it in advance. (Even with a little bit of standing, it does start to form a skin, but a quick stir—just with the serving utensils—gets rid of that.) I can't stop making it. I certainly can't stop eating it.

I know we generally can't buy this brand of butter in cans but, while we were shooting the photographs for this book, my sister gave me the can, opposite, as a present from Italy and I couldn't *not* picture it.

MOCK MASH

SERVES 4-6, *AS A SIDE DISH* Ⓝ
1 QUART WHOLE MILK
1 TABLESPOON UNSALTED
   BUTTER
KOSHER SALT OR TABLE SALT,
   TO TASTE
FRESHLY GRATED NUTMEG
1½ CUPS SEMOLINA
¾ CUP GRATED PARMESAN
PEPPER, TO TASTE

Heat the milk in a large, wide saucepan (you will need room to whisk later), then add the butter, a sprinkling of salt, and a good grating of nutmeg.

When the milk is just coming to a boil, pour the semolina into the pan in a steady stream, whisking as you go.

Continue to whisk the mixture until it thickens, and big bubbles come to the surface with a gentle plopping sound. This should take 3-5 minutes.

Take the pan off the heat and beat in the grated cheese, check the seasoning, then tip the mock mash into a bowl, grating a little more nutmeg over it as you serve. ■

CESARE CASELLA, A CHEF FROM LUCCA, whose family used to run the fabulous Vipore restaurant (from which the views over the Tuscan hills were more enchanting than I can say) and who is now cooking in New York, is the man who invented Tuscan Fries. Think French fries, but with garlic cloves and fresh herbs thrown into the hot oil toward the end of the cooking time.

Now, this would be too much for my nerves on a regular basis—deep-frying in anything other than small amounts, as per the Italian Tempura Shrimp on **p.84**, say, isn't for me—were it not for the fact that the always compelling *Cook's Illustrated* introduced me to a radical, new, and stress-free way of cooking fries.

It sounds crazy, but it works: you put the uncooked fries into cold oil, then heat it up. It's revolutionary. You'd think it would make the fries unbearably greasy but in fact you end up with crisp, oil-free fries of utter fabulousness. That much you can tell by taste; but I have further proof in the fact that I once measured how much oil I had left when it had cooled down, and found that the potatoes had scarcely absorbed any.

You do need, however, as I have found, to cut the potatoes more into the chunkier size of steak fries than skinny French fries. That's no punishment, however.

Cesare's fries came on a plate lined with a chic and simple piece of brown paper, but I am happy to give them a quick sit on a baking sheet lined with a double thickness of paper towels before letting them clatter out onto a platter or onto a newspaper (Italian, for preference), lined with parchment paper.

TUSCAN FRIES

SERVES 4–6
2¼ POUNDS WAXY POTATOES, SUCH AS YUKON GOLD
1½ QUARTS CORN OIL OR FLAVORLESS VEGETABLE OIL, FOR FRYING
UNPEELED CLOVES FROM 1 HEAD GARLIC
8 TENDER TOP SPRIGS THYME, ROSEMARY, AND SAGE, OR HERBS OF YOUR CHOICE
KOSHER SALT, TO TASTE

Cut the short ends off each potato (but don't peel) so that it can sit up vertically, and then slice it downwards into generous ½-inch slices. Cut these slices into fries about ½ inch thick; again, err on the generous side. Load up a clean dishcloth with the fries as you cut them.

Put the oil into a wide, heavy pan (mine is approx. 11 inches diameter and 4½ inches deep), and add the freshly cut potatoes. Then put the pan over a high heat and bring to a boil, which should take about 5 minutes. Keep a careful watch on the pan at all times.

Continue to cook the fries, without stirring them, for another 15 minutes. The pan will be bubbling vigorously. If the oil gets too hot or bubbles too hard, reduce the heat a little, and always keep a close eye on it. (If you're using a thermometer, once the oil temperature reaches 325°F, turn down the heat slightly and keep the fries cooking at between 300 and 325°F.)

Now you can very carefully give the fries a gentle stir with a pair of tongs held in an oven mitt, moving any that have stuck away from the bottom or sides of the pan. Add the unpeeled cloves of garlic to the pan, stir gently again, and cook for another 5–10 minutes (watching the temperature and making sure the garlic doesn't look burnt or the fries too dark), before testing a fry for crispness on the outside and tenderness on the inside. Do not burn your mouth, though! You might need another 5 minutes or so beyond this, but stand by your pan: the fries can turn from a cooked gold to a burnt bronze quickly.

At the point when the fries are pale gold, but crisp, toss in the herbs, then after a minute or so scoop everything out—using a couple of perforated scoops for ease, and wearing oven mitts to protect your hands—onto a baking sheet or platter lined with a double thickness of paper towels. Once any excess oil has been absorbed, tip the fries off the tray clatteringly onto the plate and sprinkle with salt to taste, serving immediately. ■

SWEET THINGS

IN ITALY, IT'S NOT HARD TO GET FIGS that are so luscious it would be a sin to do anything more than pop them plumptiously into your mouth. I don't even hold with peeling. I suppose, though, even in Italy a disappointing fig cannot be unknown; here in Britain, it is sadly routine.

So, if you are unable to resist buying figs but then go home to discover that they are either bland or grittily tough, here's how to proceed.

I find eight figs perfect for four people, but if they are small, then up quantities to twelve figs; the sauce quantities should be fine as they are. The idea is not to drown the figs in honey-scented cream, but to kiss them with it.

FIGS WITH HONEY-CREAM & PISTACHIOS

Preheat the oven to 425°F.

Take a knife and cut into the figs as if you wanted to cut them into quarters, downward, but do not cut right through to the bottom; you want to be able to open them like a flower. Arrange them in a small roasting pan—I use a tarte Tatin pan—and dribble the olive oil over them, then bake for 10 minutes (or a little less if the figs are small), until they are soft.

In a teeny-tiny saucepan, heat the cream and honey and let it bubble for about 1–1½ minutes so that it is slightly condensed and reduced. Keep an eye on it.

Remove the figs from the oven and arrange them on 1 large plate or 4 small plates, then pour the honeyed cream over them and scatter with the chopped pistachios. ■

SERVES 4

8 LARGE BLACK FIGS
2 TEASPOONS OLIVE OIL
¼ CUP HEAVY CREAM
2 TEASPOONS HONEY
2 TABLESPOONS SHELLED,
  UNSALTED, CHOPPED
  PISTACHIO NUTS

ICED BERRIES WITH LIMONCELLO WHITE CHOCOLATE SAUCE

THIS IS A CONTEMPORARY CLASSIC, INVENTED by the great British chef Mark Hix, but I have taken the liberty of speeding up the sauce-making process, and—crucially—adding limoncello for an Italian touch. It gives a real edge to the ultra-rich white chocolate and, besides, I have been longing to do something with this particular combo ever since I saw the winning Joanne Wheatley create her Limoncello and White Chocolate Croquembouche on the BBC's cooking show *The Great British Bake Off*.

Now, white chocolate is much sneered at by those who take pride in their palate, considered—as the master baker Dan Lepard wrote in the British newspaper *The Guardian*—"the Big Mac of confectionery." Even if you take a similar line, and I'm afraid I have been known to do so myself, you are just going to have to believe me when I say that this recipe will challenge any prejudice you may be harboring. This is elegant and punchy at the same time; the depth of the limoncello and the sharpness of the berries completely defuse the unsophisticated and otherwise one-note richness of the white chocolate. All the same, if in doubt, I advise telling people it's a limoncello sauce, with no mention of the white chocolate, to begin with.

I am too impatient to melt the chocolate in a double boiler, and I do like an element of risk, but heating any chocolate can be tricky and white chocolate especially so; I would totally understand it if you were to prefer to make the sauce sensibly in a heatproof bowl suspended over a saucepan of simmering water, but you must make sure the base of the bowl doesn't touch the bubbling water beneath.

I love to serve this on a rimmed cake stand, but it could make more sense to make up individual portions in saucers or salad plates with a lip. I think it's important that, however you serve it, you try to keep the berries in a single layer, give or take.

What makes this fantastic for a last-minute, even impromptu, dinner-party dessert (with interesting Christmas potential) is that you can keep the berries in the freezer until needed. I suppose you could, in summer, use fresh berries, though you would lose the contrast between warm rich sauce and sharp icy fruit.

Put the heavy cream and 2 tablespoons of the limoncello in a small saucepan, and heat it until just about to come to a boil, but not actually boiling.

Take the pan off the heat and add the white chocolate, then swirl the pan about so that it is all submerged.

Take the berries out of the freezer and arrange them in a single layer in a dish or plate that has a small lip (so that the sauce doesn't drip off later). Sprinkle with the remaining 2 tablespoons of limoncello and leave for 5 minutes, during which time you can swirl your white chocolate pan about every now and again to help the chocolate melt into the lemony cream.

Using a rubber spatula, gently stir the chocolate-cream mixture, still off the heat, until it's smooth, then pour it over the berries and serve immediately. ∎

SERVES 4–6
1 CUP HEAVY CREAM
¼ CUP LIMONCELLO (LEMON LIQUEUR)
7 OUNCES WHITE CHOCOLATE, FINELY CHOPPED
1 POUND FROZEN MIXED BERRIES (UNTHAWED)

WHITE CHOCOLATE MAY BE CONSIDERED an infra-dig ingredient, but for the self-styled tastemakers of the world, condensed milk is *really* beyond the pale. So how can you blame me for wanting to slip it into any recipe whenever possible? Not that I'm doing this simply to be kitsch: it is a strangely useful ingredient; see, too, the One-Step No-Churn Coffee Ice Cream on **p.170**. And, before you start wondering, there are many Italian recipes using *latte condensato*, but you tend to come across them in passed-down family recipe notebooks rather than in glamorous magazines or elegant books.

Not that I'm ashamed of using a can of it myself—I always have one or two in the house—but I do feel obliged to say that no one would ever guess that this no-wait, egg-free mousse contained condensed milk. And when I made this for dinner recently, an Italian friend even asked me for the recipe. That's good enough for me.

As for that other key ingredient, the bitter orange liqueur, I only have to smell Aperol and I feel I'm in Italy. But if you can't find it, then use triple sec, Cointreau, or Grand Marnier or any other orange liqueur in its place.

INSTANT CHOCOLATE-ORANGE MOUSSE

SERVES 6 Ⓝ

6 OUNCES BITTERSWEET
   CHOCOLATE (MIN. 62% COCOA
   SOLIDS), FINELY CHOPPED
2 CUPS HEAVY CREAM
⅔ CUP SWEETENED CONDENSED
   MILK
PINCH SALT
2 TABLESPOONS APEROL, TRIPLE
   SEC, COINTREAU, GRAND
   MARNIER, OR OTHER ORANGE
   LIQUEUR
2 TABLESPOONS ORANGE JUICE
   AND ZEST ½ ORANGE

6 APPROX. 6-OUNCE (¾ CUP)
   GLASSES

Melt the chocolate carefully either in an appropriate bowl in the microwave (following manufacturer's instructions) or over a saucepan of simmering water (making sure the bowl doesn't touch the water); when almost melted, stir with a rubber spatula, both to scrape down and to help the last solid bits of chocolate melt. Take off the heat and let cool a little.

Pour 1 cup of the heavy cream into a bowl with the salt. Whisk until the cream just makes soft peaks. Add the condensed milk and fold it in. The mixture should be thick but not too airy—when you lift a spoonful, it should leave a trail of ribbons.

Stir about a third of the whipped cream mixture into the slightly cooled melted chocolate; you can be fairly brutal about this. Now, slowly—in 2 or 3 batches—fold the lightened chocolate mixture back into the rest of the whipped cream mixture. Then gently stir in the orange liqueur followed by the orange juice (having first zested the orange).

When all is combined, carefully fill 6 glasses of around 6-ounce capacity to about ½ inch below the rim.

Put the chocolate mousses into the refrigerator for 1 hour (though you could serve them sooner as they're edible straightaway, and also see Notes on **p.265**). Just before serving, whip the remaining 1 cup heavy cream until it reaches soft peaks.

On serving, distribute the whipped cream equally among the glasses of chocolate mousse and top these fluffy blobs with the orange zest. ◼

I KNOW THERE ARE PEOPLE WHO, because of early over-indulgence in sambuca, maintain a shuddering revulsion for it now. Luckily, even those individuals seem to be won over by these entirely salubrious sambuca kisses.

It's hard to explain the precise nature of these: they are light, almost like doughnuts, but made of scented, sweet air rather than batter. They are called kisses (*baci*) in Italy, as they seem to caress the mouth flutteringly as you eat them; think butterfly kiss rather than smooch.

Strictly speaking, you shouldn't leave them to stand, once they've been made. But pleasurable though it is to eat them as soon as you can—once they're out of the pan—I have found they're fine for a while in a low oven. The contrast between outside and inside is lost, rather, but not so much as you gain in the convenience of being able to make them ahead.

SAMBUCA KISSES

Put the egg and ricotta into a bowl and beat together until smooth.

Add the flour, baking powder, sambuca, granulated sugar, and grated orange zest. Beat the mixture again to make a smooth batter.

Pour about 1 inch of oil into a frying pan, and heat until a small piece of bread sizzles when you drop it into the pan and browns in about 40 seconds (the temperature should be about 350°F). And keep your eye on the pan at all times.

Oil a teaspoon measure and gently drop rounded teaspoons of the ricotta batter into the pan; about 4 at a time is manageable.

The little kisses will puff up slightly and turn golden underneath, so flip them over carefully with an implement of your choice, to color the other side. Watch out that the oil doesn't get too hot: turn the heat down if they are browning too quickly.

Once they are golden all over, lift them out with a perforated spoon and place them on a plate lined with 1 or 2 sheets of paper towel, to get rid of any excess oil. Carry on cooking until all the mixture is used up, then turn off the heat under the oil.

Once the kisses have cooled a bit, push the confectioners' sugar through a small strainer to dust them thickly.

If you are not eating them straightaway, pop the pre-sugared, cooked kisses on a wire rack over a sheet pan in a 300°F oven, and keep them warm for up to 1 hour.

If so inclined, serve with a shot of sambuca or an espresso. ■

MAKES 18–20

1 EGG
½ CUP WHOLE-MILK RICOTTA
3 TABLESPOONS ALL-PURPOSE FLOUR
1 TEASPOON BAKING POWDER
2 TEASPOONS SAMBUCA LIQUEUR
1 TEASPOON GRANULATED SUGAR
1 TEASPOON GRATED ORANGE ZEST
FLAVORLESS VEGETABLE OR CORN OIL, FOR FRYING
1–2 TEASPOONS CONFECTIONERS' SUGAR, TO SERVE

LICORICE IS ONE OF THE SIGNATURE TASTES of Italy. As this is an ingredient that divides people viscerally, I've made it just for two, or possibly one very greedy licorice eater. . . .

I use the tiny licorice pellets that come, usually, from Calabria and are seen everywhere in Italy. Outside of Italy, you can find them in Italian delis and via the Internet: for those who share my love for this almost vicious aniseed flavor, there is a whole world online for you.

This is a pudding in the Italian sense of *budino*, a word that Anna Del Conte explains in her *Gastronomy of Italy* (original edition) "though hard to define . . . suggests a dish of a round shape, a soft texture and a trembling consistency." This is an easy, almost-instant version (in terms of the cooking) that bypasses the bain-marie baking normally required, and is eaten from a glass rather than turned out. I melt the pellets in hot water, and don't mind at all if a few dark splodges are detectable in the finished, silky, buff-colored cream.

I have expressed my passion for salted caramel elsewhere, but here I must declare my deep, almost deviant, love for salted licorice. I don't want the two wholly mixed in here, but prefer to have some soft, sea salt flakes (the French *fleur de sel* is my choice here) to sprinkle on as I eat. I get a frisson just thinking of it.

LICORICE PUDDING

SERVES 2 ⊘

¼ CUP WATER

1 TEASPOON PURE ITALIAN
   LICORICE PELLETS, SUCH AS
   AMARELLI ROSSANO

2 TABLESPOONS LIGHT BROWN
   SUGAR

⅔ CUP HEAVY CREAM

2 TEASPOONS CORNSTARCH

1 TABLESPOON MILK

SOFT SEA SALT FLAKES, TO SERVE

Put the water and licorice pellets in your smallest pan and bring to a boil, stirring or whisking frequently to help the liquorice melt. Once it starts bubbling, turn off the heat and leave for 5 minutes, stirring or whisking every now and again.

Turn the heat back on and whisk in the sugar, then the cream, and bring to a bubble. Remove from the heat.

Spoon the cornstarch into a little bowl, cup, or ramekin and whisk in the milk until you have a smooth paste.

Pour this, whisking as you go, into the mixture in the saucepan. Still whisking, put the pan back on the heat and bring back to a bubble, whisking all the while, for 20–30 seconds, or until thickened.

Divide between 2 heatproof glasses or cups and—unless you want to eat this hot—cover, touching the surface of the puddings, with plastic wrap or parchment paper that you've wet with cold water then wrung out (this is to prevent a skin forming, a thing I cannot tolerate), and put them in the refrigerator to chill for at least 2 hours or overnight.

Let the puddings come to room temperature before serving, and remove the plastic wrap or parchment paper and smooth the tops with the back of a teaspoon. Put the soft sea salt on the table to sprinkle over as you eat, if wished. For those of us who love licorice, this pudding is a sheer, spine-tingling joy. ■

PANNA COTTA THREE WAYS

I WROTE MY FIRST RECIPE FOR PANNA COTTA (admittedly, an anglicized version tagged Elderflower Cream) way back in my first book, *How To Eat*, published in 1998, but for me, this is a dessert that never falls out of favor. Besides, flavor not fashion is what counts in food, and I can never tire of the perfect panna cotta. Custom cannot stale its infinite variety, although I have shown uncharacteristic restraint and confined myself to a mere trio of versions.

But I do say "the perfect panna cotta," and if real cooking is all about the palate, let me say that texture is the key issue here. Consistency is crucial: a panna cotta must have a voluptuous and quivering softness, as if trembling between solid and liquid. A panna cotta must never be overset; the trick is to add just enough gelatin to keep the unmolded cream from collapsing, but it should still have just enough wibble about it to hint that it could, that its bulging form could break its borders and spill free. It won't, so don't worry. Because the point is I don't want you to feel that there is risk here, or that it is difficult to achieve the perfect set. Once you get it right, it's right. And so, so easy. You heat cream, dissolve gelatin, stir, pour, put in the refrigerator. That's taken about 5 minutes, max. And that's your work done. Now, you just leave it to set.

So here's the deal: at home I use sheet gelatin (readily available in British supermarkets) and I've worked out exactly how much is needed for this state of grace. Use ⅛ ounce platinum grade sheet gelatin and soak it in cold water until it feels soft—it should feel like a tissue made out of jellyfish. Squeeze out the sheets and drop them into the warm liquid, whisking as you go. However, I am advised, and advise you in turn, that you can substitute unflavored powdered gelatin as indicated in each recipe below.

And, although you can indeed flavor panna cotta freely (though Italian traditionalists may be reluctant to agree), it is important not to get too fanciful: this is a delicate creation, and an overwhelming flavor—anything too bold and shouty or attention-seekingly novel—will blow the balance. So my trio of flavors is simple: vanilla, coffee, Nutella. Served together, the slate-speckled ivory, manila, and hazelnut-colored creams are beautifully harmonious, not just in terms of taste, but tonally, too. The reason that the Vanilla and Coffee Panna Cotta recipes each make 4 servings and the Nutella makes 6 is because I have found (especially, but not only, when children are eating) that this best reflects the likely demand.

But it's only for a big party that I would really think of making these all together, so please read them as freestanding recipes. Accordingly, I repeat the instructions for each, even though the method doesn't change. It just makes life simpler: no fretful flicking back to check what you should be doing.

What I will state here, though, just to underscore its importance, is that you should use metal rum baba or dariole molds. There is any number of silicone panna cotta molds on the market, but it is easiest by far to unmold from metal. It's not conventional but, if you prefer, you could always pour the panna cotta mixture into small glasses to set, and dispense with the unmolding. Just an idea . . . ■

VANILLA PANNA COTTA

THIS IS THE PLAINEST OF THE TRIO, although it is still more emphatically flavored than the original Piedmontese *Crema Cotta* (as it used to be called, and which I, with my appetite for alliteration, wish it were still called), which was often nothing more than cream, cooked and set. I like to use proper vanilla, rather than extract here, even though I have never managed to make the black seeds disperse themselves equally throughout the cream—they always seem to settle in a speckled layer at the top once the creams are unmolded. Still, this doesn't bother me. (If it bothers you, I suggest you dispense with the seeds and, instead, use a vegetable peeler to shave off some strips of zest from an unwaxed lemon and add these to the cream while it's heating, then add a few drops of vanilla extract once you've heated the cream. Leave it to steep for 20 minutes, then remove the zest, reheat the cream a little, and proceed from here with the gelatin.)

Traditionally, panna cotta is served without any accompaniment but, as in language so in cooking, usage dictates form, and it is now customary to add a berry or two or some sort of contrasting partner on the plate. For me, the choice is some finely diced strawberries, macerated in balsamic vinegar (same vintage as panna cotta, in terms of first modish moment), and for the amount of people I'm feeding here, I'd go for 8 ounces of strawberries, dice them finely, put them in a bowl with ½ teaspoon each of sugar and of balsamic vinegar, cover with plastic wrap, and leave to steep for at least 15 minutes and up to 2 hours, out of the refrigerator, shaking the covered bowl to swirl the contents every now and again. This won't give you a lot of fruit, but you want only a spoonful or so on each plate. In winter, consider simply spooning some pomegranate seeds around, letting one or two drop on top. My son insists on a chocolate sauce (poured around the panna cotta, not over it) and if you feel so inclined, too, then make up half quantities of the Chocolate Sauce on **p.169**, but add a small espresso shot (about 2 tablespoonfuls) to the cream and chocolate in the pan when you kick off, and make sure the sauce is cool when you serve it.

SERVES 4 ⊘

2 TABLESPOONS WATER

1 TEASPOON UNFLAVORED
   GELATIN

⅓ CUP WHOLE MILK

1⅔ CUPS HEAVY CREAM

¼ CUP SUGAR

1 VANILLA BEAN

4 X ½-CUP METAL RUM BABA/
   DARIOLE MOLDS

Pour the water in a small bowl and sprinkle over the gelatin. Let stand until softened. This will take about 10 minutes, so get on with the rest of the recipe while the gelatin softens.

Pour the milk and cream into a saucepan and stir in the sugar. Remove the seeds from the vanilla bean (and see **p.164** for instructions should you want) and add them plus the emptied-out bean to the saucepan; put it over a low heat.

When the saucepan mixture is about to come to a boil—i.e., when it is beginning to bubble a little around the edges—take the pan off the heat and remove the vanilla bean (though rinse and dry it later to save for future use to flavor sugar).

Check that the gelatin looks soft—it should have turned translucent and absorbed all of the water—then scrape all of the soft gelatin into the saucepan and whisk until the gelatin has fully dissolved. Do not return the pan to the heat once you have added the gelatin.

Transfer the mixture to a heatproof pitcher before pouring the mixture into the 4 molds, giving the pitcher's contents a gentle whisk between each pour. Transfer to the refrigerator for at least 4 hours, or preferably overnight, until set. Let them come to room temperature before serving.

To unmold easily, dip the bottom of each mold into some just-boiled water, one at a time, and hold there for about 8 seconds; let it stand out of the water for another few seconds before wiping off the water and putting a small salad plate or saucer on top; then overturn the mold and let the panna cotta drop onto the plate. Do likewise with the remaining 3 molds and serve, with fruit or sauce as preferred. ■

COFFEE PANNA COTTA

I TRIED TO STOP MYSELF, BELIEVE ME, I did, as I realize that this book ain't light on coffee-flavored confections, but this is my all-time favorite and it would have given me too much pain to leave it out.

The depth of the coffee flavor, combined with the treacliness of the sugar and the satiny richness of the cream, make this, for me, an unbeatable combination. It's startlingly, but simply, sensational.

I use a couple of proper espresso shots, since I've got a machine that makes this easy, but otherwise make up *very* strong coffee by other means. And if you fancy a chocolate sauce alongside, then make up half quantities of the recipe on **p.169**, adding a small espresso shot —about 2 tablespoons—to the saucepan at the beginning, and make sure the sauce is cool on serving; or make up the Frangelico cream on the facing page.

SERVES 4 Ⓝ

2 TABLESPOONS WATER

1 TEASPOON UNFLAVORED GELATIN

½ CUP FRESHLY MADE ESPRESSO COFFEE

¼ CUP (FIRMLY PACKED) LIGHT BROWN SUGAR

1½ CUPS HEAVY CREAM

PINCH SALT

4 X ½-CUP METAL RUM BABA/ DARIOLE MOLDS

Pour the water in a small bowl and sprinkle over the gelatin. Let stand until softened. This will take about 10 minutes, so get on with the rest of the recipe while the gelatin softens.

Pour the hot strong espresso into a small saucepan and stir in the light brown sugar until it has dissolved. Now stir in the cream and a pinch of salt and put the saucepan over a low heat.

When the cappuccino-scented mixture is about to come to a boil—i.e., when it is beginning to bubble a little around the edges—take the pan off the heat.

Check that the gelatin looks soft—it should have turned translucent and absorbed all of the water—then scrape all of the soft gelatin into the saucepan and whisk until the gelatin has fully dissolved. Do not return the pan to the heat once you have added the gelatin.

Transfer the mixture to a heatproof pitcher before pouring the mixture into the 4 molds, giving the pitcher's contents a gentle whisk between each pour. Transfer to the refrigerator for at least 4 hours, or preferably overnight, until set. Let them come to room temperature before serving.

To unmold easily, dip the bottom of each mold into some just-boiled water, one at a time, and hold there for about 8 seconds; let it stand out of the water for another few seconds before wiping off the water and putting a small salad plate or saucer on top; then overturn the mold and let the panna cotta drop onto the plate. Do likewise with the remaining 3 molds and serve, as is, or with some cool chocolate sauce lapping around the edges. ∎

NUTELLA PANNA COTTA

THIS CHEEKY LITTLE NUMBER COMES COURTESY of Angela Hartnett, a chef with, all jokiness aside, an exquisite palate and a sensibility that is utterly unsullied by the pretension natural to many of her profession.

My recipe is not quite hers, but I am grateful for the inspiration, though not nearly as grateful as my children are. By the way, don't be alarmed that I use the same amount of gelatin for this recipe as for the two others, despite the fact that the liquid content here is higher—the Nutella itself aids the set as it chills.

I like to serve this with some heavy cream poured around the panna cotta on the plate and, if the mood takes me, and I'm catering not for children but for adults with childish tastes, I splosh in some Frangelico hazelnut liqueur as well. Actually, you could also add a slug to the Nutella mixture in the pan as you cook, and put the bottle on the table with a clutch of shot glasses, on serving.

Pour the water in a small bowl and sprinkle over the gelatin. Let stand until softened. This will take about 10 minutes, so get on with the rest of the recipe while the gelatin softens.

Pour the milk and cream into a saucepan and add the chocolate hazelnut spread, stir to combine (adding a slug of hazelnut liqueur if the fancy takes you), then put the saucepan over a low heat.

When the chocolate hazelnut spread has melted and the mixture is about to come to a boil—i.e., when it is beginning to bubble a little around the edges—take the pan off the heat.

Check that the gelatin looks soft—it should have turned translucent and absorbed all of the water—then scrape all of the soft gelatin into the saucepan and whisk until the gelatin has fully dissolved. Do not return the pan to the heat once you have added the gelatin.

Transfer the mixture to a heatproof pitcher before pouring the mixture into the 6 molds, giving the pitcher's contents a gentle whisk between each pour. Transfer to the refrigerator for at least 4 hours, or preferably overnight, until set. Let them come to room temperature before serving.

To unmold easily, dip the bottom of each mold into some just-boiled water, one at a time, and hold there for about 8 seconds; let it stand out of the water for another few seconds before wiping off the water and putting a small salad plate or saucer on top; then overturn the mold and let the panna cotta drop onto the plate. Do likewise with the remaining 5 molds and serve.

For the Frangelico cream, combine the cream and liqueur, if you wish, in a pitcher. Put the pitcher on the table to serve alongside. ■

SERVES 6 ℕ

2 TABLESPOONS WATER

1 TEASPOON UNFLAVORED GELATIN

1 CUP WHOLE MILK

1 CUP HEAVY CREAM

1 CUP NUTELLA OR EQUIVALENT CHOCOLATE HAZELNUT SPREAD

HAZELNUT LIQUER (OPTIONAL)

FRANGELICO CREAM, TO SERVE (OPTIONAL)

6 TABLESPOONS HEAVY CREAM

6 TEASPOONS FRANGELICO LIQUEUR

6 X ½-CUP METAL RUM BABA/ DARIOLE MOLDS

THESE PANCAKES ARE—WITHOUT WISHING TO OFFEND ITALIANS—what we think of as French-style crêpes. For our purposes here, though, they are Italian-style *crespelle*. Be that as it may, as a quick dinner-party dessert, I buy them ready made, to be turned easily into parcels, filled with mascarpone and ricotta, flavored with lemon, vanilla, and rum; once baked, these taste like soft, cheesecake-stuffed crêpes. The rum-soused confetti of strawberries that I dollop on top echoes the fruit toppings of retro cheesecakes; more important, the liqueur-heightened brightness of the berries undercuts the richness of the filling. One parcel per person would probably be fine, portion-wise, but I work on the principle that half those eating might have seconds. You could easily give each person two apiece if you preferred or, conversely, stretch them out to feed more if need be. Once cooked, they set and cut well, so you could even slice them into sticks or smaller squares.

MASCARPONE & RICOTTA CRÊPES WITH RUM-STEEPED STRAWBERRIES

Preheat the oven to 350°F. Hull the strawberries and cut them into small dice, then put them in a bowl and sprinkle with the 2 tablespoons sugar and 2 tablespoons rum. Cover with plastic wrap and leave to macerate—swirling once or twice—while you get on with the crêpes.

Lightly brush a jelly roll pan or similar lipped baking sheet with some of the melted butter or line with parchment paper, then stir the teaspoon of rum into the rest of the melted butter and set aside for a while.

Beat together the mascarpone and ricotta, until they are light and well combined, then beat in the egg, followed by the ¼ cup sugar, the lemon zest, vanilla extract, and the remaining tablespoon of rum.

Lay out a crêpe, pale-side up, and dollop about ⅓ cup—think of an espresso cup filled brimmingly to the rim—of the mixture onto the middle, then fold the top and bottom of the crêpe over, and do the same to the sides, to make a bulging parcel. Place, fold- or seam-side down, on your prepared jelly roll pan and proceed with the remaining 7 crêpes.

Brush the crêpes with the rum-butter and put in the preheated oven for 20–25 minutes; when cooked, they will be puffed up and, although the filling will have oozed out a little, it will be safely set.

Let them stand a minute or so before carefully transferring to a serving plate (or serve straight from the pan), and spoon a gleaming sprinkle of rum-soaked strawberries over them as you serve. ■

SERVES 4 TO 6 *(MAKES 8 CRÊPES)*
FOR THE STRAWBERRIES
1 POUND STRAWBERRIES
2 TABLESPOONS SUGAR
2 TABLESPOONS RUM

FOR THE FILLED CRÊPES
2 TABLESPOONS UNSALTED
  BUTTER, MELTED
1 TABLESPOON RUM, PLUS
  1 TEASPOON
8 OUNCES MASCARPONE, AT
  ROOM TEMPERATURE
8 OUNCES RICOTTA, AT ROOM
  TEMPERATURE
1 EGG
¼ CUP SUPERFINE SUGAR
ZEST 1 UNWAXED LEMON
½ TEASPOON VANILLA EXTRACT
6 CRÊPES, STORE-BOUGHT

1 JELLY ROLL PAN OR LIPPED
  BAKING SHEET

FOR SOMEONE WHO STARTED OFF as a tiramisu scorner, I have turned out to be its most slavish proponent, finding any excuse to whip up a new one. From Anna Del Conte's all-white meringue version, and something more trad (and I say this being well aware that tiramisu as such came into being only in the latter half of the 20th century), to one made with Frangelico and another with Baileys.

Some say, challenging more generally accepted ideas about the provenance, that it was invented in a *casa chiusa* (a house of ill repute) to give the working girls a pick-me-up, as the name (*tira-mi-su*) suggests. Whatever its inception, this one reverts to the original formulation—although in dinkier format. This is not because I am a huge fan of the cute—you know that—but because it means you have a tiramisu worth making for fewer people (you don't need a partyful), and in less time. By which I mean very much less time, since, unlike the big, trifle-style tiramisu, these tiramisini—think coffee-soaked Savoiardi cookies, topped with the familiar, whipped Marsala-spiked mascarpone in small-portioned martini glasses—don't even need to sit overnight before being ready to eat.

These are a tiny bit lighter, too, as I don't use the egg yolks—the mascarpone is plenty rich enough—but keep the whites to add moussiness and air. These I buy in a carton (pasteurized) and have always at the ready (and see Note to the Reader on **p.xiii** about eggs). I make sure the Savoiardi, mascarpone, and Marsala are also on hand; and coffee is always in the house, as well as the liqueur that echoes it, but it's fine to leave out the coffee liqueur and just bump up the coffee quotient, if you prefer.

TIRAMISINI

SERVES 4

7 TABLESPOONS ESPRESSO OR STRONG INSTANT COFFEE

2 TABLESPOONS COFFEE LIQUEUR

4 SAVOIARDI COOKIES (LADYFINGERS)

2 EGG WHITES

1 CUP MASCARPONE

2 TABLESPOONS HONEY

2 TABLESPOONS MARSALA

APPROX. 1 TEASPOON GOOD-QUALITY UNSWEETENED COCOA POWDER

4 SMALL (APPROX. ½ CUP) MARTINI GLASSES

Make your espresso and pour it into a heatproof pitcher, adding the coffee liqueur, then leave it to cool. I find 10 minutes outside the window on a cool day does it!

Break each Savoiardi cookie into about 4 and drop the pieces into the martini glasses, then pour the cooled espresso mixture over them. Tamp down gently, making sure the biscuits are soaked all over.

Using an electric hand mixer for ease, beat the egg whites until they form soft peaks, and set aside for a moment.

Scrape the mascarpone into another bowl, adding the honey; I love the way its mellow sweetness marries with the Marsala, though sugar would be fine too. Beat with the electric hand mixer (no need to clean it first) and, when smooth, slowly beat in the Marsala.

Fold in the egg whites, a third at a time, then dollop this mixture over the soused Savoiardi in each glass, using a spoon to whirl it into a swirly peak at the top.

Let these stand in the refrigerator for at least 20 minutes and up to 24 hours, then dust with cocoa, pushing it through a fine-mesh strainer, just before serving. ■

I DARE SAY THAT HAVING A TRICOLORE dessert is not terribly original, when it comes to compiling a book of Italian recipes, but I just couldn't help myself. Besides, the sharpness of the berries and the aromatic rubble of pistachios provide contrast—of taste and texture—with the light, vanilla-flecked mousse. I say mousse, but this is a simple affair, consisting of no more than whisked egg whites, folded into heavy cream whipped with sugar and the seeds from a vanilla bean. To get the seeds out of the bean, I use the point of a small, sharp knife to make a lengthwise incision all along the middle of the bean, and then use the point of the knife again to scoop and scrape all the damp black seeds out. And, if I can do that with what my TV director calls my "borderline dyspraxia," anyone can. Don't throw away the bean, by the way, but rinse and dry it later to put in a jar of sugar to flavor it for baking.

If you want to top these vanilla mousses with a fine dust of pistachio, then you'll need a coffee grinder; otherwise, chop the nuts finely by hand, and you'll probably need the extra spoonful for total coverage. As for the berries that go underneath, to keep to the *tricolore* theme, I like to use 50/50 raspberries (left whole) and strawberries (chopped to match the size of the raspberries) but, otherwise, a mixture of any berries that come your way would be fine and dandy.

I have so many recipes, as you may have noted, where I use only the egg whites that, these days, I make sure my refrigerator is always stocked with a pasteurized carton of them. In fact, I've gotten so used to this, I don't even find it strange that they do come in a carton. (And see Note to the Reader on **p.xiii** on using uncooked eggs.)

VANILLA MOUSSE WITH BERRIES & PISTACHIOS

SERVES 6

2 FREE-RANGE ORGANIC OR
  PASTEURIZED EGG WHITES

1¼ CUPS HEAVY CREAM

½ CUP SUPERFINE SUGAR

SEEDS FROM 1 VANILLA BEAN

8 OUNCES RASPBERRIES

8 OUNCES STRAWBERRIES,
  CHOPPED

1–2 TABLESPOONS CHOPPED
  SHELLED, UNSALTED PISTACHIO
  NUTS

6 APPROX. ⅔-CUP GLASSES

Whisk the egg whites in a clean, grease-free bowl until they form soft peaks.

Pour the cream into another bowl, add the sugar and vanilla seeds, and whisk until this mixture, too, forms soft peaks. Fold the whisked egg whites gently into the vanilla cream to make your mousse.

Divide the berries among 6 glasses until just under half-full and dollop the vanilla mousse on top, until every glass is softly peaked.

Chill them in the fridge for 15 to 30 minutes.

On serving, dust the tops with the ground or finely chopped pistachios. ■

I FOUND THIS RECIPE FOR one of the world's easiest but most delicious desserts in a rather fabulous book, by chef and "culinary philosopher" Gioacchino Scognamiglio, called *Il Chichibio: Ovvero Poesia Della Cucina*, which translates as "The Gallant: or the Poetry of Cooking" (and Chichibio, I should also tell you, was a rakish Venetian cook in Boccaccio's *Decameron*). At Scognamiglio's instigation, I went to great lengths to acquire a bottle of Elisir San Marzano, which has a peculiarly Italian, chocolate-coffee-herbal hit. Feel free to use coffee liqueur or rum or, better still, a mixture of the two in its place.

This, like all the other ice creams in these pages, is a no-churn affair. You mix everything together, wodge it into a loaf pan, freeze, and you're done.

I like this with a few raspberries to tumble around and a chocolate sauce to Jackson Pollock over it, the recipe for which is on **p.169**.

MERINGUE GELATO CAKE WITH CHOCOLATE SAUCE

SERVES 6–8 Ⓝ

1¼ CUPS HEAVY CREAM

1 OUNCE BITTERSWEET CHOCOLATE (MIN. 62% COCOA SOLIDS)

1 TABLESPOON ELISIR SAN MARZANO, OR COFFEE LIQUEUR AND/OR RUM

4 OUNCES STORE-BOUGHT MERINGUE COOKIES

TO SERVE (OPTIONAL)

1 BATCH CHOCOLATE SAUCE (SEE PAGE 169)

8 OUNCES RASPBERRIES

1 X 1-POUND LOAF PAN (8 X 4 X 3 INCHES OR SIMILAR CAPACITY)

Line your loaf pan with plastic wrap, making sure you have enough overhang to cover the top later.

Whip the cream until thick but still soft.

Chop the chocolate very finely so that you have a pile of dark splinters, and fold them into the cream, along with the liqueur.

Now, using brute force, crumble the meringue cookies and fold these in, too.

Pack this mixture into the prepared loaf pan, pressing it down with a spatula as you go, and bring the plastic wrap up and over to seal the top, then get out more plastic wrap to wrap around the whole pan. Freeze until solid, which should take around 8 hours, or overnight.

To serve, unwrap the outer layer of plastic wrap, then unpeel the top and use these bits of long overhanging wrap to lift out the ice-cream brick. Unwrap and unmold it onto a board and cut the frozen meringue cake into slabs to serve. I like to zigzag a little chocolate sauce (see opposite) over each slice, and sprinkle a few raspberries alongside on each plate. ◼

THIS IS A USEFUL BLUEPRINT FOR a chocolate sauce; it is gloopily thick, but intentionally so. If pouring over an ice cream, as here or on **pp.170** or **254**, you want to leave this until only subtly warm; if to accompany panna cotta (and see **pp.155–159**), then leave it to cool to room temperature. In either case, whisk well before bringing to the table. If you feel that the sauce has become too solid, then stand the pitcher in a bowl of warm water for a few minutes, whisking frequently, before pouring. Or I whisk in a small shot—about 2 tablespoons—of hot espresso to make it a little more fluid.

CHOCOLATE SAUCE

Pour the cream into a saucepan and add the tiny bits of chocolate.

Put over a gentle heat and whisk as the chocolate melts, taking the pan off the heat once the chocolate is almost all melted. If the mixture gets too hot, the chocolate will seize, whereas it will happily continue melting in the warm cream off the heat.

Add the liqueur, still off the heat, and whisk again to amalgamate the sauce completely. Pour into a pitcher, whisking every now and again until it cools to the desired temperature. ■

MAKES APPROX. 1¼ CUPS Ⓝ

1 CUP HEAVY CREAM

⅔ CUP (5 OUNCES) BITTERSWEET CHOCOLATE (MIN. 62% COCOA SOLIDS), FINELY CHOPPED OR IN CHIPS MADE FOR MELTING

2 TABLESPOONS ELISIR SAN MARZANO, OR COFFEE LIQUEUR AND/OR RUM

I'M ALMOST EMBARRASSED AT HOW EASY this is but, as you will find out, simple though it is to make, its flavor is deep, complex, and utterly compelling.

So, here's how it goes: you don't make a custard and you don't need an ice-cream maker. You could (and I often do) serve it with a chocolate sauce (see previous page) but my absolute favorite way of eating this is by squidging it into little brioches, like sweet burger buns, as they do in the south of Italy. Luckily, I live near an Italian *caffè* that will sell them to me, but I am also searching dutifully for an online source.

I use Illy espresso liqueur here, but any coffee liqueur would do, even if it weren't quite as strong. I have never tried using regular instant coffee granules in place of the instant espresso powder stipulated, though I dare say if you boosted quantities and dissolved the granules in a little boiling water first, you could make it work for you.

But this works so perfectly for me that I have no desire to meddle. And I whip up this ice cream so often, it makes comforting sense for me to keep the key ingredients in stock.

Maybe I don't have to add this but as a security measure, let me remind you that 1 tablespoon is 3 teaspoons. My instant espresso powder comes with a teaspoon measure inside, so, if it helps, use 6 of these to make sure you are adding the right amount.

ONE-STEP NO-CHURN COFFEE ICE CREAM

MAKES 1 PINT Ⓝ

⅔ CUP SWEETENED CONDENSED
  MILK
2 TABLESPOONS INSTANT
  ESPRESSO POWDER
2 TABLESPOONS ESPRESSO
  LIQUEUR
1¼ CUPS HEAVY CREAM

1 X 1-PINT AIRTIGHT CONTAINER

Put the condensed milk in a bowl and stir in the espresso powder and liqueur. In a separate bowl whisk the cream until it reaches soft peaks. Fold the cream into the condensed milk mixture, then pour this gorgeous caffe-latte–colored airy mixture into an airtight container and freeze for 6 hours or overnight. Serve straight from the freezer. ■

THE "DOUBLE AMARETTO" PART OF THE title refers to the fact that both amaretti biscuits and amaretto liqueur are included; *"semifreddo,"* which simply means "semicold," indicates that although this is an ice cream, it has a soft rather than frozen-solid texture. (Please take note that the biscuits are the crunchy amaretti, not those labeled *morbidi* or soft; and see Note to the Reader on **p.xiii** about eggs.)

This is very much a shortcut semifreddo, incidentally; I have given recipes before that—divine though they are—involve much beating of egg yolks and sugar in a heatproof bowl suspended over a pan of simmering water. And as far as ice creams go, this is a double-doddle: no effort to whip up and no machine to churn it. You just fill some dainty dariole molds (not really me, generally speaking, though see also Panna Cotta Three Ways on **p.155**) and stash them in the freezer for at least 6 hours or overnight.

To unmold, dip the bottom of the dariole molds into a cup or bowl of hot water for 30 seconds, then clamp a small plate or saucer over the top, upend, and turn out. But you could simply line the molds with plastic wrap (leaving an overhang for pulling out the semifreddo later), if you prefer. The apricot amaretto sauce is for pouring over each little semifreddo, as you serve. You don't need much sauce, so don't worry about the scant quantity below. Also, the sauce must not be hot, so make it early. I like to get it done at the same time as the semifreddi go into the freezer, and then leave it in a milk pitcher, plastic wrapped and out of the refrigerator until required.

I know smart Italians consider amaretto to be too frightfully déclassé for words, but surely that is part of its charm?

DOUBLE AMARETTO SEMIFREDDO WITH GOLDEN-GLEAMING SAUCE

SERVES 6 Ⓝ

2 OUNCES AMARETTI COOKIES
  (CRUNCHY NOT *MORBIDI*)

1 EGG WHITE

1 CUP HEAVY CREAM

2 TABLESPOONS
  CONFECTIONERS' SUGAR

3 TABLESPOONS AMARETTO
  LIQUEUR

▶

Put the amaretti cookies into a resealable plastic bag and bash them with a rolling pin until you have crumbs: you should end up with a mixture of coarse and fine crumbs but don't be so brutal that you end up with sand.

Put the egg white in a bowl and whisk to soft peaks. In a separate bowl whisk the cream until soft peaks form, then fold in the egg white. You can use a hand mixer for speed and you don't need to wash the beaters between whisking the whites and the cream.

Fold in the confectioners' sugar and amaretto liqueur, then fold in the cookie crumbs.

Fill 6 dariole molds, packing in the mixture, tamping it down, and smoothing the top. Then cover each one with plastic wrap and place in the freezer, leaving for at least 6 hours or overnight (and not longer than 1 week).

To make the sauce, put the preserves and amaretto liqueur into a small saucepan and bring to a boil, whisking together.

Boil for 1 minute, then take off the heat and let cool slightly before pouring into a small milk or cream pitcher. Leave to cool, then cover and set aside.

When you are ready to serve the semifreddo, sit the bottom of each dariole mold, one at a time, in a bowl of just boiled water for a brief 30-second dip, wipe off the water, then put a small plate or saucer on top, upturn the mold, and turn out the semifreddo (dip again if it won't come out first time), and spoon a little of the golden, gleaming sauce over it. I'd put the bottle of amaretto and 6 shot glasses on the table, too. ■

FOR THE SAUCE
¼ CUP APRICOT PRESERVES
¼ CUP AMARETTO LIQUEUR

6 ½-CUP METAL RUM BABA/
DARIOLE MOLDS

I DON'T KNOW IF I SHOULD apologize for this or boast about it. Either way, I feel you will thank me for it. The thing is that it's embarrassingly easy and, although I first started making it last Christmas—a lot—reckoning that it was just the sort of count-no-calorie indulgence that the season demands, I have since decided that something this good, and this speedily simple to conjure into being, needs to be in our lives all year round.

Don't be tempted to let the cheesecake come to room temperature before serving. It slices and eats better with a bit of refrigerator chill on it.

However, you must have both Nutella and cream cheese at room temperature before making it. To simplify your life a little, try to buy the hazelnuts already chopped and toasted.

CHOCOLATE HAZELNUT CHEESECAKE

Break the crackers into the bowl of a food processor, then add the butter and 1 tablespoon of Nutella and blitz until the mixture starts to clump. Add 3 tablespoons of the toasted hazelnuts, and continue to pulse until you have a damp, sandy mixture.

Tip this into your springform pan and press it into the base, using either your hands or the back of a spoon. Place in the refrigerator to chill while you get on with the filling.

Beat together the cream cheese and confectioners' sugar until smooth and soft, then patiently scrape the rest of the Nutella out of its jar and into the cream cheese mixture and continue beating until combined.

Take the springform pan out of the refrigerator. Carefully scrape and smooth the Nutella mixture over the cracker crumb base and scatter the remaining chopped hazelnuts on top to cover. Place the pan in the refrigerator for at least 4 hours or overnight.

Serve straight from the refrigerator for best results, unspringing the cake from the pan, still on its base, just before you eat. To cut it, dip a sharp knife in cold water, wiping it and dipping again between each cut. And don't worry: it may look disappointingly flat when whole, but when sliced, its dark depths are revealed. ∎

SERVES 8–12 Ⓝ

10 OUNCES GRAHAM CRACKERS (ABOUT 16 SHEETS OR 2½ CUPS CRUMBS)

5 TABLESPOONS SOFT UNSALTED BUTTER

1 X 13-OUNCE JAR NUTELLA OR EQUIVALENT CHOCOLATE HAZELNUT SPREAD, AT ROOM TEMPERATURE

¾ CUP CHOPPED TOASTED HAZELNUTS

1 POUND CREAM CHEESE, AT ROOM TEMPERATURE

½ CUP CONFECTIONERS' SUGAR, SIFTED

1 X 9-INCH SPRINGFORM CAKE PAN

THERE IS SOMETHING SO COZY-MAKING ABOUT the way new technology re-creates the recipe-sharing traditions of older communities. This recipe is a case in point. Francesca Petracca, one of my Italian Twitter followers, tweeted a picture of her family's *Torta di Mele* and I asked her to post the recipe on my website. She did, I made it—or a version of it—and here we are.

The English title Francesca gave to her *Torta di Mele* was Italian Apple Pie, and I have stayed faithful to it, although the finished product is really more of a cake. Whatever it is, it is just wonderful: simple to make, and alluringly rustic. I like it best served still warm, as a kind of pudding cake, with crème anglaise, mascarpone, or heavy cream (whipped or runny), but *la famiglia* Petracca prefer to eat slices as an accompaniment to a cup of tea or an espresso "in the company of lovely friends." Who can argue with that?

I used Pink Lady apples here, as I don't peel the slices that go on top of the cake, and a firm, red-skinned apple works well and looks pretty. But it's not worth going for a red-skinned apple that won't hold its shape—such as a Red Delicious—so bear that in mind while shopping; the color of the skin is not the crucial factor here. Perhaps I should mention that the original recipe, as posted on my website, stipulates that all the apples be peeled; what follows is my lazy version. . . .

As ever with baking, all the ingredients should, of course, be at room temperature.

ITALIAN APPLE PIE

SERVES 8 Ⓝ

7 TABLESPOONS SOFT UNSALTED
  BUTTER, PLUS MORE FOR
  GREASING
1²/₃ CUPS ALL-PURPOSE FLOUR
2 TEASPOONS BAKING POWDER
PINCH SALT
¾ CUP SUPERFINE SUGAR
2 EGGS
ZEST 1 UNWAXED LEMON
1 TEASPOON VANILLA EXTRACT
5 TABLESPOONS WHOLE MILK,
  AT ROOM TEMPERATURE
3 PINK LADY APPLES, OR ANY
  CRISP EATING APPLES (APPROX.
  1 POUND TOTAL)

▶

Preheat the oven to 400°F. Butter your springform pan and line the bottom with parchment paper.

Into a food processor, put the flour, baking powder, pinch of salt, 7 tablespoons soft butter, superfine sugar, eggs, lemon zest, and vanilla extract, and blitz till it forms a thick, smooth batter. Then, with the motor still running, pour the milk gradually down the funnel to lighten the mixture.

To do this by hand, if you prefer, beat the butter and sugar together until pale and creamy, then beat in the eggs, followed by the flour, baking powder, salt, vanilla, lemon zest, and milk, till you have a batter with a soft, dropping consistency.

Halve 1 of the apples, then peel, core, and chop one half into approx. ½-inch cubes, add these to the batter, and either pulse to mix, or beat in. Pour your batter into the springform pan.

Quarter and core the remaining apples (including the unused half apple, above), leaving the skin on, then finely slice them and arrange in pleasing concentric circles on top of the cake batter.

Mix together the brown sugar and cinnamon and sprinkle this over the apples, then bake for 40–45 minutes, by which time the cake should be risen and golden. Pierce with a cake tester, which should have only a few crumbs sticking to it when removed.

Let cool for 1 hour, before springing it out of the pan to cut and serve warm, or leave to cool completely once out of the pan. ∎

1 TEASPOON LIGHT BROWN OR
  TURBINADO SUGAR
½ TEASPOON GROUND
  CINNAMON

1 X 9-INCH SPRINGFORM
  CAKE PAN

THE BEST WAY TO DESCRIBE CROSTATA is to say that it's like a giant jam tart, only instead of having to roll out pastry, you can make a dense sponge cake. This, anyway, is the homestyle *crostata*; storebought ones tend to involve the more labor-intensive pastry process, with a lattice-weave effect on top.

I find that some almond meal added to the mixture stops the sponge casing from being too dry; you cannot, of course, make too damp a batter, as it needs to be firm enough to hold its shape on baking—not too firm, however. Gratifyingly, it does still have a tender, marzipanny center beneath the preserves. Speaking of which: once I'd added almonds, the apricot preserves seemed an obvious pairing, but use any preserves you please. I have a hankering after a filling of gleaming ruby black currant preserves: I think it would have a charming, but still majestic, queen of tarts look to it. Whatever preserves you use, it's important that they're not too sweet. Failing that, there's always the juice from the lemon, whose zest has given up its ultra-Italian aroma in the sponge, so squeeze some in if you want to sour it up. As with most sponges, this really should be eaten on the day it's made.

APRICOT & ALMOND CROSTATA

SERVES 6–8

7 TABLESPOONS SOFT UNSALTED
   BUTTER, PLUS MORE FOR
   GREASING
¾ CUP SUPERFINE SUGAR
2 EGGS
ZEST 1 UNWAXED LEMON, PLUS
   (OPTIONAL) JUICE
1 CUP ALL-PURPOSE FLOUR
½ CUP ALMOND MEAL (FLOUR)
PINCH SALT
1 TEASPOON BAKING POWDER
1¼ CUPS GOOD-QUALITY
   APRICOT PRESERVES

1 DEEP, 10-INCH FLUTED TART PAN
   WITH LOOSE BASE (MEASURE
   FROM THE FLUTED EDGES)

Preheat the oven to 350°F. Butter a 10-inch tart pan that is approximately 2 inches deep, getting into all the crevices, or use a specially made baking spray.

Beat together the butter and sugar until pale and fluffy. Add the eggs, one at a time, continuing to beat the mixture as you go, then beat in the lemon zest.

Mix together the remaining dry ingredients and fold into the mixture.

Pour or scrape the batter into the tart pan, and spread it with a silicone spatula to make an even layer, pushing the batter into the sides. Then, using a smaller metal spatula or the back of a spoon, make a shallow circular indentation in the middle of your batter—for the jam—leaving a thicker raised border about 1¼ inches wide all around it.

Measure the preserves into a bowl and whisk to make it looser, squeezing in some lemon juice now, if you want to offset the sweetness. Then spread the preserves into the indentation in the middle of the tart base, leaving the raised edge clear all around.

Bake for 25–30 minutes, until the sponge around the edges is risen, golden brown, and firm to the touch and a cake tester comes out clean when inserted into the edge. Remove with care from the oven.

Let it cool in its pan on a wire rack for about 15 minutes or so, then very carefully ease the tart out of the fluted sides, still on its base. If you leave it to get too cold, it will be harder to get out of the pan. Do not even attempt to get it off the base.

Slip a cake slicer between the bottom of the *crostata* and the pan base to loosen it, then slice it still on the base and eat it warm with ice cream, whipped cream, or mascarpone, as dessert, or cold with a cup of tea or coffee. ◼

ALONG WITH A LOT OF NOT traditionally Italian baking, the good old English crumble has seemed to be gaining popularity—even modishness—in Italy. *"Il crumble,"* as it is called there, is described as fruit covered with *briciole croccanti* or crunchy crumbs, and I have added to the crunch factor here by incorporating—in the spirit of harmony between two great nations—crushed-up amaretti cookies, letting some fall into the stove-softened fruit first, to bring a little thickness to the ruby juices without adding cornstarch.

By all means, use other-colored plums—or indeed any other fruit you feel like—but be prepared to modify lemon and sugar content accordingly. You should also know that I like the fruit beneath the sweet crunchy crumbs to have a tanginess that could, for some people, be thought to verge on the sharp. For me, contrast is key; but if you want to keep sourness in stricter check, add more sugar to taste.

RUBY-RED PLUM & AMARETTI CRUMBLE

Preheat the oven to 375°F, and slip in a baking sheet at the same time. Put the amaretti into a resealable plastic bag and bash with a rolling pin or similar, until reduced to coarse crumbs, then decant them into a bowl.

Melt the 2 tablespoons of butter in a large saucepan (that comes with a lid), add the prepared plums, sprinkle in the 2 tablespoons of sugar, add the lemon zest and juice, and shake the pan over the heat, cooking for 2 minutes without a lid and 2 further minutes with the lid on. These timings are based on having plums that are ripe; if the fruit is disappointingly unyielding, be prepared to cook for longer with the lid on, checking frequently. You may need to add the juice of the remaining half lemon—and more sugar—if cooking for much longer.

Pour the plums (with care—they're hot) into your pie dish and set to one side. Already the red skins will have made a gorgeous garnet gravy. Sprinkle in 2 tablespoons of your amaretti crumbs.

To make the crumble topping the easy way, put the flour and baking powder into the bowl of a freestanding mixer, shake to mix, then add the small, cold butter cubes and beat, not too fast, with the flat paddle until you have a mixture rather like large-flaked oatmeal. Or you can do this by hand, just by rubbing the butter into the flour with your fingers.

Add the sugar and mix with a fork, then tip in the rest of the amaretti crumbs and fork to mix again. Pour the mixture over the waiting fruit in its pie dish, making sure you cover right to the edges to stop too much leakage; although for me, some of the rich-hued syrup spurting out over the crumble topping is essential.

Place on the baking sheet in the oven and bake for about 30 minutes; by which time you should see some ruby bubbling at the edges, and the top will be scorched gold in places. If you can bear it, let this stand for 10–15 minutes before eating, with ice cream, whipped cream, or mascarpone. ■

SERVES 6–8 ℕ

4 OUNCES AMARETTI COOKIES (CRUNCHY NOT *MORBIDI*)
2 TABLESPOONS UNSALTED BUTTER
2¼ POUNDS RED PLUMS, QUARTERED IF LARGE, HALVED IF SMALL, PITS REMOVED
2 TABLESPOONS SUGAR
ZEST AND JUICE ½ UNWAXED LEMON

FOR THE CRUMBLE TOPPING
1 CUP ALL-PURPOSE FLOUR
1 TEASPOON BAKING POWDER
7 TABLESPOONS COLD UNSALTED BUTTER, CUT INTO SMALL DICE
3 TABLESPOONS SUGAR

1 X 9-INCH OVENPROOF PIE DISH (APPROX. 2 INCHES DEEP)

YOGURT CARTON CAKE

IF THERE'S A FAMILY IN ITALY that doesn't have a recipe for yogurt carton cake, then I've yet to meet them. And I love this plain cake with perhaps disproportionate intensity. There is something so quintessentially Italian about its scent—as it bakes, I think I'm in a kitchen in Italy—and its taste—that combination of lemon and vanilla—and even the old-fashioned charm of its method.

This is it: your yogurt carton is your unit of measurement. And even though I saw from the original recipe that I copied down (from some scrawled piece of paper in the kitchen of a house I'd rented one summer) that the specified yogurt carton had a 4-ounce capacity, I have kept the same number of eggs for my 6-ounce yogurt carton. I work on the principle that eggs these days are larger than when the cake first came into being. Anyway, it works, and that's the main thing. And this is the way it works: for 1 cake, you need 1 carton of yogurt, 2 cartons of sugar, 1 carton of oil, 1 carton of potato starch or cornstarch, and 2 cartons of flour. In keeping with this style of measuring, you will see that I have even stipulated 2 capfuls of vanilla extract.

Although potato starch is the norm in Italy, it isn't easily available in Britain, which is why I have substituted cornstarch. Bear in mind that potato starch is denser, or rather weighs more per carton than cornstarch does. I've specified cup measures in the ingredients list, not only so that you can make this even if you're working from a jumbo carton of yogurt, but also because I feel the ingredients list should double as a shopping list, too.

I know this cake best in a ring shape, *ciambella* (pronounced "chambella") as it's known in Italy, and a 9-inch savarin or plain-sided tube pan can be found fairly easily online in the United States, too, but do use a 9-inch springform pan if that's easier for you: the cake won't be as high, but don't use a smaller diameter because, without the hole in the middle, the cake wouldn't cook properly in the center if the pan were any deeper.

Finally, I'm aware it may sound a bit of a bore having to whisk the egg whites, but it only *sounds* it; in the days of electric hand mixers, it really isn't any trouble.

This is my favorite weekend breakfast, or—indeed—anytime treat.

Preheat the oven to 350°F, and grease your ring mold (or springform pan); you can use vegetable oil for this or a special baking spray.

Separate the eggs and put the whites in one bowl and the yolks in another. Whisk the whites until you have firm peaks, then set aside while you get on with the rest of the cake.

Scrape the yogurt out of its carton and onto the egg yolks, then use the emptied yogurt carton to measure out your other ingredients—so, next, add 2 cartons (just) of sugar and whisk with the egg yolks and yogurt until airy and light.

Now fill up your yogurt carton with vegetable oil and, beating all the while, slowly add this to the egg yolk mixture. Then beat in 2 capfuls of vanilla extract and the zest of half a lemon.

Still beating, add 2 yogurt cartonfuls of flour followed by 1 yogurt cartonful of cornstarch or potato starch, then scrape down and fold in with a rubber spatula. Now, with a large metal spoon, dollop in the whisked egg whites, and fold them in with the spatula.

Fill the prepared savarin mold with the smooth, soft batter—it will come right to the top— and bake in the oven for 30–35 minutes; when cooked, the sides will be coming away at the edges and a cake tester will come out clean.

Remove it from the oven to a wire rack, letting the cake sit in the pan for 10 minutes before turning it out.

Once cooled (although I love this still slightly warm), transfer it to a serving plate or stand and dust with confectioners' sugar. Traditionally, this cake would be placed on the plate with the smooth side on top, but I rather like it turned back up the way it was baked, with its rustic cracks and uneven surface visible. ■

CUTS INTO 16 SLICES, *BUT IT WOULD BE EASY TO EAT 3 OR 4 AT A SITTING* Ⓝ

⅔ CUP PLAIN WHOLE-MILK YOGURT

⅔ CUP FLAVORLESS VEGETABLE OIL, PLUS SOME FOR GREASING

3 EGGS

1¼ CUPS SUPERFINE SUGAR

2 CAPFULS (1½ TEASPOONS) VANILLA EXTRACT

ZEST ½ UNWAXED LEMON

1⅓ CUPS ALL-PURPOSE FLOUR

⅔ CUP CORNSTARCH

1 TEASPOON CONFECTIONERS' SUGAR, TO SERVE

1 X 9-INCH (AND APPROX. 2-INCH-DEEP) SAVARIN MOLD OR PLAIN TUBE PAN

ALTHOUGH I FIRST CAME UP WITH THIS RECIPE because I had someone coming for supper who—genuinely—couldn't eat wheat or dairy, it is so meltingly good, I now make it all the time for those whose life and diet are not so unfairly constrained, myself included.

It is slightly heavier with the almonds—though not in a bad way—so if you want a lighter crumb, rather than a squidgy interior, and are not making the cake for the gluten-intolerant, then replace the 1½ cups almond meal with ¾ cup plus 1 tablespoon of all-purpose flour. This has the built-in bonus of making it perhaps more suitable for an everyday cake.

Made with the almonds, it has more of dinner-party pudding feel about it and I love it still a bit warm, with some raspberries or some such on the side, as well as a dollop of mascarpone or ice cream.

CHOCOLATE OLIVE OIL CAKE

CUTS INTO 8-12 SLICES Ⓝ

⅔ CUP REGULAR OLIVE OIL, PLUS MORE FOR GREASING

6 TABLESPOONS GOOD-QUALITY UNSWEETENED COCOA POWDER, SIFTED

½ CUP BOILING WATER

2 TEASPOONS BEST VANILLA EXTRACT

1½ CUPS ALMOND MEAL (FLOUR) OR ¾ CUP PLUS 1 TABLESPOON ALL-PURPOSE FLOUR

½ TEASPOON BAKING SODA

PINCH SALT

1 CUP SUPERFINE SUGAR

3 EGGS

1 X 9-INCH SPRINGFORM CAKE PAN

Preheat your oven to 325°F. Grease your springform pan with a little oil and line the base with parchment paper.

Measure and sift the cocoa powder into a bowl or pitcher and whisk in the boiling water until you have a smooth, chocolatey, still runny (but only just) paste. Whisk in the vanilla extract, then set aside to cool a little.

In another smallish bowl, combine the almond meal (or all-purpose flour) with the baking soda and pinch of salt.

Put the sugar, olive oil, and eggs into the bowl of a freestanding mixer with the paddle attachment (or other bowl and whisk arrangement of your choice) and beat together vigorously for about 3 minutes, until you have a pale-primrose, aerated, and thickened cream.

Turn the speed down a little and pour in the cocoa mixture, beating as you go, and when all is scraped in, you can slowly tip in the almond meal (or all-purpose flour) mixture.

Scrape down, and stir a little with a spatula, then pour this dark, liquid batter into the prepared pan. Bake for 40–45 minutes or until the sides are set and the very center, on top, still looks slightly damp. A cake tester should come up mainly clean but with a few sticky chocolate crumbs clinging to it.

Let it cool for 10 minutes on a wire rack, still in its pan, and then ease the sides of the cake with a small metal spatula and spring it out of the pan. Leave to cool completely or eat while still warm with some ice cream, as a dessert. ■

YOU MIGHT THINK THAT BANANA BREAD was not an Italian recipe and you'd be right, of course. It is, however, hugely popular in Italy right now, as are many recipes that emanate from the baking canon of North America and the UK. Still, I wanted to introduce an Italian element (ironic, as Italians are keener not to) and I've done that by adding some instant espresso powder. And, even though I add quite a bit, the flavor doesn't overwhelm at all: it's there, but as a hint, and the subtle bitterness of the coffee undercuts, most elegantly, the creamy sweetness of the banana.

The Italians like something sweet for breakfast, which is more than I do, so this is only mutedly so. But feel free to smooth some chocolatey spread—or mascarpone dusted with cinnamon—over a damp slice or two.

This banana bread is best if you can bear to let it stand a day after baking. Actually, I find this makes life easier: you can throw it together on Sunday, say (and it is the work of moments to make the batter), and then you have a delicious stash of breakfast slices waiting for you in the week. But, please, just because it says "breakfast" in the title, don't disregard it for any other time of the day; it's perfect for a teatime treat—and is my stepdaughter's perennial favorite.

You can also make 12 muffins out of this mixture: they will need 20 minutes in a 400°F oven.

ITALIAN BREAKFAST BANANA BREAD

CUTS INTO 8-10 SLICES Ⓝ
⅔ CUP FLAVORLESS VEGETABLE
  OIL, PLUS SOME FOR GREASING
3 MEDIUM BANANAS, VERY RIPE
  INDEED (APPROX. 14 OUNCES
  TOTAL WITH SKIN ON OR
  1⅓ CUPS MASHED)
2 TEASPOONS VANILLA EXTRACT
PINCH SALT
2 EGGS
¾ CUP SUPERFINE SUGAR
1 CUP PLUS 2 TABLESPOONS
  ALL-PURPOSE FLOUR
½ TEASPOON BAKING SODA
4 TEASPOONS INSTANT
  ESPRESSO POWDER

1 X 1-POUND DEEP LOAF PAN

Slip a baking sheet into the oven, and preheat to 325°F. Get out a deep 8½-by-4½-inch loaf pan, and line it with parchment paper or a paper loaf pan liner, or lightly oil it. I find that the bananas create a non-stick bouncy surface, though, rather like prunes do on baking, so don't fret if you don't have a liner.

Mash the bananas with the vanilla extract and salt and then beat in the oil. After I've used the oil, I use any residue in the cup measure to grease my loaf pan.

Now, beat in the eggs, one by one, followed by the sugar.

Mix the flour with the baking soda and espresso powder, and beat these dry ingredients into the runny batter.

Pour the batter into your prepared loaf pan, and put it into the oven, on the baking sheet, and bake for 50–60 minutes, or until slightly coming away at the sides and bulgingly risen: a cake tester should come out clean, barring the odd crumb. I urge you exercise restraint and wait for a day or at least half a day before slicing into it. If I can do that, so can you. ∎

THE WARM SCENT OF ANISEED in the air is, for me, the smell of Italian baking. And while I willingly concede that licorice is one of those love-it-or-loathe-it tastes (those on the positive side of the divide can turn briskly to **p.152**), for some reason this anise-flavored shortbread has even made greedy conquests of those who have promised me in advance that they don't like anything aniseedy or licorice-linked. It's true to say that I wouldn't have minded in the least had they insistently resisted; all the more for those of us who are grateful for the offering in the first place. Still, it is useful to know that this recipe does not rely on a niche-market following. I'd rather hope it could be considered a safe bet all round: perfect for snacks, teatime, or to be brought out with after-dinner coffee. But for those closest to my heart, the hard-core licorice-lovers: can I just plead with you to consider this as an accompaniment to that pudding on **p.152**?

Do make sure you buy aniseeds or anise seeds—i.e., the seeds themselves—and if you have trouble finding them locally, look online.

ANISEED SHORTBREAD

Preheat the oven to 325°F, and get out your springform pan. Line the base with parchment paper.

Put the flour, cornstarch, confectioners' sugar, and butter in a food processor and blitz till combined and just clumping into a pale dough.

Remove the lid, add the aniseeds, then put the lid back on and pulse until the aromatic seeds are well mixed in.

Tip the mixture into the prepared pan and press it out smoothly and patiently until you have an even layer at the bottom of the pan. (Yes, I do know that the aniseeds are indistinguishable from mouse droppings, but I really don't know what can profitably be said on the matter; so ignore it.)

Put it in the oven and bake for 20–25 minutes, until the shortbread is cooked through, slightly gold at the edges but still pale on top.

Remove to a wire rack, and if you want that familiar dotty-patterned shortbread look, gently use the tines of a fork to dimple the surface straight after it comes out of the oven (taking care—the pan is hot); then leave it in the pan for 10 minutes before cutting into 16 slender wedges, still in its pan. Cool for another 20–30 minutes, before lifting out the base of the pan and gently transferring the shortbread wedges to a wire rack or plate. Serve cool, or eat as warm as you like. ■

MAKES 16 SLICES Ⓝ
½ CUP ALL-PURPOSE FLOUR
⅔ CUP CORNSTARCH
½ CUP CONFECTIONERS' SUGAR
9 TABLESPOONS SOFT UNSALTED
   BUTTER
2 TEASPOONS ANISEEDS

1 X 8-INCH SPRINGFORM
   CAKE PAN

NOT LONG AGO ANNA DEL CONTE, who for me represents authentic Italy in England, emailed me a recipe—for chocolate tagliatelle—that she'd made with her granddaughter, Coco (and this is where I must interrupt myself to tell you that Anna's *Cooking with* Coco is not only a contemporary classic but an absolute must-have, though without her chocolate pasta recipe, which came after). "So," she said in her email: "I am become a Britalian cook, too." I took this as permission to make a chocolate dessert pasta. This is really Anna's recipe, only I in slovenly fashion use store-bought chocolate pasta. Well, this is a book that emphasizes speed and simplicity, so it would seem not in the spirit of things to instruct you to make homemade cocoa pasta. The ready-made stuff is not available everywhere, but it is worth tracking down (and can be found online) for this unconventional but intriguing sweet treat.

CHOCOLATE PASTA WITH PECANS & CARAMEL

SERVES 2

4 OUNCES COCOA OR
  CHOCOLATE PASTA, SUCH AS
  COCOA FUSILLI

PINCH OR TWO OF SALT

½ CUP UNSALTED PECAN NUTS,
  ROUGHLY BROKEN UP

3 TABLESPOONS SOFT UNSALTED
  BUTTER

¼ CUP DARK BROWN SUGAR

7 TABLESPOONS HEAVY CREAM,
  PLUS MORE (OPTIONAL),
  TO SERVE

Put water on to boil for the pasta and, when it's boiling, add a pinch of salt and cook the pasta, setting a timer for 2 minutes before the package instructions say it will be ready.

Put a medium-sized, non-stick frying pan on the stove and tumble in the pecans, then toast them over a medium heat. Once you can smell their scent wafting up from the pan, remove them to a cold plate.

Now stir the butter and sugar together in the frying pan over a low heat, until you have a hot, thick syrup. Carefully, pour in the cream, stir, and let the caramel mixture bubble up, add the toasted pecans and a pinch of salt, then turn off the heat.

Just before draining the pasta, lower in a cup to remove a little pasta-cooking water, then toss the drained pasta back into the frying pan with the dark and nutty caramel sauce, adding a tablespoon or two of the cooking water, if needed, to help coat the pasta. Stir to combine before dividing between 2 bowls. Serve with a little extra cream in a small pitcher to pour over as you eat, if wished. ■

AN ITALIAN-INSPIRED CHRISTMAS

THIS MAY SEEM A MODEST RECIPE with which to open the great celebratory Christmas chapter—more exuberantly expansive than all those preceding it—but it is indicative of the approach I recommend throughout the season: low-effort yet uplifting. Even in festive mood, I prefer an informal approach.

Actually, I blush to call this a recipe, but it is too useful a part of my repertoire for me to exclude it. Think, rather, of this as a blueprint for the perfect, no-cook pre-dinner or party *cicchetti*. The word *"cicchetti"* is the Venetian term for little snacky nibbles, only so much more glamorous and enticing than any English term.

All you have to know about my wrapped grissini is this: you need equal weights of Parma ham (or my preferred version, prosciutto di San Daniele from the Friuli-Venezia Giulia region) and of the chunkier Italian breadsticks, often labeled "grissini rustici." Should you be using the more industrial-looking, streamlined grissini, then you'll probably need slightly less ham.

And by the way, if you're interested, when we see a tall, skinny model-type person, we might call them a stick insect; an Italian would label them a "grissino." Not that this will ever overly concern me. Besides, I think that the grissini rustici I use are rather more plus size.

PROSCIUTTO-WRAPPED GRISSINI

Get out your grissini and break them into irregular lengths, then wrap strips or pieces (depending on how the ham comes out as you unpeel the slices) of pink prosciutto around each breadstick bit and arrange them on plates for people to pick at. ∎

SERVES 10

8 OUNCES GRISSINI RUSTICI OR OTHER ITALIAN BREADSTICKS
8 OUNCES PROSCIUTTO DI SAN DANIELE, OR PARMA HAM, DELI-SLICED VERY THIN

CRAB CROSTINI

IN MY VERY FIRST BOOK, *How To Eat*, I dedicated many, many pages (well, it was a very long book) to crostini, and I still can't stop with them. If you're new to the crostini caper, let me fill you in briefly: get a baguette or slim stick of bread, slice it, toast it in oven till pale gold, let it cool, and then spread with toppings of your choice. It's that simple. As you may know, I am not a great formal appetizer person, but a plate of these with cocktails has kicked off many a supper of mine.

Crab, chilis, lemon: three ingredients; one deep joy. Toss them in spaghetti or linguine for the ultimate no-cook sauce (a recipe I've given before, which is why it doesn't feature here) or into creamy rice for a dreamy risotto (see **p.40**). Here, they are garnered together for just about the most low-effort antipasti possible. And I do mean low-effort: I like to use the fabulous Italian crackers *lingue di suocera*—they translate as mother-in-law's tongues. I buy a package, break them into pieces, and smear them, just before serving, with the spicy crab. For more traditional crostini, cut a baguette or ficelle (so called because it is thinner, like "string," and I know both terms are French, but there it is) into slices about ½ inch thick, leaving both "elbows" out (cook's treat: eat immediately or they'll stale), and brush them with garlic-flavored oil; then arrange them on a wire rack above a baking sheet, bake in an oven preheated to 400°F for 5–7 minutes a side, and leave to cool. I keep bags of these plain bread slices in the freezer (or they will keep in an airtight box for 2–3 days) so that I have them ready to be oiled and toasted without notice.

Now for the chili-crab topping: I use a 50/50 mix of white and brown crabmeat. And I'm not expecting you to start cooking and picking over crabs yourself. I go to Rex my fishmonger for this, or even the supermarket, as I now find little containers of fresh crabmeat, either all white, half-white and half-brown, or all brown. Actually, I'd really love these made with nothing but the rich, almost pâté-like, brown meat but I know this is strong medicine for most people. Half and half works perfectly, not least because the soft brown meat helps you spread the crab topping on the bread and helps it to stick. If you won't eat brown crabmeat or can't find it, then you will have to think of some other fixative for the sweet, white flakes. I am presuming a spoonful or so of mayonnaise would do it, but I am not enough of a (store-bought) mayonnaise person myself to champion this tack.

Be that as it may, the amount here is enough to cover 35 little slices or cracker pieces.

If you are using bread rather than crackers, see the introduction to this recipe and proceed as directed.

Check the white crabmeat for stray pieces of shell, then put all the crabmeat into a bowl, and add the finely grated zest and juice of 1 lemon.

Tip in the chopped red chili and the chopped parsley, and stir to mix thoroughly. You can mix this up, cover it and sit it in the refrigerator for up to 24 hours, then stir before using.

Spread onto the toasts (prepared as suggested in the intro) or crackers: a scant teaspoon on each one is enough, as the brown meat provides richness and the chili, fire. ■

MAKES 35

1 BAGUETTE OR FICELLE LOAF, OR 1 PACKAGE LINGUE DI SUOCERA OR OTHER CRACKERS

8 OUNCES CRABMEAT, HALF-WHITE AND HALF-BROWN, FOR CHOICE

ZEST AND JUICE 1 UNWAXED LEMON

1 RED CHILI, SEEDED AND FINELY CHOPPED

1 TABLESPOON CHOPPED FRESH PARSLEY

GORGONZOLA & CANNELLINI DIP WITH A TRICOLORE FLOURISH

I LOVE THIS COMBINATION OF BLUE CHEESE AND WHITE BEANS, but I have to say its gorgeousness is due in no small part to the mascarpone and Marsala that add creaminess of texture and smoky depth of tone respectively.

I like this dip to have real tang: I need to feel that burning, blue-cheese buzz. If you want something milder and maybe with more universal appeal, simply reduce the amount of cheese. I started with 6 ounces (rindless weight), and bumped it up until I felt its fierceness, which made me end up with double that amount; you could stop anywhere along the route.

The dip itself does have a corpse-like gray-blue pallor, I don't deny it, but not for long: I cover it with a sprinkling of finely chopped scallion—chives would do as well—and seeded red chili and then, with a further flourish, serve it with a platter of *tricolore* crudités. For the amount of dip below, I'd core, seed, and slice up 2 red bell peppers, take the florets from a small head of cauliflower, and tumble these alongside, then add about 10 ounces of raw sugar snaps. (Speaking of which: apologies to all Italians for picturing your flag at the wrong angle here.) But I do also add some breadsticks and crackers, mainly the mother-in-law's tongues I used for the Crab Crostini on the previous page, for dipping in, as well as and sometimes instead of the raw veggies.

When I halve this (as I often do) I still use the whole can of beans, as having half an empty can sitting around would be too annoying.

MAKES 3⅓ CUPS (SERVES AT LEAST 12 PEOPLE AS APPETIZER, MANY MORE AS PART OF A BUFFET) Ⓝ

1 X 15-OUNCE CAN CANNELLINI BEANS, DRAINED AND RINSED

12 OUNCES GORGONZOLA PICCANTE (RINDLESS WEIGHT)

½ CUP MASCARPONE

⅔ CUP PLAIN YOGURT

3 TABLESPOONS GRATED PARMESAN

FRESHLY GROUND PEPPER

2 TABLESPOONS MARSALA

2 TABLESPOONS EXTRA-VIRGIN OLIVE OIL, OR TO TASTE

TO SERVE

1 RED CHILI

1 SCALLION (GREEN PART ONLY), OR 1 TABLESPOON CHOPPED CHIVES

Put the beans, drained and rinsed, into a food processor (or you could mash everything by hand or with an immersion blender) and drop in the Gorgonzola, broken loosely into chunks. Add the mascarpone, yogurt, and Parmesan and grind in some pepper enthusiastically. Put on the lid and blitz to mix.

When it's a stiff purée, still slightly grainy, blitz again, pouring the Marsala and then the olive oil down the funnel. Taste for seasoning (remembering that the top is to be sprinkled with chili) and texture; you may want to add extra oil for a more fluid, dressing-like, smoothness.

Remove the blade carefully, then scrape the dip into a bowl or divide between as many little bowls as you want (and see Notes on **p.266** if you want to pause here).

Just before serving, seed and finely chop a shiny red chili and slice the green part of a scallion into teeny-tiny pieces (or just finely slice some chives), and sprinkle both red and green dip-decorations over the waiting dip. Serve with the crudités and other accompaniments noted in the introduction, or with whatever takes your fancy. ■

I HAVE WRITTEN A RECIPE FOR PANETTONE DRESSING BEFORE: the sweet seasonal fruit bread was cubed, toasted, and mixed with Italian sausage; this is very different, not least because I see it not as an accompaniment to the turkey on **p.221** (which has its own interior stuffing) but to be served, at parties or over cocktails, in small squares, like savory brownies.

As ever, feel free to substitute the plainer pandoro if you wish, though I do think the rich fruitiness is part of this unconventional appetizer's charm.

PANETTONE DRESSING SQUARES

Peel and halve the shallots (or peel and quarter the onions) and quarter and core the apples, and roughly cut up the pancetta (or bacon). Drop the shallot or onion and the apple pieces into the bowl of a food processor along with the celery stalks, snapped in half, and the sage leaves, and process in a short burst to start the chopping, before adding the roughly cut pancetta (or bacon), and then blitz at full speed until finely chopped. Don't worry about the mixture's wetness; mush is what I expect. You can chop everything by hand, though; in which case, don't expect to get everything as ground up as it would in the processor. Anything goes.

Heat the garlic-flavored oil in a wide, heavy frying pan and fry this mixture, stirring every now and again, for 10–15 minutes, until the vegetables et al. have softened.

Remove the fried mixture to a large bowl, crumble in the chestnuts, grate in the lemon zest and squeeze in the juice, then tear and crumble in the panettone, and—I use my hands for this—combine everything into a squidgy, fragrant paste. (If you're making this in advance, leave it to cool at this stage, then cover and transfer to the refrigerator where it can stand for up to 2 days—and see Notes on **p.266** if you want to freeze it.)

When you are ready to cook this, preheat the oven to 400°F and let the dressing come to room temperature. Uncover the bowl, beat the eggs and mix them in, then spread the mixture into a foil pan or lightly greased ovenproof dish, and bake for 25–30 minutes, until the edges brown and begin to come away from the pan or dish and a cake tester comes out clean.

For appetizers, let the pan cool for 30 minutes and then cut into 48 little bite-sized squares—or into 24 larger pieces to accompany roasted meat, if you'd prefer. ■

MAKES 48 LITTLE SQUARES Ⓝ

4 ECHALION OR BANANA
   SHALLOTS, OR 2 ONIONS
   (APPROX. 8 OUNCES TOTAL)

2 APPLES (APPROX. 8 OUNCES
   TOTAL)

14 OUNCES PANCETTA SLICES OR
   RINDLESS STREAKY BACON

2 STALKS CELERY

4 LARGE FRESH SAGE LEAVES

3 TABLESPOONS GARLIC-
   FLAVORED OIL

1½ CUPS (APPROX. 7 OUNCES)
   VACUUM-PACKED CHESTNUTS

ZEST AND JUICE 1 UNWAXED
   LEMON

1 POUND PANETTONE (OR
   PANDORO), SLIGHTLY STALE,
   SLICED

2 EGGS

OLIVE OIL, FOR GREASING

ALUMINUM FOIL PAN OR
   OVENPROOF DISH APPROX.
   9 X 13 INCHES

THIS IS AN ITALIAN-INSPIRED RECIPE that comes to me from Australia via Brazil. To explain: a Brazilian friend, and the best cook I know, Helio Fenerich, made it for me, and I had to keep (rudely) asking him to carry on making it for me. Eventually, I begged him for the recipe, which he told me he'd found in Australia. The journey was certainly worthwhile: it is a complete winner; I go into auto-Parmesan-shortbread mode whenever I have friends coming for dinner, as not only is it perfect with cocktails, but it can be made in advance.

Indeed, you can make the dough, wrap it, and then leave in the refrigerator for up to 3 days before slicing and baking it as instructed below, although you will need to let these cheese-scented cylinders sit out on a kitchen surface just long enough to get the fridge chill off them before slicing. Sometimes, I freeze a cylinder for later use (and see Notes on **p.266**).

PARMESAN SHORTBREADS

MAKES 35–40 Ⓝ
1 CUP ALL-PURPOSE FLOUR
¾ CUP GRATED PARMESAN
7 TABLESPOONS SOFT UNSALTED
  BUTTER
1 EGG YOLK

Mix all the ingredients together—using bowl and spoon, electric mixer, or food processor as wished—until a golden dough begins to form a clump.

Turn it out onto a surface and knead for about 30 seconds, until smooth, then divide into two.

Take the first half and, using your hands, roll it into a cylinder, as uniform as possible without stressing over it, about 1¼ inches in diameter. Make sure the ends are flat, too, so that the cylinder resembles a roll of coins. Now roll this up in a piece of plastic wrap, twisting the plastic wrap at the ends, like a Christmas cracker, and put the roll in the refrigerator, then proceed in the same way with the remaining half of the dough.

Preheat the oven to 350°F while the wrapped cylinders of dough rest in the refrigerator for about 45 minutes, by which time you should be able to cut them into thick slices easily: aim for about ½ inch thick.

Arrange on a baking sheet lined with parchment paper, and put in the oven for 15–20 minutes, when they should be just beginning to turn a pale gold at the edges.

Remove from the oven, then leave to cool (if you can) before eating. ■

ALTHOUGH THESE CHEESE-INFUSED, CRISP, AND GOLDEN polenta triangles with their tangy tomato dipping sauce are perfect for party picking, I have to say that in Casa Mia we like them mighty fine, too, at breakfast time as an Italianate version of hash browns or fried slice, depending on where you're coming from.

I've given a range of cheese quantity to add: if I'm eating the polenta triangles as either a breakfast add-on or supper accompaniment, I stir in ½ cup of Parmesan; when I'm treating the triangles as antipasti to be eaten alone or, rather, dipped into the tomato sauce, I add ¾ cup of the cheese. To make the polenta is not exactly hard, since the polenta I use here is the instant or quick-cook kind. All packages come with instructions, but bear in mind—should you want to fiddle with amounts—that you should stick to the ratio of 2½ cups water to every 1 cup polenta.

This is a real party pleaser: cozy but with the glamor of the not-entirely familiar.

POLENTA TRIANGLES WITH CHILI TOMATO SAUCE

MAKES 30 TRIANGLES Ⓝ
2½ CUPS WATER
1 TEASPOON KOSHER SALT OR
  ½ TEASPOON TABLE SALT,
  OR TO TASTE
1 CUP INSTANT OR QUICK-COOK
  POLENTA
½–¾ CUP PARMESAN, GRATED
OLIVE OIL, FOR COOKING THE
  TRIANGLES

1 ALUMINUM FOIL OR BROWNIE
  PAN APPROX. 9 X 13 INCHES

TO SERVE
CHILI TOMATO SAUCE
  (SEE P.209)

Put 2½ cups water in a large saucepan and bring to a boil. Add the salt and then whisk in the polenta in a steady stream. Cook the polenta, stirring constantly, for 1–3 minutes, until it is thick. When it is the required consistency, it should take 3–4 seconds to flow back when you pull a wooden spoon through the polenta.

Once it is thickened and has cooked for the required time, take off the heat, then beat in the Parmesan and check the seasoning.

Dampen a foil pan or brownie pan, by letting some water from the cold tap splash it a bit, and then spread the polenta out in an even layer in the pan, smoothing the top with a wet spatula.

Leave to cool and set, which should take about 1 hour. Once the polenta is cold, cut the panful into 15 squares (3 columns long ways by 5 columns short ways). Then cut each square into triangles; i.e., halved diagonally.

When you are ready to cook the triangles, preheat the oven to 425°F or heat the broiler.

Arrange the triangles on a baking sheet, lined with aluminum foil or parchment paper, and drizzle each triangle with about ½ teaspoon olive oil, then cook for 10–15 minutes, until hot through and a deeper gold in parts; or cook under the broiler for 5 minutes, until they begin to crisp—and don't leave the broiler.

Let cool slightly, then arrange on a plate ready to serve with the tomato dipping sauce on **p.209**. ∎

I LIKE A LOT OF TANG in my tomato sauce, but if you feel that you need to make it more universally appealing, you may want to reduce, or even eliminate, the red pepper flakes.

Don't take alarm at the 2 cloves of garlic: they are left whole and then removed, so that they infuse the sauce rather than stomp all over it.

Although this amount of sauce is—provided no double dipping, of course—enough for the Polenta Triangles on the previous page, I like to dot a couple, or more, of bowls around for people to dip in, so I sometimes make a double batch. This is also a quick and simple, piquant sauce for pasta, when hot; cold, it is an accompaniment well worth considering for the butterflied lamb on **p.58** and many other meats besides.

CHILI TOMATO SAUCE

Put the oil and garlic cloves into a small saucepan that has a lid and heat until the garlic becomes golden, at which point remove the pan from the heat, stir in the red pepper flakes, and let the oil cool slightly.

Now—standing well back in case of spitting—add the white wine or vermouth.

When any spitting has died down, put the pan back on the heat and add the canned tomatoes and the salt.

Let everything come to a boil, then turn the heat to the lowest possible setting, put the lid on, and let cook for 10 minutes.

Pour the sauce into a heatproof bowl and let it cool, at which point remove the garlic cloves and check for seasoning. If you wish to serve this warm, by all means do of course. Similarly, should you want a smooth, rather than rustically chunky, sauce, get out an immersion blender and blitz or push through a food mill. ◼

MAKES ENOUGH FOR 30 POLENTA TRIANGLES Ⓝ

2 TABLESPOONS OLIVE OIL

2 CLOVES GARLIC, PEELED BUT LEFT WHOLE

½ TEASPOON CRUSHED RED PEPPER FLAKES

2 TABLESPOONS DRY WHITE WINE OR VERMOUTH

1 X 14-OUNCE CAN DICED TOMATOES

½ TEASPOON KOSHER SALT OR ¼ TEASPOON TABLE SALT, OR TO TASTE

BECAUSE OF THE TIME OF YEAR I first made this, I think of it as my Christmas Caprese, but I didn't want its title to shackle it seasonally. Not least, you could argue, because nobody's really got any business buying cherry tomatoes in December. But, frankly, if you don't live somewhere warm, the tomatoes you buy in August are not necessarily any sweeter or juicier than those bought in the bleak midwinter. Anyway, I can't start apologizing for my unseasonal and unlocal approach now. I buy the tomatoes from my local greengrocer and that's good enough for me. I mean, do I want to be eating nothing but cabbage and parsnips all winter?

I had thought that this approach to the simple tomato, mozzarella, and basil salad would not have much currency in Italy, but I hear that Italian supermarkets now stock tomatoes in winter, even if their greengrocers—quite rightly—won't. So, for anyone who buys tomatoes when they shouldn't, and wants to help them up their game: this is the recipe for you. But you have to know that if I didn't feel it was a bonus in its own right, I wouldn't include it here.

In short, I roast the tomatoes to intensify their flavor, let them cool, and then dot these sweet and sticky heat-wilted blobs of red around some of the best mozzarella I can get my hands on. Instead of strewing basil leaves (also unseasonal) around, I blend a cupful of them to a pool table-baize green purée with a little olive oil; you'll need an immersion blender for this, or at least I do.

TOMATOES, MOZZARELLA & BASIL, MY WAY

Preheat the oven to 425°F.

In a small roasting pan in which the tomatoes will fit snugly (I use a tarte Tatin pan) arrange the tomatoes cut-side up. Going over each tomato half, one by one, grind a little pepper and sprinkle on a little salt and the oregano, then dribble the tablespoon of olive oil over and transfer the pan to the oven to cook for 25 minutes, though check at 20 just in case they are softened and heat-wilted by then. Remove and let cool to room temperature or just above. (They can be left at room temperature for about 4 hours.)

To make the sauce, put the basil leaves and 2 tablespoons extra-virgin olive oil and 1 teaspoon vinegar and a small sprinkle of salt into a suitable bowl or cup, and blend to a deep-green purée with an immersion blender. Add another 1–2 tablespoons extra-virgin olive oil as needed to form a not-entirely-smooth brilliant green paste that can be poured; taste to see if you want the remaining ½ teaspoon vinegar or more salt, and blend in if you do.

Take the mozzarella out of any liquid, drain, tear into pieces, and, on a platter, arrange the mozzarella blossoms and the cooked, cooled tomato halves, then drizzle the basil dressing over them, and your beautiful creation is ready to be served, preferably with bread. ■

SERVES 6, *OR MORE AS PART OF*
 AN ANTIPASTI TABLE OR BUFFET
11 OUNCES (1 DRY PINT) CHERRY
 OR GRAPE TOMATOES, HALVED
½ TEASPOON DRIED OREGANO
1 TABLESPOON REGULAR
 OLIVE OIL
KOSHER SALT AND GROUND
 PEPPER, TO TASTE
APPROX. 1 CUP BASIL LEAVES
4–5 TABLESPOONS EXTRA-VIRGIN
 OLIVE OIL
1–1½ TEASPOONS GOOD RED
 WINE VINEGAR
8 OUNCES FRESH MOZZARELLA
 (PREFERABLY BUFFALO)

THIS IS A WARMLY BUT NONETHELESS ELEGANTLY ROBUST winter pasta, salty with the bacon and grainily sweet with chestnuts, bound in a scant and glossy sauce infused with the mellow, musky grapiness of Marsala. It is not an appetizer—though of course it could be—but a relaxed entrée, both for those cooking and those eating: an ideal state of affairs all round, and a comforting showcase for the seasonal chestnuts, even if they do come out of a vacuum package. You can get the pancetta out of a package, too, but for this festive special, I do try and get a slab of pancetta and chunk it up generously myself: pre-cut pancetta tends to come in tiny dice—they're not called *cubetti* for nothing.

PAPPARDELLE WITH CHESTNUTS & PANCETTA

SERVES 6, *DEPENDING ON AGE AND APPETITE*

1 POUND EGG PAPPARDELLE

SALT FOR PASTA WATER, TO TASTE

2 TEASPOONS GARLIC-FLAVORED OIL

14-OUNCE SLAB PANCETTA, CUT INTO APPROX. ½-INCH DICE

3 TABLESPOONS BUTTER, PLUS MORE ON SERVING, AS DESIRED

1½ CUPS (APPROX. 7 OUNCES) VACUUM-PACKED COOKED CHESTNUTS

7 TABLESPOONS MARSALA

2 TABLESPOONS FINELY SNIPPED CHIVES

2 TABLESPOONS FINELY CHOPPED FRESH PARSLEY

Put a large pot, filled abundantly with water, on the stove to heat for the pasta, and when it comes to a boil, salt generously and confidently.

Meanwhile, in a wok or large flameproof Dutch oven, heat the garlic-flavored oil, then tip in the pancetta cubes and cook over a high heat until they are bronzed and crisp.

At the appropriate moment, according to how long the pasta needs (egg pappardelle is quick), add the pasta to the bubbling salted water and cook following the package instructions, but make sure to start testing a minute or so before it should be ready.

Returning to the pancetta pan, add the butter and, when it has melted, tumble in the chestnuts, released from their vacuum-packed captivity, then, using a wooden spoon or other implement of your choice, squish them down so each chestnut crumbles into a good 4 pieces, and stir everything to mix.

Pour in the Marsala, letting it bubble up, then, just before you drain the pasta, lower in a ladle or measuring cup to remove a cupful of the starchy cooking water and tip about half of it—aim for ½ cup or think 1 small wineglassful—into the pancetta and chestnut pan and stir well, letting it bubble and reduce down a little.

Drain the pasta and add it to the wok or pan of sauce, followed by just under half the prepared chives and parsley, then mix gently but firmly together so that all ingredients are equally dispersed and the light sauce is clinging to the thick ribbons. You may need to stir in some more of the pasta-cooking water, and a little extra butter if you like.

If you're not serving from the pan you cooked it in, transfer the pasta to a warmed bowl, sprinkle with the remaining herbs, and serve. If you're dishing out from the pan, just sprinkle and serve. ■

HEARTY WHOLE WHEAT PASTA WITH BRUSSELS SPROUTS, CHEESE & POTATO

IT IS NOT QUITE NORMAL TO FEEL AS JOYOUS as I do when saying the words "Brussels sprouts," but this recipe does not merely use said much-denigrated ingredient, it also celebrates it. Brussels sprouts are nutty, fresh, and gorgeous, and I regard this recipe as their seasonal showcase. Not Italian, you might say. Well, my inspiration for it is the one authentically defining dish of Valtellina, in Lombardy, up toward the Swiss border. That dish is *pizzoccheri*, a traditional winter-warmer hodgepodge of homemade buckwheat tagliatelle, potatoes, Savoy cabbage, and Taleggio or fontina cheese, baked and flavored with sage, garlic, and Parmesan. You can buy *pizzoccheri* in boxes, with dried short lengths of buckwheat pasta, but for me it is too gummy and tastes nothing like the *pizzoccheri* I've eaten in Italy. I thought it better to do an Anglo version and very happy I am with it indeed. This is no self-aggrandizing boast: it's a tribute to the ingredients, rather than the cook (as all food should be).

I do understand that Gruyère cheese is not English but its nuttiness matches that of the Brussels sprouts—if you avoid picking ones that have moved toward blowsiness—and the sweet richness appeals. Feel free to use a mild Cheddar, if the spirit—or appetite—moves you.

Don't be modishly alarmed by the double-carb combo; it can be an alcohol-sopping salve, much appreciated at this time of year. Besides, it is important to remember that the original predates central heating.

SERVES 8 AS AN ENTRÉE, *OR MORE AS PART OF A BUFFET*

1¾ POUNDS BRUSSELS SPROUTS, TRIMMED AND HALVED

1 X 8-OUNCE BAKING POTATO, PEELED AND IN 1-INCH DICE

1 POUND WHOLE WHEAT OR SPELT TORTIGLIONI OR PENNE

SALT FOR VEGETABLE AND PASTA WATER, TO TASTE

½ CUP RICOTTA

8 OUNCES GRUYÈRE, IN ½-INCH DICE

3 TABLESPOONS UNSALTED BUTTER

1 TABLESPOON GARLIC-FLAVORED OIL

4 SAGE LEAVES, SHREDDED

½ CUP GRATED PARMESAN

1 ROASTING PAN APPROX. 10 X 15 INCHES OR 1 LASAGNA DISH APPROX. 9 X 13 INCHES

Preheat the oven to 400°F, and fill a large pot with water to cook the Brussels sprouts, potato, and pasta.

When the water boils, salt it generously, tip in the prepared Brussels sprouts, the potato dice, and the pasta and let the water come back to a boil, then cook for about 8–10 minutes, or until the potato is tender and the pasta *al dente*. Just before draining, remove 2 cupfuls of the cooking liquid and put to one side.

Tip the drained pasta, Brussels sprouts, and potato pieces into a roasting pan (or a lasagna dish), then add the ricotta and diced Gruyère and a cupful of cooking water, and toss well to combine. Add more liquid if you feel the pasta is too dry.

Warm the butter and garlic-flavored oil in a small saucepan and, when melted and beginning to sizzle gently, add the shredded sage and fry for about 30 seconds before spooning or dribbling the butter and crisp sage over the pasta bake. Sprinkle with the Parmesan and bake in the oven for 20 minutes, by which time the surface will be scorched a light gold. I like this best if it's left to stand for at least 15 minutes before eating. ■

ASTUTE READERS WILL BE ABLE TO SPOT straightaway that the pasta I have used is not macaroni but, in fact, penne. But Mountain Macaroni is the name of this dish, partly due to the alliterative allure, but more pointedly because it is adapted (in much-simplified fashion) from the Alpen Magrone recipe I found in the quite beautiful and altogether inspiring book *Winter in the Alps*, by Swiss-born cook and food writer Manuela Darling-Gansser.

I have specified pancetta below, as it's easier to come by than the speck that I think would be more commonly used in the region. Jamon Serrano would be good here, too. Similarly, you can use the more accessible corrugated penne (*rigate*) if you can't find the smooth penne (*lisce*). Or, of course, just use elbow macaroni.

By the way, my children love this best—and it is one of their top favorites in this book of mine—when it's cooked ahead and (once cooled) left to stand for a day or so in the refrigerator before being brought to room temperature and blitzed in a hot oven.

MOUNTAIN MACARONI

SERVES 6–8

1 POUND (2) BAKING POTATOES, PEELED AND CUT INTO APPROX. 1½-INCH CUBES

2 TEASPOONS KOSHER SALT OR 1 TEASPOON TABLE SALT, OR TO TASTE

1 POUND PENNE LISCE OR PENNE RIGATE

2 TEASPOONS GARLIC-FLAVORED OIL

12 OUNCES CUBED PANCETTA

2 ECHALION OR BANANA SHALLOTS, PEELED AND CHOPPED

1½ TEASPOONS DRIED THYME

7 TABLESPOONS DRY WHITE WINE OR VERMOUTH

1¼ CUPS HEAVY CREAM

FRESH NUTMEG

2 CUPS GRATED GRUYÈRE

Preheat the oven to 425°F, unless you are making this up ahead.

Fill a large pot of water to cook the pasta in and add the potato cubes and salt and put it on to boil. When it's come to a boil, let it bubble away for 5 minutes to help cook the potatoes a bit more before the pasta goes in. Once the pasta is in, cook for a little less time than it says on the package; my penne stipulated 12 minutes, so I set my timer to 10. You need the pasta slightly more *al dente* than you would otherwise eat it.

On the stove, heat the garlic-flavored oil in an ovenproof pan that can later take all the cooked pasta and other ingredients, and add the pancetta cubes.

Cook for 4–5 minutes, stirring frequently, until the fat begins to render, although the pancetta will be far from crisp, and add the chopped shallots and thyme.

Stirring the pan every now and again, cook the shallots and pancetta together for another 4–5 minutes, or until the pancetta is crisping up and the shallots are soft. You can take the pan off the heat at this stage, and keep it to one side until the pasta is nearly ready.

When you're a couple of minutes away from draining the pasta, put the pancetta pan back on the heat and when it begins to sizzle again, add the wine or vermouth and let it bubble away in the heat. Now add the cream and a good grating of nutmeg and stir well. Take off the heat.

Check that the potatoes are just tender and the pasta still slightly *al dente*, then remove and reserve a good cupful of the cooking water. Drain the pasta and the potatoes and put them back in the pan they were cooked in.

Pour the creamy pancetta-shallot mixture over the pasta and toss well together, adding about half your cup of pasta-cooking liquid as you go. Keep the rest in case you need more; I tend to use it all. The sauce should be quite runny at this point—the pasta will soak it up as it bakes.

Now add half the cheese and toss again, and when it is pretty well incorporated add most of the remaining cheese, leaving just enough to sprinkle on top before the assembled dish goes into the oven.

Toss again and tip everything into the pan that the pancetta and shallots were cooked in. (If you're making this up ahead, you can let it cool now and leave it to stand, covered in the refrigerator, for up to 2 days, bringing it to room temperature before cooking.)

Now sprinkle with the remaining cheese and put it straight into the preheated oven for 20 minutes or until the top is a pale gold. (If the pasta is cold when you put it in the oven—but winter room temperature, please, not fridge cold—it will probably need 30 minutes, and check that it is piping hot all the way through.) Once cooked, let it stand out of the oven for 10 minutes or so before serving. If you can wait . . . ■

IT'S ALWAYS WISE, WHEN HAVING PEOPLE OVER for cocktails, to make sure there is something to absorb excess alcohol at the end of the evening. I don't mind if this is a phoned-in pizza but I'd much prefer it to be this rich plate of pork belly, cut into slices, then slow-roasted with that familiar southern Italian pairing of fennel seeds and crushed red pepper flakes.

All you need to do, frankly, is put these slices in the oven. Once they're cooked, drain off most of the fat, and serve them with hunks of bread and, should vegetable accompaniment be required, some thinly sliced fresh fennel.

As far as I know, you need to go to a butcher to get the pork belly cut into slices. Do request that the rind be scored and the rib bones be left attached. It's up to you whether you ask for them by weight or by number of pieces; any way you slice it, it's a bit of a lottery as to how big each piece is, as pigs are not necessarily uniform in size.

PORK BELLY SLICES WITH CHILI & FENNEL SEEDS

SERVES 6–8 *(MAKES 12 SLICES)*
¼ CUP GARLIC-FLAVORED OIL
2 TABLESPOONS FENNEL SEEDS
2 TEASPOONS CRUSHED RED
  PEPPER FLAKES
1 TABLESPOON KOSHER SALT OR
  ½ TABLESPOON TABLE SALT,
  OR TO TASTE
5 POUNDS (12) BELLY PORK
  SLICES

Preheat the oven to 325°F.

Put the garlic-flavored oil, fennel seeds, red pepper flakes, and salt into a wide, shallow dish, and stir to mix.

Rub all the belly slices in this mixture on both sides, and then sit them in a roasting pan, with the rind on top, leaning the slices against each other snugly like a line of fallen dominoes. If it works in your pan, then do 2 lines of pork slices, even if the second line might have to be at a slight angle. I prefer doing it this way rather than using 2 pans.

Roast the belly slices for 2 hours, turning the pan, though not the slices, around halfway through. If they have not crisped up completely then give them another 30 minutes.

Take the belly slices out of the pan carefully: I use tongs and apply more care than is characteristic; the pork belly may have given out a lot of fat as it cooked, and caution is needed with the hot pan.

When the belly slices are arranged to your satisfaction—on a platter or a wooden board— then take them to the table, breathing in the warming and heady aroma, and dig right in. ∎

TURKEY BREAST STUFFED WITH ITALIAN SAUSAGE & MARSALA-STEEPED CRANBERRIES

AS WITH THE BISCOTTI on **p.238**, there is an undeniable American-Italian influence at play here but, once again, I embrace this. Actually, though, American-Italian food has had its own influence on the cooking of the Old Country: these days, I am reliably informed by my Italian publisher and celebrated food writer, Csaba dalla Zorza, you can find dried cranberries with relative ease in Italy.

The true Italian Christmas dinner is very much about the capon. Yes, you can find capons outside of Italy, although not everyone can quite cope with the idea of eating a castrated cockerel. Many understandably view old-school caponization with distaste, although it is considered ethically acceptable if the rooster has been chemically rather than surgically castrated. I don't know about you, but the idea of eating meat that has been flooded with the types of hormones necessarily involved here gives me the willies.

Besides, my Christmas Dinner is my Christmas Dinner: unchanging, ritualistic, an intrinsic part of me. When in Rome, and all that, but if I'm cooking at home, I don't fiddle with my time-honored menu. I'm not going to give an evangelical tub-thump about my turkey brining techniques, as I've done enough of that in the past, but I am still open to other ways of celebrating the Big Bird and this recipe is a case in point. For me, it is perfect for any sort of seasonal supper party, but really comes into its own on a buffet table, as it carves fantastically and is as good (maybe even better) cold than hot, so you can make it in advance and then be the world's most unharried host on the night.

You need to go to a butcher to get a whole breast joint and you need to ask for it to be butterflied and boned and make sure the skin is left on.

I know it might sound a bit of a faff, but take it from me that stuffing a whole double breast joint is very much easier than stuffing and rolling a single breast joint, as is more commonly found in supermarkets. Basically, all you're doing here is opening out your boneless turkey joint, smothering it with stuffing, and folding it over. What you end up with, for all the ease of its creation, is nothing short of a showstopper.

SERVES 12, *OR MANY MORE AS*
PART OF A BUFFET Ⓝ
FOR THE STUFFING
⅔ CUP DRIED CRANBERRIES

7 TABLESPOONS MARSALA

2 TABLESPOONS OLIVE OIL

2 ECHALION OR BANANA
  SHALLOTS, PEELED AND FINELY
  CHOPPED

¼ TEASPOON GROUND CLOVES

½ TEASPOON GROUND ALLSPICE

2 TEASPOONS CHOPPED FRESH
  SAGE

2¼ POUNDS ITALIAN SAUSAGES

2 EGGS, BEATEN

APPROX. ½ CUP GRATED
  PARMESAN

APPROX. 1 CUP BREAD CRUMBS

FOR THE TURKEY JOINT

1 X 11-POUND BONELESS (DOUBLE)
  TURKEY BREAST, BUTTERFLIED,
  WITH SKIN LEFT ON

¼ CUP DUCK OR GOOSE FAT

Put the cranberries and Marsala into a small saucepan and bring to a boil, then take off the heat and leave to one side.

Put the oil into a large frying pan or similar heavy pan, and fry the shallots for a minute or so, then add the spices and chopped sage, turning them in the soft shallots.

Squeeze the sausage meat out of its skins, add to the pan, and break it up—using a wooden fork and spatula for ease—turning it in the hot pan until it loses its pinkness. This will take about 5 minutes.

Take the frying pan off the heat and turn the contents into a large bowl, mixing in the steeped cranberries and any Marsala clinging to them, and leave to cool. You can cover with plastic wrap and put in the refrigerator for up to 2 days at this stage.

When you are ready to stuff the turkey breast, take the bowl of sausage meat out of the refrigerator.

Preheat the oven to 400°F.

Uncover the bowl of sausage meat, add the eggs, Parmesan, and bread crumbs and—I use my hands for this—mix well.

Lay the butterflied turkey joint out in front of you. It really does look like a butterfly, though admittedly a fleshy one. Spread the stuffing out first in the slight cavity in the center of the butterfly and then outward onto the wings though not going right up to the edge (or it will squidge out when cooking) but as evenly as possible over the whole joint.

Carefully, in one swift but steady movement, fold one "wing" over the other to close the joint, and then sit the turkey in a large roasting pan, breast bone (or where the breast bone would be) on top as it would look were it the whole bird, with the pointier bit farthest away from you. Thread 2 skewers through the base—i.e., the widest part that is nearer you—to keep it closed, and smear it all over with the duck or goose fat.

Roast the turkey breast for 2–2½ hours, then check it is cooked with a turkey or meat thermometer. When cooked, it should read 165°F in the center. (If you're leaving it to rest, as you should, or to cool, you could take it out at 160°F—it will retain heat and continue to cook for a short while once out of the oven.)

Flex your muscles, then lift out onto a cutting board, and leave to rest for at least 20 minutes. Or leave to get cold if you are eating it as part of a cook-ahead buffet.

Cut through the whole joint in wide slices right across; they will need to be quite thick, at least ½ inch, maybe 1 inch, to keep the stuffing intact within the slice.

As you place it on table or sideboard, dot around it the condiments of your choice: I revert to Christmas in Italy here by putting a lusciously extravagant pot or two of Italian *mostarda di Cremona* on the table alongside: this is a hot and sweet preserve of mustardy candied fruits that gleam beautifully and taste both festive and fabulous. ∎

THIS IS SUCH A BASIC RECIPE of mine, but I still felt it had a place here. A roasted potato is always celebratory but often labor-intensive; here, life's easy as I don't go in for peeling and I don't turn the potatoes over as they cook. Actually, it's better that way as they've really had time to crisp up on the bottom and therefore don't stick to the pan as you take them out.

I have a very large roasting pan, so can fit all the potatoes in, but it would be fine to use 2 pans; just cook them for 15–30 minutes longer and swap the pans over halfway through. In which case, too, you may as well bump the spuds up to 4½ pounds.

I love serving these on platters lined with my favorite lettuce, escarole, thus providing potatoes and salad on one easy-serving dish.

ITALIAN ROASTED POTATOES

Preheat the oven to 425°F.

Dice the potatoes, with their skins on, roughly into about 1 inch chunks, and then spread them out on a large but shallow roasting pan or lipped baking sheet.

Break up the garlic heads into cloves, keeping their skins on too, but discarding the loose papery outside layers. Arrange the garlic among the potato pieces.

Sprinkle with the chopped rosemary and then drizzle the oil over, turning everything in the pan to coat well.

Cook in the hot oven for 1 hour, by which time the potatoes should be golden on the outside and tender within. Lift or scrape the potatoes off the pan with the implement of your choice, and put onto a couple of salad-lined plates or a warmed platter, sprinkling with sea salt flakes to taste, then serve. ■

SERVES 8, *OR 10 IF MIXED WITH LETTUCE*

4 POUNDS WAXY POTATOES, SUCH AS YUKON GOLD

2 HEADS GARLIC

2 TEASPOONS CHOPPED FRESH ROSEMARY NEEDLES

⅔ CUP OLIVE OIL

1 HEAD ESCAROLE LETTUCE (OPTIONAL), TO SERVE

SEA SALT FLAKES OR KOSHER SALT, TO TASTE

IN MY HEAD—AND IN MY HOME—This recipe is known as Fir-Tree Romanesco. Admittedly, the epithet "fir-tree" is a seasonally induced fantasy; I came across a beautiful display of Romanesco last Christmas and it seemed to me that, once dismembered, this dazzling, bright-green vegetable had the look of fir trees in tiny, squat form. Actually, as you can see from the still life on **p.195**, it more closely resembles the cartoonily sci-fi landscape of the film *Avatar*. There is something about the whirls and whorls of its orderly design that could make you think it was a newfangled, genetically engineered breed of vegetation altogether, but in fact Romanesco predates broccoli and cauliflower (to both of which it is related) having been established in Italy in the 16th century. I call it (as do the stores that stock it) by its majestic Italian name, but I have seen references to it both as caulibroc and broccoflower.

I like best to eat this nuttily flavorsome Romanesco at room temperature (which makes life easier when staggering your cooking for seasonal meals) but it is good—of course—when hot, too, and I know that not everyone shares my taste (acquired from living in Italy) for room-temp veggies.

ROMANESCO WITH ROSEMARY, GARLIC, LEMON & PECORINO

SERVES 4–6, *OR MORE AS PART OF A BUFFET*
1 HEAD ROMANESCO
KOSHER SALT OR TABLE SALT, TO TASTE
¼ CUP EXTRA-VIRGIN OLIVE OIL
1 TABLESPOON FINELY CHOPPED FRESH ROSEMARY NEEDLES
1 CLOVE GARLIC, PEELED
ZEST AND JUICE 1 UNWAXED LEMON
2–3 TABLESPOONS GRATED PECORINO (OR PARMESAN) CHEESE

Fill a large pot with water and put on to boil.

Remove the top floret/fir tree of the Romanesco in its entirety, and the larger of the remaining florets, and when the water comes to a boil, add salt according to your taste, then drop in (gently) the big central floret and cook for 2 minutes.

Now add the other large florets and cook for another 2 minutes. Meanwhile, cut off all the remaining Romanesco florets. Add all these to the pot and bring back to a boil. Let everything bubble for a final 3-5 minutes, until the florets are tender, but still with a bit of crispness about them, then drain and tip gently into a shallow serving bowl.

In a very small saucepan, heat the olive oil, then add the chopped rosemary needles and let them sizzle for a few seconds. Then grate in (or mince and add) the garlic, stir it in, and turn off the heat.

Add the lemon zest and now take the pan away from the stove altogether and let the contents cool slightly before whisking in the lemon juice and salt to taste (remembering that you are adding salty cheese in a moment), then pour this over the Romanesco in its bowl. Toss again gently and then, as soon as it's all touchable, turn the little florets of Romanesco to stand up so they look like a bowlful of small fir trees (as best you can!).

Grate a "snow" of pecorino (or Parmesan) over them and serve—although I love this best once it's all stood together for a while (30-60 minutes) and is at room temperature. ■

RENAISSANCE SALAD

IN OLD-FASHIONED WOMEN'S MAGAZINES, writers used to advise their readers to create a signature vinaigrette to charm their guests and polish their hostessly credentials. I'm not sure about any of that, but if I don't have a signature dressing, I most certainly have a signature salad, and it's this.

I hesitate even to give a recipe, I throw it together in so—intentionally—slapdash a fashion, but I have no doubt at all that I need to tell you about it. I call it my Renaissance Salad, sometimes my Red Renaissance Salad, quite simply because the deep, garnet tones of the ivory-veined Treviso and tardivo radicchio have something of the glorious colors in the paintings that line the walls of the Uffizi; though, really, I should have called this Late Renaissance Salad, as the glowing dark reds bring to my mind even more vividly the Caravaggio paintings I remember seeing in Rome. Though I should tell you that actually these beauteous lettuces come from around Venice.

I ought to mention, too, that if you don't come across the beautifully bitter Treviso or the sweeter tardivo, simply use a couple of the more accessible round radicchio, instead. I sometimes add some blushing spears of red endive, too.

Radicchio, Treviso, and tardivo are the names these red lettuces are sold by in American grocery stores. In Italy, they'd be identified as—going from top to bottom (see left)—*radicchio di Chioggia*, *radicchio precoce di Treviso*, and *radicchio tardivo di Treviso*. These days, both early (*precoce*) and late (*tardivo*) Treviso varieties can be found together for an overlapping period.

I use a ludicrously vast platter for this—about 16 inches in diameter—which means I can get all the red leaves in a single layer, with a frame of plate around them, before I sprinkle sprouts and seeds over, but you can use a regular salad bowl and toss everything together if you prefer.

Tear the Treviso into ragged rough pieces and pull the tardivo off its stalk into fronds, then strew a large platter with them. Leaves from round radicchio can be left whole or treated like the Treviso.

Sprinkle with salt, then drizzle with the oil and vinegar, in a roughly zigzag fashion, and scatter the pomegranate seeds on top. And that is that. Just beautiful! ∎

SERVES 8–10

1 HEAD TREVISO RADICCHIO
AND 1 HEAD TARDIVO
AND 1 HEAD ROUND RADICCHIO
OR 3 HEADS ROUND RADICCHIO
SCANT TEASPOON KOSHER SALT
  OR SCANT ½ TEASPOON TABLE
  SALT, OR TO TASTE
2 TABLESPOONS EXTRA-VIRGIN
  OLIVE OIL
2 TEASPOONS BALSAMIC
  VINEGAR
½ CUP POMEGRANATE SEEDS

FIG & OLIVE CHUTNEY

THE SCRAWL ON MY KITCHEN NOTEBOOK under this recipe reads: Ancient Italian flavors, English recipe; that just about sums it up.

I often give homemade chutneys to Italian friends when I visit, as I'm proud of our traditional recipes and know that an English chutney can pair magnificently with an Italian cheese. Italians themselves are not averse to a condiment or two of their own, either. But I love bringing the two strands of our differing cultures together—and this fig and olive chutney is a marriage made in *paradiso*.

The quantities below are modest, but then this is not a chutney that can be kept for long, so I don't make a lot at a time. Plus, it is so quick and easy that there is no need for old-school "putting down," as preserving used to be known in the kitchen, or even for sterilizing your jars (unless you especially want to make a longer-life version described just below).

I cannot cope without a few jars of pitted oil-cured black olives in the cupboard; you don't find them everywhere, so it's worth getting a stash in when you do come across them. And if you don't have these, then you will need 1¾ cups of black olives with pits in—the kind that are stored in vacuum packs or in jars (without liquid)—and will have to pit them yourself. Do not use cans of pitted olives in brine, please, as you won't get the depth of flavor or the right consistency.

Should you be inclined to store this chutney for longer, up to 3 months or thereabouts (in which case you'll need sterilized jars—see Notes on **p.267**), then you should return the processed chutney to the saucepan, put it over a medium heat, and bring it back up to a boil; it will bubble at the edges and be steaming slightly. Transfer it to warm, sterilized jars, seal, and let them to cool, then store in a cool, dark place. I tend not to bother with this fandango but warn friends who are the recipients of my chutney as a gift that they must keep it in the refrigerator and eat within the month; they don't find this problematic at all. Nor will you.

I use the amount below to fill three preserving jars of 1-cup capacity or six tinier ones.

MAKES APPROX. 750ML Ⓝ

12 OUNCES SOFT DRIED FIGS, SNIPPED IN HALF (2 CUPS)

1¼ CUPS PITTED OIL-CURED BLACK OLIVES

½ CUP (PACKED) DARK BROWN SUGAR

1 TEASPOON FENNEL SEEDS

1 TEASPOON GROUND CINNAMON

PINCH GROUND CLOVES

¼ CUP MARSALA

⅔ CUP RED WINE VINEGAR

7 TABLESPOONS WATER

3 X 1-CUP OR 6 APPROX. ½-CUP SEALABLE JARS WITH VINEGAR-PROOF LIDS

Put all the ingredients into a smallish (approx. 7-inch diameter), heavy saucepan that has a lid, bring to a bubble, and when it starts boiling, clamp on the lid, turn down the heat, and simmer for 15 minutes.

Remove from the heat, take off the lid, and let it stand to cool a little for 5 or so minutes, then tip into a food processor and blitz until finely chopped: this does not take long.

Spoon the chutney into clean, warm jars, then seal with their lids and leave to cool for about 3 hours before transferring to the refrigerator. ■

WHENEVER I'M IN ITALY, I buy and bring back bulging cellophane packages of herb mixes to keep in a cupboard at home so I can turn some plain pasta into an instant Italian-scented supper. All of them contain dried parsley, red pepper flakes, garlic granules, and salt, though others add oregano and crumbled dried tomatoes, too. I thought I'd stick to the simpler version myself, as it makes it actually more versatile.

The reason I give the recipe—more of a blueprint—for it here is that I find a small jar makes for a charming present. I attach a label to the jar, with instructions for use, namely that for each 4 ounces of spaghetti (uncooked weight), 2 teaspoons of the mix should be sprinkled in a tablespoonful of olive oil in the still-hot pan once the pasta's drained, then the spaghetti should be tossed back in, along with 2–4 tablespoons of starchy cooking water.

I have given precise measures below in an effort to be helpful, but basically you need to think of using (by weight) 1 part dried parsley and garlic to 2 parts red pepper flakes and 3 parts sea salt flakes. I know this sounds as if the red pepper will dominate but remember that the red pepper flakes weigh more, as it were, than the dried parsley, so that even though you have double the weight of red pepper flakes, the volume of parsley is greater.

It goes without saying—or ought to—that you should try to get the best-quality dried herbs that you can find.

SPAGHETTI SPICE

Mix the ingredients in a bowl and then, when you're happy everything's thoroughly combined, fill your waiting containers, close tightly, and attach instructions for use, if so desired. ■

**MAKES ENOUGH TO FILL
4 ½-CUP JARS** Ⓝ
1⅓ CUPS DRIED PARSLEY
1½ TABLESPOONS GARLIC
   GRANULES
⅓ CUP CRUSHED RED PEPPER
   FLAKES
⅓ CUP SEA SALT FLAKES OR
   KOSHER SALT

4 X ½-CUP AIRTIGHT JARS

WHILE I WAS TEMPTED TO CALL THIS ITALIAN TOAST, rather than the almost tactless Panettone French Toast, I felt the latter title had the benefit of conveying to you exactly what this is. You can certainly make it with plainer golden pandoro, but it may also be useful to know that should you have made, or be making, the Italian Christmas Pudding Cake on **p.250**, the amount of panettone specified below is pretty much what you'll have left over if you started with a 2-pound panettone. Besides, the panettone with its spicy studding of sweet fruits does make this feel like a fully festive breakfast. Dried- and candied-fruit phobes should obviously take the pandoro path.

Either way, you don't really need to start measuring and weighing, though: I just cut four slices, cutting each in half so I end up with eight small-loaf-sized slices. If need be, and with a lot of extra fruit about, you could easily stretch this to feed eight for breakfast. Especially if you give in to requests (as I have done) for some crisp-cooked, wafer-thin rashers of pancetta on top. For me, though, this needs no more than a scant sprinkling of sharp, fragrant, festive pomegranate seeds.

If you cook these, as I do, for 1 minute a side, the egg will be soft inside, so some eaters may want them cooked longer (and see also Note to the Reader about eggs on **p.xiii**).

PANETTONE FRENCH TOAST

In a dish that will take half the panettone pieces easily—I use a 9-inch square glass dish—whisk the eggs together with the mascarpone and milk; you will have to be a bit patient to smooth out the mascarpone—not that a normal person would register this, but my impatience colors my judgment.

Dunk 4 of the panettone slices in the egg mixture and leave to soak for 1 minute.

Put half of the butter and ½ teaspoon oil in a large frying pan, and set over a low heat to melt. Turn the panettone slices in the egg mixture, and soak the other side for another minute, by which time the bread should have soaked up enough to soften it and the butter should have melted in the pan.

Turn up the heat, then add the soaked slices to the frying pan and cook for 1 minute on each side, so that their egg-soaked surfaces are golden, and browned in part. Meanwhile, soak the remaining 4 slices in the egg mixture for their 1 minute a side.

Remove the first batch of Panettone French Toast from the pan to a large plate, add the remaining butter and oil to the pan, and cook the second batch as you did the first.

When all the pieces are cooked and on the platter, scatter with pomegranate seeds, then dust thickly with the confectioners' sugar pressed through a tea strainer, letting the "snow" fall mostly on the golden sweet-bread slices rather than on the fruit. ∎

SERVES 4–6

4 EGGS
2 TABLESPOONS MASCARPONE
½ CUP MILK
APPROX. 12 OUNCES PANETTONE
 (OR PANDORO), SLIGHTLY STALE,
 CUT INTO 8 EQUAL PIECES
3 TABLESPOONS UNSALTED
 BUTTER
1 TEASPOON FLAVORLESS
 VEGETABLE OIL

TO SERVE
APPROX. ⅓ CUP POMEGRANATE
 SEEDS
1 TEASPOON CONFECTIONERS'
 SUGAR

I READILY CONCEDE that, what with the addition of dried cranberries, this is rather more of an Italo-American recipe than an Italian one, but this is not a bad thing: Italian-Americans bring a lot of vigor and expressiveness to the traditional canon. In any event, the story of Italian food is inextricable from the history and mores of the Italian diaspora.

Biscotti, so named because they are cooked (*cotti*) twice (*bis*) are not tricky to make, but it's not a fast job. Still, you need do nothing while they get their double-baking in the oven, and this kind of cooking can be very calming.

The method below follows traditional lines, and brings you bold, golden biscotti, gorgeous wrapped or in a jar for a Christmas present.

But even if I do like to give these as presents (in which case it may be simpler to make more than one batch at a time), I certainly keep some back for Personal Use. And just as I embrace the American influence behind this recipe, so I like to bring a little Anglo touch to the table when I eat them. The Italians dip their biscotti into the sweet dessert wine, vin santo; I dip my cranberry-studded ones in a glass of color-coordinated ruby port.

CRANBERRY & PISTACHIO BISCOTTI

MAKES 15, *EXCLUDING THE END PIECES* ◐

1 EGG

⅓ CUP SUPERFINE SUGAR

2 TEASPOONS FINELY GRATED ORANGE ZEST

⅔ CUP PLUS 2 TABLESPOONS ALL-PURPOSE FLOUR, PLUS MORE FOR ROLLING

½ TEASPOON BAKING POWDER

FRESH NUTMEG

½ CUP UNSALTED SHELLED PISTACHIO NUTS

⅓ CUP DRIED CRANBERRIES

Preheat the oven to 350°F.

Whisk the egg and sugar until pale and moussy: the mixture should leave a ribbon-like trail when you lift the beater. Beat in the orange zest, and then slowly fold in the flour, baking powder, and a good grating of nutmeg.

Fold in the whole pistachios and dried cranberries, then flour your work surface well, and you may find it helpful to dust your hands lightly with flour, too, as the dough is quite sticky. Now form the dough into a flattish, oval ciabatta-like loaf, approx. 10 x 2 inches, tapering the ends slightly.

Lay the biscotti dough loaf onto a piece of parchment paper on a baking sheet and cook for 25–30 minutes, or until it is a pale brown color. It may help to rotate the baking sheet halfway through the cooking time, as the base can brown quickly; this reduces the risk of the base scorching at one end.

Transfer to a wire rack and leave for 5 minutes to harden slightly, and then—using a bread knife or similar stout serrated-edged knife—cut the baked loaf diagonally into slices about ½ inch thick.

Put these back onto the parchment-covered sheet and cook again for another 10 minutes, then turn the biscotti over and cook for yet another 5 minutes. Let the golden-brown biscotti cool on a rack and then store them in an airtight container. ■

CHRISTMAS IN ITALY WOULD NOT BE COMPLETE without *torrone*, that slab of dentist-defying chewiness made with egg white, honey, toasted nuts, and, often, orange blossom, that we know by the French word *nougat*. I considered making some, I really did, but I came to the conclusion that it involved too much precision-heat measuring and a degree of patience that eludes me at any time of year, but most specifically at Christmas. (You should know that most Italians buy rather than make their own *torrone*, too, no shame attached.) One day I hope to overcome my visceral anxiety and become a serene if—by necessity—energetic *torrone* maker, but until then I wanted a way to incorporate the shop-bought version into my own seasonal festivities. This is what I present to you here and now.

Before I felt I could go public with it, I tested it on a number of Italians—a small sample, I concede, but not an irrelevant one—and was gratified, or rather relieved, by the enthusiastic response. It's always a risk playing about with time-honored traditions. But Italians are, as I've mentioned elsewhere in these pages, embracing the Anglo-American baking tradition and are cupcakes and cookies a-go-go right now, so this recipe seems a timely marriage of kitchen customs. In fact, it was an Italian friend, admittedly one who's been resident in London for over a decade, who gave me the idea in the first place.

If you're cooking for those who can't or won't (that's my children, actually) eat nuts, then you will have to give up any aspiration toward Italianness and use 1 cup white chocolate chips, instead. This is how my daughter loves these cookies, and has insisted they be part of her birthday (which is around Christmas) celebrations from now on. When I make them with chocolate chips, I think they should be eaten still warm; if using nougat, then they are best cold, as the firmness of the cooled cookies contrasts best with the still chewy chunks of *torrone*. And to cut up the sticky nougat first (if you're including it) into the required 1/2–3/4-inch pieces, it helps to use a heavy knife, spraying the blade with baking spray, or you could dip it in cold water every so often.

CHOCOLATE NOUGAT COOKIES

MAKES 25 ⓝ

9 TABLESPOONS SOFT UNSALTED BUTTER

1/2 CUP SUPERFINE SUGAR

1/3 CUP LIGHT BROWN SUGAR

1 EGG

1 1/3 CUPS ALL-PURPOSE FLOUR

3 TABLESPOONS BEST-QUALITY UNSWEETENED COCOA POWDER, SIFTED

▶

Preheat the oven to 350°F, and line a baking sheet.

Beat together the soft butter and white and brown sugars until creamy, then add the egg, beating quickly to incorporate it well.

In another bowl, mix together the flour, cocoa, baking soda, salt, and coffee. Then slowly add the dry ingredients to the wet ingredients in a couple of batches, tossing the chopped nougat pieces into the second batch of flour before you add it. Mix to combine, but don't overbeat as it will make the mixture too sticky.

Using a lightly oiled rounded tablespoon measure, take out a scoop of the cookie mixture, flatten off the top, and ease out the round dome of cookie dough onto a tray you can fit in your refrigerator. Repeat until all the dough is used. Let the cookie dough mounds chill in the refrigerator for 30 minutes. This is not crucial but it helps keep the inside of the cookies chewy; if you like yours crisp, go straight to oven. You could always freeze them at this stage, too (see Notes on **p.267**).

When you are ready to bake the cookies, gently transfer them to your lined baking sheet, spacing them about 2 inches apart. Bake in the oven for 12–15 minutes, then carefully move the cookies to a wire cooling rack—they will be firm on the outside but still soft inside. Let cool. Push the teaspoon of confectioners' sugar through a fine strainer to decorate the cookies before serving proudly on a stand or platter. ■

½ TEASPOON BAKING SODA
SMALL PINCH TABLE SALT
2½ TEASPOONS ESPRESSO
   POWDER
7 OUNCES NOUGAT, CHOPPED
   INTO ½–¾-INCH PIECES
FLAVORLESS VEGETABLE OIL,
   FOR GREASING SPOON
1 TEASPOON CONFECTIONERS'
   SUGAR, FOR DUSTING

1 ROUND-SHAPED TABLESPOON
   MEASURE
1 BAKING SHEET

I'VE ENCOUNTERED QUITE A FEW VERSIONS of chocolate salami in Italy—coming to the conclusion that it's really an Italian version of our chocolate refrigerator cake—and although I am not normally a huge fan of the culinary pun, this does seem the right time of year for such whimsical enterprises. And, I admit, the chocolate salami does have a certain charm, especially when dusted with confectioners' sugar, tied like a proper salami with string. (I am grateful here to Jacob Kenedy for his instructions on how to string up a *finocchiona* in the *Bocca Cookbook*.) If I can do the stringing up, then you can, honestly, but if you prefer, you can just dust the unstrung salami with confectioners' sugar and leave it picturesquely on a board. (And please see Note to the Reader on **p.xiii** about eggs.)

CHOCOLATE SALAMI

In the microwave (following manufacturer's instructions), or in a heatproof bowl suspended over a saucepan of simmering water (but not touching the water), melt the chocolate until smooth. While the chocolate's melting, put the crackers into a resealable bag, seal, and bash them with a rolling pin until you have a bag of rubble—not dust. When the chocolate's melted, remove it to a cold place (not the refrigerator) and set aside to cool.

Cream the butter and sugar together; I do this in a freestanding mixer, but you don't have to. You just need to use a large bowl and make sure the mixture is soft and superlight.

Gradually, and one by one, beat in the eggs. (Don't worry if the mixture looks curdled at this stage: all manner of ills will be righted once the chocolate is added later.) Then beat in the amaretto liqueur.

Push the cocoa powder through a little strainer into the cooled chocolate and, with a small rubber spatula, stir till combined, then beat this into the egg mixture, too.

When you have a smooth chocolate mixture in front of you, tip in the chopped nuts and crushed graham crackers. Fold these in firmly but patiently to make sure everything is chocolate covered. Transfer this mixture, still in its bowl, to the refrigerator to firm up a bit for 20–30 minutes. Don't leave it for much longer than this or it will be difficult to get out of the bowl to shape.

Unroll and slice off 2 large pieces of plastic wrap, overlapping them, so that you have a large wrap-covered surface to roll the chocolate salami out on. Tip the chocolate mixture out in the middle of this and—using your hands, messy though this is—mold the mixture into a fat salami-like log, about 12 inches long.

Cover the chocolate log completely with the plastic wrap, and then firmly roll it, as if it were a rolling pin, to create a smooth, rounded cylinder from the rough log you started with. Twist the ends by grasping both ends of the plastic wrap and rolling the sausage

MAKES APPROX. 20 GENEROUS SLICES Ⓝ

9 OUNCES GOOD-QUALITY BITTERSWEET CHOCOLATE (MIN. 62% COCOA SOLIDS), ROUGHLY CHOPPED

9 OUNCES AMARETTI COOKIES (CRUNCHY NOT *MORBIDI*) OR GRAHAM CRACKERS

7 TABLESPOONS SOFT UNSALTED BUTTER

3/4 CUP SUPERFINE SUGAR

3 EGGS

2 TABLESPOONS AMARETTO LIQUEUR

2 TABLESPOONS UNSWEETENED COCOA POWDER

1/2 CUP RAW ALMONDS (UNSKINNED), ROUGHLY CHOPPED

1/2 CUP HAZELNUTS, ROUGHLY CHOPPED

1/3 CUP UNSALTED SHELLED PISTACHIO NUTS, ROUGHLY CHOPPED

1-2 TABLESPOONS CONFECTIONERS' SUGAR, TO DECORATE

log toward you several times. Then put it in the refrigerator for at least 6 hours—though preferably overnight—to set.

Now—once it's set—for the exciting bit: tear off a large piece of parchment paper and lay it on a clear kitchen surface. Take the salami out of the refrigerator and sit it on the paper. Measure out a piece of string at least 6 times longer than the length of the salami, and tie one end of the string firmly around the twisted knot of plastic wrap at one end of the salami. Then trim away as much plastic wrap as you can, but without cutting either of the tapered, nose ends, so that you can attach the string to these.

Dust your hands with a little confectioners' sugar and then rub 2 tablespoons of confectioners' sugar (more if needed) over the unwrapped salami to stop it getting sticky as you string it up. Plus it makes it look more like a salami!

Make a loop with the string, a little wider than the salami, and feed it over the end of the salami, close to where it is tied on. Pull on the trailing end to tighten (but not too tightly) and form another loop of string as before. Work this second loop around the sausage, 1½ inches or so farther along from the first, tighten again, and repeat until you reach the far end of the salami, then tie the string firmly round the other twisted nose of plastic wrap.

With your remaining length of string, start to feed it back along the salami, twisting it around the encircling string each time it crosses a loop, then tie it again when you come to the end. Repeat these lengths as many times as you want, to make the authentic-looking pattern, but two or three times would be enough to get the effect.

Transfer it to a wooden board, and cut some slices, fanning them out as if they were indeed slices of salami, leaving a knife on the board, too, for people to cut further slices, as they wish. Obviously, when you cut the salami, you will cut through the string, but the many knots and twists keep it securely tied. Serve refrigerator cold, or very near to it. ■

THIS TIME OF YEAR IS SO FILLED with rich confections, fruited and larded and celebratory (not that this is a bad thing), that I am drawn to the underplayed hand of this only deceptively plain cake. It is not one of those high-rise spectaculars, but rather a modest shallow cake; at least insofar as appearances go. To taste, it is meltingly damp, and fragrantly redolent of marzipan—not surprising, since it is made with almond meal. So, yes, it's a plain cake, but it has a restrained richness of its own: small cinnamon-scented slices suffice.

Although a grating of clementine (or orange) zest and a sprinkling of ground cinnamon confer Christmas status, and the confectioners' sugar dusted on top makes it look seasonally snowy, I do make it all year round and it's wonderful in summer with fresh, sharp raspberries. Also in its favor, for any time of year, is that it is gluten- and dairy-free, though not in a special-pleading kind of way.

Normally, when using olive oil in cakes, I am happy to use regular, non-extra-virgin, but for this cake, which has only egg whites rather than the rounded fullness of yolks, I feel it's better to go for olive oil specifically labelled "mild and light." Also, I use free-range pasteurized egg whites out of a carton, rather than leaving myself with 8 egg yolks gazing reproachfully from the refrigerator afterward.

CINNAMON ALMOND CAKE

CUTS INTO 8–12 SLICES Ⓝ

8 EGG WHITES
¾ CUP SUPERFINE SUGAR
FEW DROPS ALMOND EXTRACT
ZEST 1 CLEMENTINE OR
  ½ ORANGE
½ CUP MILD AND LIGHT
  OLIVE OIL, PLUS MORE FOR
  GREASING PAN
1½ CUPS ALMOND MEAL (FLOUR)
1 TEASPOON BAKING POWDER
1 CUP SLICED ALMONDS
1 TEASPOON GROUND
  CINNAMON
APPROX. 2 TEASPOONS
  CONFECTIONERS' SUGAR, TO
  DECORATE

1 X 9-INCH SPRINGFORM
  CAKE PAN

Preheat the oven to 350°F, and grease a 9-inch springform cake pan (or use a special baking spray) and line the base with parchment paper.

In a clean, grease-free bowl, whisk the egg whites until they are opaque and start to hold their shape, then slowly add the sugar, whisking until it's all incorporated and the mixture is thick and shiny.

Add the almond extract and the clementine or orange zest. Then, in about 3 goes each, alternately whisk in the oil and the almond meal (mixed with the baking powder) until they are both smoothly incorporated into the meringue.

Pour the mixture into the prepared pan, then mix together the sliced almonds and cinnamon and sprinkle them over the top of the cake.

Bake for 35–40 minutes (though start checking at 30), by which time the top should have risen and be set and the almonds become golden, and a cake tester should come out clean, barring the odd almondy crumb.

Remove from the oven and let the cake cool, in its pan, on a wire rack. Once it is no longer hot, spring open the sides of the pan, but don't try to remove the cake from the base until properly cool.

When you are ready to serve, push the confectioners' sugar through a small strainer and over the cake to create a snowy effect, and take to the table. ◼

I AM INORDINATELY PROUD OF THIS, and am not ashamed to say so. I have long been a Pavaholic but this is my first venture into a fruit-free, though far from fruitless, version. The instant espresso powder (do not use regular instant coffee granules) gives bitter oomph to the sweet, marshmallowy meringue, which (as with the Cinnamon Almond Cake on the previous page), which I make with free-range pasteurized egg whites from a carton.

I feel disinclined to labor any Italian *bona fides* here, but the cappuccino element—in flavor and form—is self-explanatory and we could always think of it not as a Cap Pav (as it's known in my house) but as *meringa al caffè con panna montata*. Not that I feel the need: I declare its inspiration, not its identity, to be authentically Italian.

CAPPUCCINO PAVLOVA

Preheat the oven to 350°F, and line a large baking with parchment paper and—if it helps— using a 9-inch cake pan as a guide—draw a circle on it with a pencil.

In a smallish bowl, mix the sugar with the instant espresso powder, and set aside for the moment.

In a clean, grease-free bowl, preferably metal (and wipe the inside with a piece of paper towel dipped in vinegar first, if you want) whisk the egg whites with a pinch of salt until they are holding soft peaks and keep whisking while you gradually add the sugar-coffee mixture, 1 tablespoon at a time.

When all this mixture is incorporated and you have a firm, gleaming écru-colored meringue, fold in—using a grease-free metal spoon—the cornstarch and vinegar.

Dollop large spoonfuls of the meringue mixture inside the drawn circle (or make a circle shape freehand if you prefer) on the parchment paper, and smooth and shape it with a spatula so that it looks rather like the crown of a straw boater hat: it must be flat on top.

Put this in the oven and *immediately* turn the oven down to 300°F, and cook for 1 hour. The meringue's outer shell should be crisp, but only just. When it's ready, turn off the oven and leave the Pavlova base inside it until it's cool.

Once the Pavlova base is cool, lift it carefully in its paper and place it, top-side down, on a large, flat plate, then gently peel off the paper.

Whip the heavy cream until thickened and airy, but still soft, and spread this delicately over the top (which previously was the bottom) of the meringue. With a teaspoon, push the cocoa powder through a fine strainer to decorate—cappuccino-style—the top. ∎

SERVES 8 Ⓝ

1¼ CUPS SUPERFINE SUGAR

4 TEASPOONS INSTANT ESPRESSO POWDER (*NOT* INSTANT COFFEE GRANULES)

4 EGG WHITES

PINCH SALT

2 TEASPOONS CORNSTARCH

1 TEASPOON WHITE WINE VINEGAR

1¼ CUPS HEAVY CREAM

1 TEASPOON GOOD-QUALITY UNSWEETENED COCOA POWDER

ITALIAN CHRISTMAS PUDDING CAKE

THIS RECIPE IS MY OWN BUT at the same time a conflation of a couple of Italian Christmas must-haves: the glorious, fruit-studded panettone and *crema di mascarpone*, which is best described as tiramisu without the Savoiardi layer, and sometimes with pieces of chocolate stirred through the mascarpone mixture. I have brought in a cassata element, which means I add, along with the chocolate, some crumbled *marrons glacés* (though any candied or dried fruits could do) and chopped pistachios. The pomegranate seeds I tumble over the top at the end are there for their beauty as well as to add a further seasonal touch but, importantly, are (according to my Italian publisher) thought to bring luck and should therefore be an indispensable part of the Christmas table.

With all the liqueur, chocolate, mascarpone, and other sweetmeats involved here, you'd think it would be unbearably rich: instead, it is curiously elegant. If *sophisticated* weren't such an unsophisticated term, I'd be tempted to use it to describe this glorious creation.

I've called it Italian Christmas Pudding Cake because, while it does possess very much the elements of an Italian Christmas and is presented in cake form, for me it also invokes the liqueur-laden fruitiness—in lighter guise—of a traditional British Christmas pudding.

I use Tuaca to soak the panettone slices, as this Italian vanilla liqueur with its citrus essences and brandied undertones has always seemed to me to be panettone in alcohol form (and I also tend to put a splosh of it in Prosecco to create an aromatic and festive cup of seasonal cheer), but really you can use rum, brandy, or Grand Marnier in its place. Indeed, if you don't want to splash out on more than one bottle for this dessert, simply use the Marsala that's in the mascarpone mixture.

Naturally, you can substitute pandoro for the panettone if you want to do away with the dried-fruit element, and you can also dispense with the *marrons glacés*—the beautiful ones on **p.253** are from the venerable Giovanni Galli in Milan—not by replacing them with other candied fruits, but by upping the quantities of chocolate and nuts instead. Speaking of which, I found some adorable mini chocolate chip morsels and they are my chocolate of choice here, but regular chocolate chips, or finely chopped chocolate—bittersweet, milk, or white—can be used without anxiety. Still on the chocolate theme: although this magnificent pudding cake needs absolutely no accompaniment, if you have an excess of chocolates that people have given you at Christmas, you can chop them up (crumble them into the cream if they're chocolate liqueurs) and use them in place of the chopped chocolate in the sauce on **p.169**; it must be at room temperature when serving.

I've written at length about the cake, and there may seem to be many steps to the recipe on **p.253**. This conceals the fact that it is ludicrously, dazzlingly easy to make: it doesn't require cooking or technical brilliance; it is merely an assembly job. Not that you need to be advertising this fact to appreciative eaters.

One thing I must be strict about, is that the eggs, mascarpone, and cream be at room temperature. (And, as the eggs are not cooked, see Note to the Reader on **p.xiii**.)

Using a serrated knife, cut the panettone roughly into ½-inch slices, then use about a third of these to line the bottom of the springform pan. Tear off pieces to fit so that there are no gaps; panettone is fabulously soft and moldable, so this isn't a hard job. Drizzle 2 tablespoons of the Tuaca (or other liqueur of choice) over it so that the panettone lining is dampened. It looks like a beautiful golden patchwork made out of cake.

Now get on with the luscious filling. Whisk—using a standing mixer for ease—the eggs and sugar until very frothy and increased in volume and lightness.

More slowly, whisk in the mascarpone and heavy cream, then gradually whisk in the Marsala and carry on whisking until the mixture is thick and spreadable. Remove a good cupful to a bowl or other container, cover and put in the refrigerator; this is for the top layer, which is not added until you serve the cake.

Crumble the *marrons glacés* into the big bowl of mascarpone cream mixture, followed by three-quarters each of the chocolate chips and the chopped pistachios, and fold in. Use half of this creamy filling to top the panettone layer that is lining the cake pan.

Use another third (approx.) of the panettone slices to cover the cream filling, again leaving no holes for the cream to escape through. Dampen with another 2 tablespoons of liqueur.

Spoon on the other half of the cream mixture and spread it evenly. Then top with a third and final layer of panettone, covering the cream as before, and drizzle over it the last 2 tablespoons of liqueur.

Cover tightly with plastic wrap, pressing down on the top a little, and put in the refrigerator overnight or for up to 2 days.

When you are ready to serve, take the cake out of the refrigerator, unmold and sit it on a flat plate or cake stand, then spread with the reserved mascarpone mixture. Don't try to lift the cake off the base, as the panettone slices at the bottom are too delectably damp.

Scatter the top—and all around the cake, if wished—with the remaining chocolate chips and chopped pistachios and your pomegranate "jewels." These sprinklings also provide beauteous camouflage for any less than aesthetically uplifting edges of the springform base which may be visible. ∎

CUTS INTO 12–14 SLICES Ⓝ

APPROX. 1½ POUNDS PANETTONE (OR PANDORO)

⅓ CUP TUACA LIQUEUR (SEE INTRO FOR OTHER OPTIONS)

2 EGGS, AT ROOM TEMPERATURE

⅓ CUP SUPERFINE SUGAR

2 CUPS MASCARPONE, AT ROOM TEMPERATURE

1 CUP HEAVY CREAM, AT ROOM TEMPERATURE

½ CUP MARSALA

APPROX. ⅓ CUP PIECES MARRONS GLACÉS

⅔ CUP MINI (OR REGULAR) CHOCOLATE CHIPS, OR 5 OUNCES FINELY CHOPPED CHOCOLATE

⅔ CUP UNSALTED SHELLED PISTACHIO NUTS, CHOPPED

2 TABLESPOONS POMEGRANATE SEEDS

1 X 9-INCH SPRINGFORM CAKE PAN

I ADORE ALL CHRISTMAS AND WINTRY FOODS but my chief joy is the chestnut. In my view, there is no bad way to eat chestnuts, ever: my greatest—and exquisitely extravagant treat—is a *marron glacé*, as dispersed prodigally and festively within the mascarpone cream that is layered with panettone in the Italian Christmas Pudding Cake on **p.250**; but I adore them just as much when, unglacéd, they add their waxen sweetness to savory pasta or stuffings and dressings (see **pp.212** and **203**). Nothing, though, gives me quite the same frisson of intense, sugary delight as a can or jar of sweetened chestnut purée. I know I've told you about my Ma's Quickly-Scaled Mont Blancs before, but I need to tell you how to make them again here. Get out six smallish glasses, with a capacity of about ½ cup each, and into them drop a layer of chopped bittersweet chocolate (you'll need a 4-ounce bar altogether); on top of the rubbly shards of chocolate, dollop some sweetened chestnut purée from a can (a 1-pound can is more than generous); then whip 2 cups heavy cream until thick but still soft, fold in a couple of crumbled meringue cookies (storebought) and spoon this on top of the chocolate and chestnut layers; finally, crumble another couple of meringue cookies in a snowy layer on top.

Frankly, I wouldn't complain about having to eat the sweet grainy purée from a spoon straight out of the can, but this ice cream is perhaps a more elegant showcase for it. If you have any *marrons glacés* (and this is a particularly good use for broken pieces) you could crumble some as you serve; otherwise make the chocolate sauce from **p.169**, using rum as your liqueur of choice. I couldn't resist the chocolate spoon, pictured, though it's better to eat than to eat with.

NO-CHURN CHESTNUT ICE CREAM

MAKES ENOUGH FOR 2 1-PINT CONTAINERS, *FILLED JUST UNDER CAPACITY* Ⓝ

1 CUP SWEETENED CHESTNUT PURÉE, FROM A CAN OR JAR
2 TABLESPOONS DARK RUM
1¼ CUPS HEAVY CREAM
½ CUP CONFECTIONERS' SUGAR

2 X 1-PINT AIRTIGHT CONTAINERS

Mix the chestnut purée and rum together until gloopily smooth.

Whip the cream with the confectioners' sugar until it forms soft peaks, then fold into the chestnut mixture, or pour the chestnut mixture into the cream and fold to combine. Either way works.

Spoon into airtight containers, cover, and freeze for 12 hours or overnight. Serve straight from the freezer. ∎

STRUFFOLI

IF YOU'VE NEVER ENCOUNTERED *STRUFFOLI* BEFORE, they are best described—visually at any rate—as the *croquembouche* of southern Italy: small dough balls, and I mean really small, the size of marbles, that are deep-fried and then rolled in honey before being assembled into a cone—as in the French piled-up profiteroles model—or a bulging wreath. Since I was taught the recipe by a pair of Calabrian sisters, I make mine as their *mamma* makes hers; and this takes the wreath form.

I'll be honest: you don't make these because you're seeking some exquisite taste sensation; *struffoli* are about custom, celebration, and sweetness. This, in effect, is *the* festive centerpiece of Christmas in the south of Italy.

You get a very real sense of this if you make the *struffoli* not alone, but in company, with other hands to roll out the dough with you. Children love doing this, by the way, and their little hands are much better suited for rolling the small marble-sized dough balls you need. Obviously, children are best kept away from the deep-frying part of the operation.

As for the decoration, I've seen not only the regular cake-decorating sprinkles used but also candied fruit, glacé cherries, almond *dragées*, and cinnamony-preserved pumpkin pieces. It's the former, solely, for me. And although I've seen only the multicolored ones in Italy, I go for the festive and flag-resonant Christmas sprinkles in red, white, and green. The *struffoli* would look more beautiful, perhaps, left burnished but otherwise unadorned, although gaudiness not elegant restraint—I'm firmly told—is in order here; I have tried to maintain some balance between the two.

Get out a large, rimmed baking sheet and shake the semolina over the base. And get out another tray (it doesn't have to be a baking sheet) and line it with a double layer of paper towels. Set both aside while you get on with the dough.

Beat the eggs, sugar, finely grated lemon zest, and 2 tablespoons of olive oil until frothy.

Gradually add about 2⅔ cups of the flour and the baking powder, and mix to a dough. If it is too sticky, then add more flour and keep kneading, using either your hands or a freestanding mixer fitted with a dough hook, until you have a smooth, pliable dough. This doesn't take very long: probably around 3 minutes or 5 by hand.

Flour your work surface and turn out your dough. Then divide the dough into 10 roughly equal pieces, each about the size of a golf ball. Take 1 ball and roll it into a rope approx. ½ inch thick, then with floury hands divide this into about 20 small pieces, and roll each piece between your hands (flouring them again if this helps) to make marble-sized balls. Place the formed balls of dough on the semolina-sprinkled baking sheet, as you shape them. Repeat the process with the remaining golf-ball-sized portions of dough: you should make a staggering 200 of the tiny balls!

Heat the vegetable oil in a wide, heavy pan—about 11 inches diameter and at least 6 inches deep—and then when the oil is at 375°F but no higher (you can leave a preserving or candy thermometer in, if you want), or a piece of bread sizzles and browns immediately when dropped in the pan, you can begin to cook the dough balls. Regulate the temperature and keep a careful eye on the pan and the oil all the time.

Gently lower, using a mesh scoop or perforated spoon, about 15 little dough balls at a time. At first they will sink and then, as they cook, they'll float to the surface and begin to turn golden brown. This will take up to about 1 minute depending on how many you have in at a time, but be ready to fish them out with your mesh scoop or perforated spoon onto the paper towel–lined tray as soon as they become the right golden color. And keep watching your pan.

Continue to cook them in batches—making sure the oil returns to the correct temperature but doesn't get too hot or bubble too vigorously—until they are all fried; you can pile them up on the tray without harm. Now turn off the heat under the oil pan, and move on to the adhesive and assembly stage.

Pour the honey into a roasting pan that can go on the stove, and heat very gently until it becomes runny—a matter of moments, so do not leave the pan—then take it off the heat.

Tip all of the fried dough balls into the warmed honey and, using a soft spatula, turn them gently to coat them. Get out a large plate or cake stand with a slight lip or rim and, with wet hands, check the balls are not too hot then pick up the sticky balls and arrange them around the outer edge of the plate in the shape of a bobbly wreath, leaving just a small empty circle in the middle. Do not worry about symmetry or perfection or counting dough balls here, please.

Wash the honey from your hands and shake your chosen sprinkles over the sticky wreath, then stand back and admire, before placing your creation where others can do likewise. These struffoli are best, to my mind, eaten on the day they're made. Use a scoop or spoon and fork to serve. It will be a sticky affair, but that's part of their charm. ∎

SERVES 10 OR UP TO 16;
ESSENTIALLY A CHRISTMAS CENTERPIECE
2 TABLESPOONS SEMOLINA
6 EGGS
1 TABLESPOON SUGAR
ZEST 1 UNWAXED LEMON, FINELY GRATED
2 TABLESPOONS OLIVE OIL
3–3⅓ CUPS FLOUR, PLUS MORE FOR ROLLING
½ TEASPOON BAKING POWDER
2½–3 QUARTS FLAVORLESS VEGETABLE OIL, FOR FRYING
1½ CUPS HONEY
APPROX. 2 TEASPOONS CHRISTMAS SPRINKLES, TO DECORATE

...TO START THE NEW YEAR

EGGS IN PURGATORY

...OR WHAT TO EAT WHEN YOU'RE FEELING LIKE HELL.

I'm not saying that New Year's Day has to mean you have a hangover, but after that evening of almost-enforced carousing, this dish of eggs cooked in a fiery tomato sauce can feel like heaven.

I feel I should address this recipe's name, but I have nothing conclusive to offer you. The heat of the red pepper and the red of the tomato might more plausibly have led this to be called *uova in inferno* rather than *in Purgatorio*. Purgatory is the place where those who die in a state of grace but are not ready for ascension into Heaven must wait, in a long-suffering limbo. This, I do appreciate, is a simplistic categorization, but please: I'm writing an introduction to an egg recipe, here, not a work of doctrinal history. Besides, not being Catholic, all I know about Purgatory I learned from reading Dante. So I particularly liked the hopeful literary attribution which suggests that said dish of golden egg yolks rising out of Parmesan-hazy tomatoes might be a reference to Dante's having reached Purgatory at dawn, and later hailing the advancing sun as the "cheeks of beautiful Aurora...changing into orange." Yes, I know, I wouldn't push it too far either, but you can't blame a person for trying.

Let's put questions of attribution and whimsical theories aside, for we have the pure and pleasurable physicality of the dish to consider. Now, normally I have an almost hysterically inflexible no-red-with-egg rule: I can't bear to see so much as a blob of ketchup or broiled tomato near (let alone mixed with) an egg on someone's plate. But these heavenly Eggs in Purgatory utterly challenge and overturn my previously rigid prejudice.

To the cooking itself: if I use my little cast-iron skillet, only 7 inches in diameter, there is really only room for 1 egg; but generally, a small frying pan tends to come in at about 8 inches in diameter, in which case you can easily fit 2 eggs in. Or you could always do 1 egg and drop the yolk of the second egg on the white of the first.... Either way, this is so easy and speedy to make, I can find time to rustle it up for breakfast, brunch, lunch, supper, or late-night snack, whatever state I'm in.

If solo salvation turns into brunch for a roomful of people, obviously use a bigger pan and I would think 2 cans of tomatoes could provide enough liquid—if there's room in the pan—for up to 8 eggs (but do see Note to the Reader on **p.xiii** about eggs).

Pour the olive oil into a frying pan, then grate in (or mince and add) the garlic, scatter in the red pepper flakes, and put the pan over a medium heat, stirring, for 1 minute.

Tip in the tomatoes, stir in the salt, and let it come to a bubble. It's got to be hot enough to poach an egg in.

Crack in the egg (or eggs), sprinkle the Parmesan over it, leaving some of the yellow yolk still exposed, and partially cover with a lid. Let it bubble for 5 minutes, by which time the white should be set and the yolk still runny, but keep an eye on it.

Remove from the heat and serve—if so wished—sprinkled with a little more Parmesan and some chili oil, and some bread to dunk in. ■

SERVES 1

1 TABLESPOON OLIVE OIL
1 SMALL CLOVE GARLIC, PEELED
¼ TEASPOON CRUSHED RED
   PEPPER FLAKES
1 X 14-OUNCE CAN DICED
   TOMATOES
½ TEASPOON KOSHER SALT OR
   ¼ TEASPOON TABLE SALT,
   OR TO TASTE
1–2 EGGS
2–3 TEASPOONS GRATED
   PARMESAN

TO SERVE
GRATED PARMESAN (OPTIONAL)
CHILI OIL (OPTIONAL)
BREAD (MANDATORY)

THIS IS EITHER A LENTIL SOUP WITH PASTA, or a dish of pasta with lentils, depending on where you are in Italy. And when I say that, I don't mean so much where you are geographically: this differs from house to house, family to family, day to day. My version is on the soupy side, or at least it is on its first outing; any leftover soup will thicken on cooling.

This recipe does double duty for the New Year: on the one hand, it is carbohydrate dense and well suited to sopping up seasonal excess; on the other, lentils are customarily eaten on New Year's Day in Italy as their coin-like shape is thought to bring prosperity for the year ahead. Since I have given a recipe for a New Year's Day lunch of lentils and sausage before, this recipe simply begged to be included here in its stead.

PASTA & LENTILS

Put the onion, bacon or pancetta, parsley, and garlic into the bowl of a food processor and chop finely.

Heat the oil in a Dutch oven that has a lid (I use an enameled cast-iron one measuring 11 inches in diameter and 4 inches deep). Add the contents of the processor and stir to cook over a medium heat for 5–7 minutes, or until softened.

Stir in the lentils and then the tomatoes, then fill the emptied tomato can with cold water and add this, too. Throw in the bay leaves.

Stir again and pour in the broth and bring to a boil, then turn down the heat, cover, and let the lentils simmer, with the lid on, for 30 minutes, by which time they should be soft.

Remove the lid, turn up the heat so that you've got a bubble, then add the pasta and cook it in the pan, with the lid off, for 10 minutes, until the pasta is *al dente*. Season to taste, then put the lid on, turn off the heat and let stand for 10 minutes.

Serve with chili oil, or some extra-virgin olive oil, for people to drizzle over each bowl as they eat. ∎

SERVES 8–10 Ⓝ

1 ONION, PEELED AND
    QUARTERED

6 OUNCES (APPROX. 11 SLICES)
    BACON OR PANCETTA

SMALL HANDFUL FRESH PARSLEY

1 CLOVE GARLIC, PEELED

2 TABLESPOONS OLIVE OIL

3 CUPS LENTILS, BROWN OR
    GREEN, RINSED

1 X 14-OUNCE CAN DICED
    TOMATOES, PLUS 1⅔ CUPS
    COLD WATER TO RINSE OUT

2 BAY LEAVES

2½ QUARTS CHICKEN OR
    VEGETABLE BROTH

8 OUNCES PASTA *MISTA* (MIXED),
    OR ANY BROKEN OR SMALL
    PASTA SHAPES

SALT AND PEPPER, TO TASTE

CHILI OIL, OR EXTRA-VIRGIN
    OLIVE OIL, TO SERVE

NOTES

Make-ahead dishes and leftovers (except cakes) should be cooled and refrigerated as quickly as possible, and always within 2 hours of making. Foods should be stored in the refrigerator in airtight containers, or tightly covered or wrapped with plastic wrap, as appropriate.

PASTA

SICILIAN PASTA WITH TOMATOES, GARLIC & ALMONDS

Refrigerate leftovers as soon as possible. Will keep in the refrigerator for up to 3 days.

MINI MACARONI & CHEESE ALL'ITALIANA

You can also cook all of the pasta in a larger dish (approx. 7 x 11 x 2 inches/ 5 cups). Bake for 20–25 minutes in an oven preheated to 400°F, until golden brown on top and bubbling around the edges.

TORTELLONI MINESTRONE

Refrigerate leftovers as soon as possible. Will keep in the refrigerator for up to 3 days. Reheat gently in a saucepan until piping hot.

SQUID SPAGHETTI

Tomato sauce can be made ahead up to the end of step 4. Cool and refrigerate, or freeze, as quickly as possible. Will keep for 3 days in the refrigerator or 3 months in the freezer (thaw overnight in the refrigerator before using). Reheat gently until just boiling then add squid and continue as directed in the recipe.

CHILI CRAB RISOTTO

It is not advisable to reheat leftovers of crabmeat or rice.

FARRO RISOTTO WITH MUSHROOMS

Can be made ahead up to the end of step 7. Cool and refrigerate as quickly as possible. Will keep in the refrigerator for up to 2 days. Return to the pan, cover, and reheat gently until piping hot, stirring occasionally and adding a splash of extra water or broth if needed. Continue as directed in the recipe. Leftovers should be refrigerated as quickly as possible; will keep in the refrigerator for up to 3 days and are best eaten as a salad. It is not advisable to keep leftovers from reheated farro risotto.

MEAT, FISH & FOWL

BUTTERFLIED LEG OF LAMB WITH BAY LEAVES & BALSAMIC VINEGAR

Refrigerate or freeze leftovers as quickly as possible, wrapped tightly in aluminum foil. Will keep for 2 days in the refrigerator or 2 months in the freezer (thaw overnight in the refrigerator before using).

ITALIAN TRAY BAKE

This is an easy recipe to scale up for a large crowd, if you have enough pan and oven space—just make sure you swap the pans and turn them around in the oven at halftime.

VEGETABLES & SIDES

CHERRY TOMATOES WITH OLIVES

Can be made ahead up to the end of step 3. Cool and refrigerate as quickly as possible. Will keep in refrigerator for up to 2 days. Return to pan and reheat gently until piping hot, then continue as directed in the recipe. Leftovers should be refrigerated as quickly as possible, will keep in the refrigerator for up to 2 days and are best eaten as a pasta sauce. It is not advisable to keep leftovers from reheated tomatoes.

PEAS WITH PANCETTA

Can be made ahead up to the end of step 4. Cool and refrigerate as quickly as possible. Will keep in refrigerator for up to 2 days. Return to pan and reheat gently until piping hot, then continue as directed in the recipe. Leftovers should be refrigerated as quickly as possible and will keep in the refrigerator for up to 2 days. It is not advisable to keep leftovers of reheated peas.

BRAISED FAVA BEANS, PEAS & ARTICHOKES WITH THYME & MINT

Can be made ahead up to the end of step 3. Cool and refrigerate as quickly as possible. Will keep in refrigerator for up to 2 days. Return to pan and reheat gently until piping hot adding a splash of extra water if needed, then continue as directed in the recipe. Leftovers should be refrigerated as quickly as possible and will keep in the refrigerator for up to 2 days. It is not advisable to keep leftovers of reheated beans.

ROAST RED ONIONS WITH BASIL

Can be made ahead up to the end of step 3. Cool and refrigerate as quickly as possible. Will keep in refrigerator for up to 2 days. Remove the onions from the refrigerator about 1 hour before serving, to allow to come to room temperature, then continue as directed in the recipe.

SAVOY CABBAGE WITH POTATOES, FENNEL SEEDS & TALEGGIO

Leftovers should be refrigerated as quickly as possible and stored in a non-metallic container. Will keep in the refrigerator for up to 2 days.

SICILIAN CAULIFLOWER SALAD

Can be made ahead up to the end of step 6. Cool and refrigerate as quickly as possible. Will keep in refrigerator for up to 3 days. Remove the cauliflower from the refrigerator about 1 hour before serving to allow to come to room temperature, or leave chilled, and continue as directed in the recipe. Leftovers should be refrigerated as quickly as possible and will keep in the refrigerator for up to 3 days from day of making.

CANNELLINI BEANS WITH ROSEMARY

Leftovers should be refrigerated as quickly as possible and will keep in the refrigerator for up to 2 days. Eat at room temperature or return to the pan and reheat gently until piping hot.

ITALIAN GOLDEN LENTILS

Can be made ahead, omitting chopped herbs. Cool and refrigerate as quickly as possible. Will keep in refrigerator for up to 2 days. Return to pan and reheat gently until piping hot then add herbs; or remove from refrigerator about 1 hour before serving, to allow to come to room temperature, and add herbs. Leftovers should be refrigerated as quickly as possible, will keep in the refrigerator for up to 2 days, and are best eaten cold. It is not advisable to keep leftovers of reheated lentils.

MASCARPONE MASHED POTATOES

Leftovers should be refrigerated as quickly as possible and will keep in the refrigerator for up to 2 days. Reheat gently in a small saucepan until piping hot, adding a splash of extra milk if needed. Can also be reheated in a microwave, following the manufacturer's instructions.

SAFFRON ORZOTTO

Can be made ahead omitting Parmesan. Cool and refrigerate as quickly as possible. Will keep in the refrigerator for up to 2 days. Return to the pan, cover, and reheat gently until piping hot, stirring occasionally and adding extra water or broth as needed to loosen the orzotto. Add Parmesan and continue as directed in the recipe.

MOCK MASH

Leftovers should be refrigerated as quickly as possible and will keep in the refrigerator for up to 2 days. To reheat, transfer to an ovenproof dish, dot with butter, grate some Parmesan on top, and cook in an oven preheated to 400°F for 20–30 minutes, until piping hot in the center and golden brown on top.

SWEET THINGS

INSTANT CHOCOLATE-ORANGE MOUSSE

Can be made ahead up to the end of step 4. Cover and refrigerate. Will keep for up to 2 days in refrigerator. Remove from refrigerator about 30 minutes before serving to take some of the chill off. Continue as directed in the recipe.

LICORICE PUDDING

Can be made ahead to the end of step 5. Will keep for up to 3 days in refrigerator. Serve as directed in the recipe.

PANNA COTTA THREE WAYS

Can be made ahead. Will keep for up to 3 days in the refrigerator. Serve as directed in the recipe.

MERINGUE GELATO CAKE WITH CHOCOLATE SAUCE

Cake can be made ahead. Best if eaten within 1 week but can be kept for up to 1 month in the freezer. Sauce can be made ahead. Cool and refrigerate as quickly as possible. Will keep in refrigerator for up to 3 days. Remove the sauce from the refrigerator 1 hour before serving to allow it to come back to room temperature; if necessary rewarm as directed in the recipe.

ONE-STEP NO-CHURN COFFEE ICE CREAM

Can be made ahead. Best if eaten within 1 week but can be kept up to 1 month in the freezer.

DOUBLE AMARETTO SEMIFREDDO WITH GOLDEN-GLEAMING SAUCE

Semifreddo can be made ahead. Best if eaten within 1 week but can be kept up to 1 month in the freezer. Sauce can be made ahead. Cool and refrigerate as quickly as possible. Will keep in refrigerator up to 1 week. Remove sauce from refrigerator about 1 hour before serving to allow it to come back to room temperature.

CHOCOLATE HAZELNUT CHEESECAKE

Can be made ahead. Will keep for up to 4 days in refrigerator. Leftovers should be kept refrigerated and eaten within 4 days of making.

ITALIAN APPLE PIE

Can be made ahead. Cool and freeze on day of making, wrapped tightly in a double layer of plastic wrap and a layer of aluminum foil. Unwrap and thaw at room temperature for 4 hours. Best on day of making or as soon as thawed. Leftovers will keep for up to 1 day in the refrigerator, tightly wrapped in plastic wrap.

RUBY-RED PLUM & AMARETTI CRUMBLE

Crumble topping can be made ahead. Store in the refrigerator for up to 3 days or freeze in a plastic bag and use directly from frozen. Leftovers should be refrigerated as quickly as possible and will keep in the refrigerator for up to 2 days.

YOGURT CARTON CAKE

Can be made ahead. Store in an airtight container in a cool place for 2–3 days or freeze for up to 3 months, wrapped in a double layer of plastic wrap, followed by a layer of aluminum foil. Unwrap and thaw at room temperature for about 2 hours.

CHOCOLATE OLIVE OIL CAKE

Can be made ahead. Store in an airtight container in a cool place for 2–3 days or freeze for up to 3 months, wrapped in a double layer of plastic wrap, followed by a layer of aluminum foil. Unwrap and thaw at room temperature for about 3 hours.

ITALIAN BREAKFAST BANANA BREAD

Can be made ahead. Store in an airtight container in a cool place for up to 5 days or freeze for up to 3 months, wrapped in a double layer of plastic wrap, followed by a layer of aluminum foil. Unwrap and thaw at room temperature for about 4 hours. If the bread is to be toasted it is best to store it in the refrigerator.

ANISEED SHORTBREAD

Baked shortbread will keep in an airtight container for up to 5 days.

AN ITALIAN-INSPIRED CHRISTMAS

GORGONZOLA & CANNELLINI DIP WITH A TRICOLORE FLOURISH

Can be made ahead to end of step 3. Refrigerate for up to 1 day and serve as directed in the recipe.

PANETTONE DRESSING SQUARES

Can be made ahead to end of step 3. Cool and refrigerate as quickly as possible, or freeze. Will keep for up to 2 days in the refrigerator or 3 months in the freezer (thaw overnight in the refrigerator before using). Continue as directed in the recipe. Leftovers should be refrigerated as quickly as possible and will keep in the refrigerator for up to 2 days.

PARMESAN SHORTBREADS

Can be made ahead to end of step 3 and kept in the refrigerator for up to 3 days or frozen, wrapped in a double layer of plastic wrap and a layer of aluminum foil, for up to 3 months (thaw overnight in the refrigerator). Bake as directed in the recipe. Sliced dough can also be frozen on parchment-lined baking sheets until solid, then transferred to plastic bags and kept in the freezer for up to 3 months. Bake from frozen as directed in the recipe. Baked shortbreads will keep in an airtight container for up to 5 days.

POLENTA TRIANGLES

Can be made ahead. Cool and refrigerate triangles as quickly as possible, or freeze on parchment-lined baking sheets until solid, then transfer to plastic bags and keep in the freezer for up to 3 months and bake from frozen. Chilled and frozen triangles should be baked as directed in the recipe, but add an extra 5–10 minutes to the baking time.

CHILI TOMATO SAUCE

Can be made ahead. Cool and refrigerate, or freeze, as quickly as possible. Will keep for 3 days in the refrigerator or 3 months in the freezer (thaw overnight in the refrigerator before using). If serving warm, return to saucepan and reheat gently until piping hot then cool slightly before serving.

TURKEY BREAST STUFFED WITH ITALIAN SAUSAGE & MARSALA-STEEPED CRANBERRIES

Can be made ahead to end of step 4. Cool and refrigerate as quickly as possible. Will keep in refrigerator for up to 2 days. Continue as directed in the recipe.

Cooked breast should be cooled and refrigerated, or frozen, as quickly as possible, wrapped in a double layer of plastic wrap and a layer of aluminum foil (thaw overnight in the refrigerator and make sure it is thoroughly thawed before serving). Cooked breast will keep in refrigerator for up to 2 days and in freezer for up to 3 months.

FIG & OLIVE CHUTNEY

The chutney will keep for up to 1 month in the refrigerator, or for up to 3 months if prepared as described in the recipe's introduction. For the longer-life version, I consider a jar straight from a dishwasher (as long as I don't touch the inside) to be a sterilized jar, but those with higher standards should wash their jars in warm, soapy water before rinsing and letting them dry in a cool (275°F) oven for 10 minutes. After opening, the chutney keeps for up to 1 month in the refrigerator.

SPAGHETTI SPICE

The spice mix will keep for up to 1 year if stored in a cool, dry place.

CRANBERRY & PISTACHIO BISCOTTI

The biscotti will keep for up to 1 month in an airtight container. If baking 2 batches on different shelves of the oven at the same time, switch the baking sheets about halfway through each of the cooking times; they may take a minute or two longer to bake.

CHOCOLATE NOUGAT COOKIES

Can be made ahead to the end of step 5 and stored in the refrigerator for 24 hours. Bake as directed in the recipe. Unbaked cookies can also be frozen on parchment-lined baking sheets until solid, then transferred to plastic bags and kept in the freezer for up to 3 months. Bake from frozen as directed in the recipe, adding an extra 1–2 minutes to the cooking time. Baked cookies will keep for up to 5 days in an airtight container in a cool place.

CHOCOLATE SALAMI

Can be made ahead, wrapped in the plastic wrap , then tied with string just before serving. Store in refrigerator and eat within 4 days of making. Can also be frozen on day of making, wrapped in a double layer of plastic wrap and a layer of aluminum foil, for up to 1 month. (Thaw overnight in the refrigerator, remove foil and tie with string before serving. Eat within 2 days.)

CINNAMON ALMOND CAKE

Can be made ahead. Store in an airtight container in a cool place for 2–3 days or freeze for up to 3 months, wrapped in a double layer of plastic wrap, followed by a layer of aluminum foil. Unwrap and thaw at room temperature for about 3 hours.

CAPPUCCINO PAVLOVA

The Pavlova base can be made ahead to end of step 7. Keep in an airtight container for up to 2 days and serve as directed in the recipe. Leftovers should be kept refrigerated and eaten within 2 days.

ITALIAN CHRISTMAS PUDDING CAKE

Can be made ahead to the end of step 7. Will keep in refrigerator for 2 days. Serve as directed in recipe. The cake can also be frozen for up to 3 months. Spread the reserved layer of mascarpone cream on top of the cake and chill for 6 hours. Unmold the cake, leaving it on its base, and open-freeze until solid. Wrap in a double layer of plastic wrap and a layer of aluminum foil then return it to the freezer. Unwrap and thaw on a serving dish overnight in the refrigerator, sprinkling with chocolate chips, pistachios, and pomegranate seeds before serving. Leftovers should be kept refrigerated and eaten within 4 days of making, or within 2 days of thawing if frozen.

NO-CHURN CHESTNUT ICE CREAM

Can be made ahead. Best if eaten within 1 week but can be kept up to 1 month in the freezer.

PASTA & LENTILS

Refrigerate leftovers as soon as possible. Will keep in the refrigerator for up to 3 days. Reheat gently in a saucepan, adding a little extra broth or water if liked, until piping hot.

INDEX

ACKNOWLEDGMENTS

I always both look forward to and dread writing the acknowledgments, being at once eager to give thanks and yet uncomfortable that the extent of my gratitude can never be amply conveyed in such a short space. So, please forgive my terseness and know that the list which follows is a poor reflection of my expansive thanks.

I start off, gladly, by thanking Charles Saatchi, Ed Victor, Gail Rebuck, and Mark Hutchinson, whose enthusiasm for this project before I'd even begun, helped propel it into life. My girls know how grateful I am to them, but it would be mawkish for me to express just how thankful here. Let me say simply that I couldn't have managed without Hettie Potter—yin to my yang, bread to my butter, and my Constant Kitchen Companion—and hope I never have to. Zoe Wales's meticulous research was a joy and an inspiration and I am indebted to her for it. Similarly, I am shored up, supported, and super-efficiently served here by my "A" team, namely Anzelle Wasserman and Alice Binks. Without Caz Hildebrand there would have been no book, or at least no book I could be happy with. And here I must warmly thank Petrina Tinslay, too, for her glorious photographs, which are exactly what that book, in my mind's eye, needed.

Being something of a clutter queen, I have—over the years—obsessively acquired most of the plates and bowls and so forth that you see in these pages, but clutter needs management and I am not the person for that. Luckily, I had props stylists Lucy Attwater and Emily Penrose to marshal my mess, fill in the gaps, and generally make sure every picture had what it needed. Accordingly, I would like to thank, in particular, Willer, Brickett Davda, David Mellor, and Georg Jensen for their generous loans.

All those contributions, immeasurable though they are, take us only so far. Those who have made sure that this is the book you have in your hands are Alison Samuel, an editor whose sensitivity matches her acuity and (as important when dealing with me) her resilience; Clara Farmer, Caroline Stearns, Parisa Ebrahimi, Jan Bowmer, Jane Sharp, Nicky Nevin, and Julie Martin.

Finally, to my children, Mimi, Phoebe, and Bruno: all these recipes are written chiefly with them in mind; which is to say, I've cooked this book for them and they have been most excellent eaters. They tell me that this is their favorite of my books so far, and for that, and for them, I am very, very happy.